# WARRIORS IN KHAKI

## Native American doughboys from North Dakota

Second Edition

by

Michael J. Knudson

& Ann G. Knudson

**Warriors in Khaki**

© 2012 Michael J. Knudson and Ann G. Knudson

ISBN: 978-1-61170-101-2

Library of Congress Control Number: 2014942301

Although the authors have made every effort to ensure the accuracy and completeness of information contained in this book, we assume no responsibility for errors, inaccuracies, omissions, or any inconsistency herein. Any slights of people, places, or organizations are unintentional.

Corrections or additions are welcome, especially photos of veterans, in or out of uniform. All photos used will receive proper credit. Contact the authors at **mikeannknudson@msn.com**

Front cover, photo of Jacob Douglas, courtesy of Todd Hanson. (Read about Douglas on p. 37.) Back cover, photo of Thomas Rogers, courtesy of Four Bears Museum. (See page 105.)

The authors are grateful to Louise Erdrich for permission to quote three lines from her poem, "Indian Boarding School: The Runaways."

*~ Second Edition ~*

Printed in the USA and UK on acid-free paper.

**Rp** Robertson Publishing™
www.RobertsonPublishing.com

To purchase additional copies of this book go to:

amazon.com

barnes&noble.com

www.rp–author.com/knudson

*Dedicated to the families of those who served.*

# Table of Contents

# Illustrations

# Foreword

*Warriors in Khaki* brings the history of WWI back to life through the biographies and photos of North Dakota's Indian men who served in "The Great War." It provides a personal link, a DNA chain, between the five or more generations of ND Indians since the time when President Wilson asked Congress to declare war on Germany in 1917.

The WWI Warriors, most born in the last decade of the 19th century, were only one generation later from the tremendous change of the landscape of the Great Plains of the United States. Their fathers saw the disappearance of the buffalo, the establishment of the reservations, the coming of the railroad, the influx of the homesteaders and all the other changes brought about by the concept of Manifest Destiny.

I grew up during the WWII years in a place called Elbowoods on the Fort Berthold Reservation. The great American patriotism of the Fort Berthold people has always manifested itself through these modern day warriors. Songs, dances, and speeches have always told the story of the bravery of the men who went to fight for their Country.

I consider myself to be very privileged to have some first-hand knowledge of WWI. Several of our neighbors were veterans of that Great War. John Bearstail, who played the bugle, lived to the north of us. Fred Wheeler, who suffered from the effects of exposure to poisonous gas, lived just to the west of our place. David Packineau lived southeast of us. My aunt was married to Albert Little Owl. Her scrapbook contained many postcards from the WWI era such as photos of Camp Dodge, the shelling of Verdun and German prisoners.

Prior to *Warriors in Khaki*, there was very little published information available on WWI and the Indian men from ND who served at that time. The Knudsons' extensive research and compilation of data of this era has now closed this void of information. They have given us a very valuable reference book. The complete biographies of the veterans must have required many, many hours making exhaustive searches through census records, newspapers, and other source documents. We are indeed indebted to Mike and Ann for their hard work, their perseverance and their obvious commitment to the Indian people of North Dakota in undertaking this daunting task. *Warriors in Khaki* is certainly a book that merits its place in homes, schools, libraries, and in all places where the history of North Dakota and its Indian people is kept.

**Marilyn Hudson**

Director, Three Affiliated Tribes Museum, New Town, ND
(also known as Four Bears Museum)

# CHAPTER 1

## Ready for Action

In January 1917, the United States government was still standing back from getting involved in the war, which had been going on in Europe since August 1914. However, many young men had enlisted to be a part of the fight to support the allies. This included residents of Indian Country in North Dakota. These men were the descendants of the first people to ever live in what is now North Dakota. Britten notes that the men enlisted for several reasons, including a desire to serve their country, to escape the restrictions of home and Indian boarding schools, and to seek adventure.[1] For many of the students, it was a matter of merely exchanging their school uniform for an army uniform.

On August 2, 1915, Joseph McCloud of Belcourt had enlisted in the Canadian Expeditionary Forces at Winnipeg, Manitoba. On July 26, 1916, he was seriously wounded in France. On October 25, 1916, John Red Bean of Cannon Ball enlisted in the Canadian Expeditionary Forces. On December 10, 1916, Roy LaVallee of Jamestown enlisted in the U.S. Marine Corps. After the war, LaValle wrote to Joseph Dixon, "The Mexican trouble brought me into the service. I went down to get Villa."[2]  Several men who lived in Bismarck had enlisted in the North Dakota National Guard in the early days of the war. Benedict D. Cloud and Alex White Feather had served with Company A of the First Infantry Regiment, North Dakota National Guard, on the Mexican Border. The commanding officer of Company A had been Captain A. B. Welch, who was well known to the people on the Standing Rock Reservation. In 1914, Welch had contacted Chief John Grass about recruiting several men from Standing Rock to serve as scouts on the Mexican border.

At the end of January 1917, Germany resumed unrestricted submarine warfare. In early February, President Wilson broke diplomatic relations with Germany, but hoped to still keep the U.S. from becoming active participants. By mid-March, the German Navy had sunk several American merchant ships. Finally, on April 2, 1917, Wilson declared war on Germany. American military planners were now developing plans to create the army needed to support the efforts in Europe.
As soon as the President declared war, men began enlisting in the First Regiment, North Dakota National Guard. In April 1917, a group of six men attending the boarding school at Wahpeton enlisted in the ND National Guard. A number of men attending boarding schools in other states also were among the early enlistees.[3] Two days after Wilson declared war on Germany, August Brought Plenty of the Standing Rock Reservation enlisted in a South Dakota National Guard unit at Flandreau, SD.

Wilson signed the Selective Service Act on May 18, 1917. A main focus of this act was to create a new national army composed of conscripted soldiers. Eventually, the National Army included 77% of the soldiers who served in the American Expeditionary Force. As part of the conscription plan, a national day of registration was scheduled for June 5, 1917. On that day, all men between the ages of 21 and 30 were asked to register at their local voting place. This was to include men who were not citizens. Nationwide, nearly 10 million men registered on that day. In North Dakota, it included many of the men in Indian Country. The U.S. Commissioner of Indian Affairs Cato Sells stated that the Native Americans should also register.[4]

On the Standing Rock Reservation, the local newspaper, the *Sioux County Pioneer,* noted that  the registration places included the Fort Yates School, the Cannon Ball School, the Solen School, and the Porcupine Hall.[5] The paper later reported that a total of 314 men registered in Sioux County.

These totals included 64 at the Fort Yates School, 39 at the Cannon Ball School, 24 at the Solen School and 16 at the Porcupine Hall.[6]

Around the time that the young men were registering for the draft, several former ND National Guard officers drew up a plan for organizing a Second Regiment of the ND National Guard. Governor Lynn Frazier supported the idea. The War Department in Washington approved the plan, but indicated that the regiment needed to be brought up to full strength by July 10, which was not a lot of time. Recruitment for the Second Regiment began, as men of local prominence worked to raise companies in various towns across the state. Cooper noted that some of the recruiters did not have any prior military experience.[7]

Recruitment offices for three of the companies were near the reservations. In April of 1917, the Rolla newspaper reported that Moses Fiddler and Moses (sic) Martin had set off for Devils Lake to enlist.[8] Martin continued on to Fargo, where he enlisted in the U. S. Army. Martin's younger brother, John, enlisted about a year later in the Canadian Army. Some of the first men to register in Company D at Devils Lake on June 30, 1917 included Charles Blackbird, Alfred Jettie, Martin Montreil, and Alex St. Arnaud. The *Turtle Mountain Star* reported that Alex and Alfred St. Arnaud had traveled from Belcourt to Devils Lake to enlist, as musicians.[9] Ironically, Sgt. St. Arnaud became a bayonet instructor stationed in the port city of Brest, France. On June 30, 1917, the *Devils Lake Daily Journal* reported that "Capt. Thos. Lonnevik was ordered to commence recruiting at once."[10] He likely contacted the boarding school at Fort Totten. Many of the men from the Turtle Mountain Reservation had been required to go to the school at Fort Totten, where they became part of the military-oriented curriculum. The *Devils Lake Daily Journal* reported that 14 men from the nearby reservations had enlisted, but following a medical examination, it was found that all but three were afflicted with trachoma, which was considered highly contagious. The paper reported that one man in particular was very upset when he was told that he would not be able to serve.[11]

These four men enlisted in Company G, ND National Guard, in Rolla in July 1917. This photo likely was taken not long after they were issued uniforms. Brien and Warren served together in France in the Tank Corps. Laderoute served as a mechanic and Jollie became a sergeant in the 26th or Yankee Division. *State Historical Society of North Dakota*

Edward Brien, Joe Warren, Luger Laderz
Dave Jollie, WWI Vets, 1918

In early July 1917, the company commander, John Grant, began recruiting in Rolla for Company G. A large group of men enlisted on July 13, including many men from the Turtle Mountain Reservation. On July 26, 1917, the *Turtle Mountain Star* published the Rolette County Roll of Honor, which included a list of 107 men from Rolette County. Almost 25% of the men were from the Turtle Mountain Reservation.[12] Most of these men grew up speaking French. They would have no problem communicating with the French people. A number of these men also had some health problems, including trachoma, which led to their medical discharge. At first, the men were quartered on the second floor of city hall where there were no toilets or facilities for cooking meals for the men. Cooper stated that the men took their meals at a local hotel at 35 cents per meal per man.[13] On August 18, Company G was transferred to Devils Lake to join Company D at the Chautauqua grounds, near the state military reservation. About a month later, the Second Regiment traveled by train to Camp Greene in Charlotte, NC. A number of men were given medical discharges after they underwent further medical exams. An officer writing about another training camp in the south mentioned the difficulty to hear roll call due to a lot of coughing.[14]

Meanwhile, recruiting for Company I began in Bismarck, with Captain Alfred B. Welch as company commander. Captain Welch had been a member of the ND National Guard since 1913, and had served with the First Regiment on the Mexican Border. Both Benedict D. Cloud and Alex White Feather had served with Welch, who was the adopted son of Chief John Grass. Welch spoke Lakota and was given the name Mato Watakpe. When recruiting began, Captain Welch was interested in forming a full company of Native Americans. In the middle of July 1917 he traveled to Fort Yates. Welch (n.d.) wrote:

> I went to the Standing Rock Reservation in uniform in order to feel out the temper of the Indians upon the point of service in the Army. I had sent a rider messenger before me and, at some distance from the camp, I was met by a committee of old men who wore the heraldry of coups won in battle, in times past.
>
> We sat together upon the grass, and then, being careful not to break any of the ceremonies and keenly upon the lookout for any 'bad sign' which might decide the question even before I might have had the time to address them, I stated my mission in the usual frank and blunt manner of speech in council – telling them that I was not Mato Watakpe, their brother that day, but was an officer of the Army and was raising a war party to go against the enemy. No one answered, but I could feel the pleasure which they suppressed.
>
> After our smoke, we proceeded toward the camp of about 100 tipis and wall tents. As we neared the entrance to the circle on the east, with the tents of the Hunkpapa on the south and the Hunkpati on the north, the traditional formation of camping, horses were brought and everyone mounted. We rode into camp and old Red Fish, the Master of Ceremonies, accompanied by singing men and women on foot, made the entire circle.
>
> Before many tents, Red Fish planted a painted red and black stick in the ground. This stick was an invitation to appear at the council; and afterwards, when the men did come, they handed the stick to Red Fish and sat down. When the man was not present or could not come, the stick was brought just the same and given to Red Fish, accompanied by a present of meat or ship's bread. Several hundred people were present. I shall never forget that council, for there was enacted that day a ceremony of the raising of a war party with all the rites of the old time Sioux--a ceremony of tremendous excitement but held in leash as no one but an old time Sioux can do.

We sat for fifteen minutes in silence; the moment was full of intense suppression. A woman in full costume was singing an old war song somewhere outside the council circle and the crowd drew nearer. An old man leaped to his feet and sung of his youth; of his bravery; he had passed the pipe then, but now he was old and feeble, and, as he painfully sat down upon the grass, he shot a glance from his blazing eyes to the hill where their last Sun Dance had taken place many years before and, unable to longer retain his composure, there burst from his throat that long, chilling, in-drawn cry of the Dakota warrior, which had been heard on many a battlefield from the Falls of St. Anthony on the Mississippi, to the Lake of the West, where the waters are salt.

I drew out my pipe, which had been used in the ceremony of adoption, and filled the bowl. I rammed the kinikinik close. Lighted it and drew it into good coals. I passed the pipe, stem first, with a quick, sure movement, to my old friend, Red Tomahawk, who sat on my right hand. I did not doubt but that he would take it, but it was a test. He took it. He smoked the two hissing draughts, and slowly returned it to me. It was passed to other old men and no one refused- I had been accepted as a fit leader of Indian soldiers.

It was important that the attitude of Chief Grass be known before proceeding to enlist the young men, and, as the old gentleman was sick at his log house nearly 50 miles away, Col. Settle, USA, and myself went down to see him next day. There on the ground upon which the Spanish trader, Manual Liza, built his first fort in 1807, we talked over the prospects of war in Germany. He was anxious that his young men go.

I was surprised at his grasp of events and I asked him to give me a message for the white people. In this he repeated what he had told me several times before, that "our real name, Dakotah, means friendly people. I never counseled war unless my people were struck first. We have been struck now and a man should fight if he is not a woman. I am not afraid for my young men to enlist. They will get chances for honor in battle, which their fathers had, in abundance. You tell the people that they must fight with happy hearts and that John Grass, the Sioux, believes our country will win with honor, because we are in the right."

When the people of the reservation learned that Grass looked with favor upon the young men going to war, there was much excitement; feasts and dancing were the order of the day and I anticipated no difficulty in obtaining as many men as were needed to fill the unit.[15]

On Thursday, July 19, 1917, the *Sioux County Pioneer* published an article that stated that the Secretary of War was opposed to exclusive Indian organizations in the new army. The article also mentioned that Welch had been recruiting in Fort Yates the previous Monday.[16] On July 22, the first two men from Standing Rock to enlist were Albert Grass and Joseph Jordan. Albert was the grandson of Chief Grass. The next day, Dick White Eagle also enlisted. Over the next several weeks, more men came to enlist in Bismarck, including a number of men from the Fort Berthold Reservation. Joe Young Hawk (Arikara) and Tom Rogers (Arikara) enlisted on August 1. John Smith (Hidatsa) from Van Hook enlisted shortly after Young Hawk and Rogers. On September 19, the National Guard received orders to travel to Camp Greene, Charlotte, NC. On October 1, 1917, a Bismarck paper, *The Palladium*, published a roster of Company I, Second ND Infantry, now designated as the First Ambulance Company, 41st Division. Among the list of privates were also Alphonse Bear Ghost, Richard Blue Earth, and Raphael Lyon from Standing Rock, and Robert Winans from Fort Berthold. Sidney McLaughlin who had enlisted with his cousin, Ray Lyon, held the rank of Corporal.[17]

Meanwhile, the men who had registered for the Selective Service on June 5 were waiting to hear when the first draftees would be announced. The *Sioux County Pioneer* announced that draft physical exams would begin on August 13, 1917.[18] Among the first men inducted into the army were Guy Chapman and James Tattoed from Standing Rock on September 18. Each county was assigned a quota of men to provide for the National Army. The draft calls in the spring of 1918 were quite heavy. The draft continued up to just before the end of the war. One of the last people drafted was Alfred Martell on Oct. 24, 1918. Alfred was the editor of the *Sioux County Pioneer*. More than half the men who served from the Reservations in North Dakota volunteered for service in the Army. It seems there were provisions for men to volunteer for induction. A much smaller number were included in the draftees. There were a number of men who enlisted toward the end of the war and even shortly after. Military service was important to these men. A number of the men who served were sons and grandsons of soldiers and scouts from an earlier era. Many families had men from each generation who served and would continue to serve to the present day.

# CHAPTER 2

## Roster of Veterans

Over 200 men from Indian Country in North Dakota served with the military during World War I. Most of these men were listed on some of the Census Rolls taken on the North Dakota reservations. Several of the men included in this roster were not enrolled, but were married to enrolled members. Other men were enrolled on a reservation outside of North Dakota. Some were students at boarding schools in North Dakota. Military service records of most of these men were published by the North Dakota Adjutant General in 1931 in the four volumes of the *Official Roster of North Dakota Soldiers, Sailors and Marines*. Also included in this alphabetical listing are a number of men from the Standing Rock Reservation who may have enlisted in the service in South Dakota, but had relatives from North Dakota. Their service records were not included in the ND Adjutant General's official report. There are also men included who were inducted and sent to training camps, according to local newspapers, but, for some unknown reason, were not included in the official roster. A number of other men, who registered for the draft but were too young to be called up, enlisted as the war was ending.

## A

**Ackerman, Charles.** Army number 3,776,125; registrant, Sioux County; born, Poplar, MT, Nov. 25, 1896, of German-American parents; occupation, laborer; inducted at Fort Yates on Aug. 8, 1918; sent to Jefferson Barracks, MO; served in Camp MacArthur, September Automatic Replacement Draft, to Oct. 13, 1918; Company C, 162$^{nd}$ Infantry, to Oct. 22, 1918; Company B, 9$^{th}$ Infantry (Second Division), to discharge; overseas from Sept. 29, 1918, to Aug. 1, 1919. Engagement: Offensive: Meuse-Argonne. Discharged at Camp Dodge, IA, on Aug. 14, 1919, as a Private.

Charles grew up in the Fort Kipp area. In the Census Roll taken in 1911 at the Fort Peck Reservation, Charles and his brother, Wesley, are shown as the adopted sons of Spotted Bull. Their mother was Sarah. When Charles registered for the draft on June 5, 1918, he was working for Jacob Jordan at Fort Yates. In August 1918, the Sioux County Draft Board received a request to furnish a recruit. Charles volunteered to go, and so was sent to Jefferson Barracks. During the war, Private Ackerman was a replacement in the 9$^{th}$ Infantry Regiment of the Second Division. Shortly after Charles joined the 9$^{th}$ Infantry, the regiment was used to support the Marine Brigade near Sommerance. Known as the Manchu Regiment, the 9$^{th}$ received the French Fourragère for gallantry during the Meuse-Argonne Offensive. The 9$^{th}$ Infantry became part of the Army of Occupation in Germany. Private Ackerman played baseball with the other American troops in Germany. The Chaplain for the 9$^{th}$ Infantry wrote,

> Men of honor, men of daring,
> Men of courage, onward faring,
> Men our nation's hearts are cheering;
> Ninth Infantry.
> From all walks of life collected,
> When poor France needs be protected,
> And ne'er ray of hope detected,
> America sent thee.

Shortly after his discharge from Camp Dodge, Charles returned to Fort Yates. While in Fort Yates, he attended the Standing Rock Indian Fair held in September. In the foot races held during the fair, he placed third in the 200-yard race. Not long after this, he moved back to the Fort Peck Reservation, according to the 1920 U.S. Census. He married Alice Shields on Nov. 8, 1920, in Poplar. In the 1930 U.S. Census, Charles was working as a section hand, most likely for the Great Northern Railway. At that time, their children included Alphe, Randolph, Geraldine, and Edwin. In 1941, the family moved to Portland, OR, where Charles worked in the shipyards for several years before going back to work for the Great Northern. In the 1962 Portland *City Directory*, Charles was working as a laborer for the Spokane, Portland, and Seattle Railway. In October 1963, he retired and moved back to the Poplar-Wolf Point area. Charles passed away in the Poplar Community Hospital on July 1, 1974. Alice had died the previous April. Their survivors included Randy, Virgil, Edwin, Frank, David, Mel, Geraldine, and Alphe. Charles is buried in the Ft. Kipp Cemetery, near Brockton, MT.[1]

**Albert, Jerome.** Army number 3,681,518; registrant, Benson County; born, Devils Lake, ND, March 12, 1893, of American parents; occupation, farmer; inducted at Minnewaukan on June 27, 1918; sent to Camp Dodge, IA; served in Battery A, 337th Field Artillery (88th Division), to discharge. Grade: Private 1st Class, Sept. 21, 1918; overseas from Aug. 18, 1918, to Jan. 19, 1919. Discharged at Camp Dodge, IA, on Jan. 31, 1919, as a Private 1st Class.

In the Census Roll for the Devils Lake Sioux taken in 1907, Jerome was listed with his parents, Henry and Lumina Zitkanakoyake. When he registered for the draft on June 4, 1917, he was living near Tokio, ND, with an occupation of farm laborer. Upon arrival in France, the 337th Field Artillery was assigned billets near Clermont-Ferrand in the southwest region. When the Armistice was signed, this unit was still in training. So, they were one of the first units to return to the U.S.

In the Census Roll of the Devils Lake Sioux in 1922, Jerome was living with his wife, Rebecca Medicine Stone, and daughter, Catherine. Jerome and Rebecca were later divorced. Jerome passed away on March 8, 1930, near Devils Heart Butte. He is buried in St. Michael's Catholic Church Cemetery in Mission Township.[2]

**Ankle, Henry Arnold.** Henry was born in North Dakota on the Standing Rock Reservation on April 5, 1893. His father, Daniel, had enlisted in the Army and served with the 22nd Infantry at Fort Yates. In the Standing Rock Census Roll for 1894, Henry is listed with his mother, Marcella, a brother, George, and an uncle, Matthew, who also served in WWI. In the 1900 U.S. Census, Henry lived with an uncle in Morton County. In the 1910 U.S. Census, he is listed as a student at the Bismarck boarding school. Before the war, he moved to Keldron, SD. He was inducted in South Dakota and sent to Camp Funston (Fort Riley, KS) on April 26, 1918. He served with Company H, 355th Infantry (89th Infantry Division). After the fighting stopped, his commanding officer, Captain Oscar B. Abel was interviewed. Capt. Abel stated that Corporal Ankle "proved himself very good at night work and on maps and buzzers." Ankle told Joseph Dixon that he was in no man's land eleven times volunteering each time. Corporal Ankle added that "in the battle of Argonne our supply wagons couldn't reach us for several days-- and some of the boys got weak and faint. I showed the boys how they could keep their strength up by eating Elm tree buds and bark while marching into the forest I observed that some of the trees were slippery Elm trees, which acted as food to all those that eat it." On Dec. 17, 1918, Henry sent a letter home that was published in the *Sioux County Pioneer*. He wrote: "We are here in a town called Cordel, having been here for a week. We don't know how much longer we will be here. I hope our next move will be towards the U.S., as I think I have seen as much of this country as I want to, although it is a beautiful country in its summer scenery, but now the leaves have fallen and it is rainy and cold but not as cold as South Dakota."

After the war, Henry married Ethel Many Deeds. They lived in Little Eagle, SD. In the Standing Rock Census Roll for 1939, Henry and Ethel are listed with their children, Jesse, Elaine, Thomas and Amelia. Henry died in a vehicle accident near Little Eagle in rural Corson County on July 27, 1954. He was riding with several friends, who were hurrying to avoid a severe storm coming across the prairie. His wife, two sons, Ted and Jesse, as well as two daughters survived Henry. Henry is buried in the Congregational Cemetery in Little Eagle.[3]

**Ankle, Matthew.** Matthew was also known as Matthew Ishkahula. He was born in what is now North Dakota in the mid-1870s. His parents were reported to have been killed in the battle at Lame Deer, MT. At the age of 12 he became a friend and protégé of James McLaughlin, who enrolled him at the boarding school in Hampton, VA. Matthew was a student there from August 1890 to 1898, when he received a carpentry certificate. One of Matthew's teachers was Annie Beecher Scoville, who corresponded extensively with him. Matthew traveled often on the East Coast and mailed his lessons to Miss Scoville for correction. In one letter he mentions ice skating in Central Park. His Hampton uniform intrigued some of the other ice skaters. On July 16, 1896, he sent her a letter from Fort Yates describing his efforts to interview some of the men who had fought at Little BigHorn. Around this time, Miss Scoville visited the Standing Rock Reservation and received an assignment as a special agent of the Commissioner of Indian Affairs. In the 1900 U.S. Census, Matthew was working as a carpenter in Stamford, CT. After leaving Hampton in 1898, Matthew studied for awhile at Union Academy in Meriden, NH. In 1901, he returned to Hampton Institute for their post-graduate business course. He worked as a clerk and general laborer until WWI began. In the Census Roll for Standing Rock taken in 1898, Matthew is listed with his nephew, Henry. In his later years, Matthew did not visit Standing Rock very often.

Matthew enlisted in the U.S. Army and was assigned to Battery B, 57th Artillery, Coast Artillery Corps. He was promoted to Private 1st Class. The 57th Artillery sailed aboard the USS *Rijndam* out of New York harbor on May 10, 1918. They arrived in France on May 25, 1918, and were stationed in St. Denis de Piles, near Bordeaux for training. Each Battery received four 155mm Grande Porte Filloux guns and two machineguns for defense against planes. In September 1918 they moved to the town of Void in the St. Mihiel region. The 57th Artillery played an active role in the Meuse-Argonne Offensive. Records indicate that the 1st Battalion, to which Battery B belonged, fired 8000 rounds of 155 mm shells against the Germans. Following the Armistice, the 57th moved back to a staging area near Brest, France, to await the availability of homeward bound shipping. The 57th returned in January 1919 aboard the USS *Huntington*.

When Matthew returned to the U.S., he was still suffering from the effects of being exposed to gas in France. He had spent time in some French hospitals as well as hospitals in the U.S. After leaving the hospital in the U.S., Mathew enrolled in the Law School of the National University in Washington, DC. While a student, Matthew did some modeling and also some acting in movies. He was associated with William S. Hart, who was a silent film actor. Matthew practiced law in Washington, DC. He passed away at his home in Washington, DC, on March 2, 1930, and is buried in Arlington Cemetery.[4]

**Azure, William.** Army number 5,074; registrant, Rolette County; born, Belcourt, ND, Dec. 18, 1890, of Canadian-American parents; occupation, farmer; enlisted in Company G, 2nd Infantry, North Dakota National Guard, at Rolla, on July 13, 1917; called into federal service, World War, on July 15, 1917; served in Company G, 2nd Infantry, North Dakota National Guard, to Oct. 5, 1917; 164th Field Hospital, 116th Sanitary Train, to March 15, 1918; Headquarters Company, Field Artillery Draft, to April 3, 1918; Tractor School, Trench Mortar No. 1400, AEF, to May 3, 1918; 32nd Brigade, Heavy Artillery, Coast Artillery Corps, to May 6, 1918; Battery E, 59th

Artillery, Coast Artillery Corps, to discharge. Grade: Private 1ˢᵗ Class, Dec. 1, 1918; overseas from Dec. 11, 1917, to Jan. 26, 1919. Engagements: Offensives: St. Mihiel; Meuse-Argonne. Defensive Sector: Lorraine. Discharged at Camp Dodge, IA, on Feb. 8, 1910, as a Private 1ˢᵗ Class.

In the Census Roll for the Turtle Mountain Band of Chippewa taken in 1906, Bill lived with his parents, Andrew and Emily Azure. When Bill registered for the draft on June 5, 1917, he was working as a day laborer at Belcourt. Bill married Beatrice Jerome (1901-1990) in Belcourt on Oct. 30, 1919. They lived in Belcourt until 1927, when they moved to Rolla. In the 1930 U.S. Census, Bill's parents were living with his family. Bill worked for the First National Bank and Hoffmeyer's Dray Line until 1938, when the family moved back to Belcourt. Bill died suddenly at his home in Couture Township on March 22, 1956. In addition to Beatrice, he was survived by his daughters, Louise, Delphine, Mildred, Rose Ann, Viola, Ruth, Delema, and his sons, William R., John and Maynard. A daughter and three sons had died previously. Bill is buried in St. Ann's Catholic Cemetery. The Belcourt American Legion Post conferred military honors.[5]

# B

**Patrick and Louise (Trottier) Baker, 1940.**
*State Historical Society of North Dakota*

**Baker, Patrick.** Army number 4,704,663; registrant, Benson County; born, Turtle Mountains, ND, Nov. 20, 1896, of American parents; occupation, farmer; inducted at Minnewaukan on Aug. 28, 1918; sent to Camp Lewis, WA; served in 166ᵗʰ Depot Brigade, to Sept. 5, 1918; Company B, 13ᵗʰ Ammunition Train, to discharge. Discharged at Camp Lewis, WA, on Jan. 23, 1919, as a Private.

In the 1900 U.S. Census, Patrick lived on the Turtle Mountain Reservation with his parents, George and Josette Baker. In the 1910 U.S. Census, Patrick was a student at the Fort Totten Boarding School. When he registered for the draft on June 5, 1918, he lived near Minnewaukan and was employed at the "Sister's School" at Fort Totten. John Landry also served with Private Baker in the 13ᵗʰ Ammunition Train at Camp Lewis, WA. In the 1920 U.S. Census, Patrick was listed as living with his parents in Benson County. He married Louise Trottier (1902-1956) in Belcourt on Nov. 8, 1920. They lived in Devils Lake from 1920 to 1923, before moving back to Belcourt. In the Census Roll for the Turtle Mountain Chippewa taken in 1928, Patrick and Louise lived with their daughter, Anna. In the 1940 U.S. Census, Patrick was working on a road construction crew. Patrick passed away at the Public Health Service Hospital in Belcourt on Dec. 26, 1963. His daughters, Agnes Poitra, Blanche Parisien, Sister Tekakewitha (Rita), and Joann

Halstengaard, as well as three sons, Morris, Joseph, and Henry survived him. He is buried in St. Ann's Catholic Cemetery in Belcourt. Military rites for the Army veteran were conducted by Lilley-Dionne American Legion Post of Belcourt.[1]

(Above) Alphonse Bear Ghost and John Brave Bull before the war. *Todd Hanson* (Right) Bear Ghost after the war. Joseph Dixon, photographer. *William Hammond Mathers Museum, Wanamaker Collection, Indiana University.*

**Bear Ghost, Alphonse.** Army number 55.085; registrant, Sioux County; born, Cannon Ball, ND, Dec. 21, 1896, of American parents; occupation, laborer; enlisted in Company I, 2nd Infantry, North Dakota National Guard, at Bismarck, on Aug. 2, 1917; served in Company I, 2nd Infantry, North Dakota National Guard, to Oct. 5, 1917; 161st Ambulance Company, Camp Greene, NC, to Oct. 15, 1917; 163rd Ambulance Company, Camp Mills, NY, to Nov. 14, 1917; Company F, 164th Infantry to Jan. 18, 1918; Company M, 26th Infantry (First Division), to discharge. Grades: Private 1st Class, March 1, 1918; Corporal, Sept. 12, 1919; overseas from Dec. 15, 1917, to Sept. 2, 1919; wounded, slightly, Oct. 9, 1918. Engagements: Offensives: St. Mihiel; Meuse-Argonne. Defensive: Mondidier-Noyon. Defensive Sectors: Ansauville and Saizerais (Lorraine); Cantigny (Picardy). Discharged at Camp Dodge, IA, on Sept. 24, 1919, as a Corporal. Cited in General Orders, Headquarters, 2nd Infantry Brigade, American Forces in Germany, Montabour, Germany, July 12, 1919, for splendid qualities of courage and bravery. During the St. Mihiel offensive, Sept. 12-13, 1918, displayed great gallantry and devotion to duty. Entitled to wear a silver star.

Alphonse is listed as Francis on the Census Rolls for the Standing Rock Reservation. In his childhood he was listed with his parents, Robert (Matowanagi) and Mary Brown Woman (Giwin) Bears Ghost. When he registered for the draft on June 5, 1917, he listed his home as Cannon Ball, where he worked as a laborer. He was described as a tall man of slender build. He enlisted with his cousin, Richard Blue Earth, on Aug. 2, 1917.

Alphonse traveled to Europe as a member of the 164th Infantry Regiment.  Shortly after arriving in France in January 1918, most of the Privates who had traveled with him were reassigned to different regiments in the First Infantry Division, which had been in France since the previous June. Alphonse was assigned to Company M, 26th Infantry Regiment, along with John Smith (Hidatsa) and Louis LaTraille (Chippewa). Alphonse's cousin, Richard Blue Earth, was assigned to Company A, 18th Infantry Regiment, also part of the First Division. The First Division participated in most of the combat until the end of the war. Alphonse, John and Louis were all cited for gallantry in battle, and all three were eligible for the Silver Star. Alphonse also received the Fourragère, a French award similar to a unit citation.

In May 1918, the *Sioux County Pioneer* published a letter that Alphonse had written in March, in which he indicated that he had received a Christmas present, but no replies to any of the letters that he had sent home. He told people not to worry about him, as he was well taken care of in every way.

When the 26th Regiment was on the Montdidier-Noyon front in May 1918, Alphonse was on the outpost, according to 1st Sergeant N. E. Heaton. 1st Sergeant Heaton added that Bears Ghost "was always considered the best man on outpost duty. An officer always felt safe when Bears Ghost was on outpost duty. They could always depend on him." Alphonse was wounded on Oct. 9, 1918, while his battalion held a position north of the Bois de Moncy, as part of the Meuse-Argonne Offensive. Alphonse's cousin, Richard Blue Earth had been killed that same day. The 18th Regiment was in line to the west of the 26th Regiment. Alphonse was wounded in the left arm by shrapnel, and was in the hospital for two months. After the Armistice, 1st Sergeant John Bilek (Co. M, 26th Infantry Reg.) provided the following testimony to Joseph Dixon.

> I have a whole lot to say about Bears Ghost. It would take whole week, but I can say he held on to that machine gun like death. He would not let go of it. Would not let anybody else handle it. He was shooting hell out of the Dutchmen. He told me he loved them when they are dead. He would rather save a dog's life than the life of a Dutchman. When he was wounded, he would not let go of his automatic rifle, but he was so badly wounded that we had to send him back. He said, "I hate like hell to go back. I'd like to get some more of them."

> After he came back from the hospital, the first thing he asked for was his automatic rifle. When he heard about the Armistice, he said he wanted to get a lot of the Dutchmen before the Armistice was signed. He said if he was in command of this army, he would wipe the German off the map. Many a time he was under heavy shellfire with me, but he never paid any attention to shells. At night, he would say, "I wish they would let me go out at night. I can find them."

> I wished many times that all the boys in the American army were Indians. We sure would have an undefeated army.

During the occupation of Germany after the Armistice, the First Division was one of the last units to return to the U.S. In April 1919, Alphonse sent a letter back to the paper in Fort Yates. He mentioned his recent stay in the hospital, as well as an earlier confinement when he had been gassed the previous June. He also mentioned that Captain A. B. Welch had not been near the front, and likely had not even seen any German prisoners of war. While Alphonse was still at Camp Merritt, NJ, Joseph Dixon, who also took his photo, interviewed him.

After the war, Alphonse married Alma Red Ears (1906-1965) at Solen in February 1925. Alphonse played baseball for the Cannon Ball team. He worked as a ranch hand, until moving to Fort Yates in March 1972. He was a member of the Cannon Ball American Legion Post. Alphonse passed away in the Fort Yates Hospital on July 4, 1972. He was survived by two daughters, Elizabeth Brings Them, and Eleanor Ross, and a son, Michael, who served in the U.S. Navy during WWII. Alphonse is buried in St. Elizabeth's Catholic Cemetery in Cannon Ball. The Cannon Ball American Legion Post performed military rites.[2]

**Bearshield, Julius.** Army number 2,558,366; registrant; Sioux County; born, Fort Yates, ND, Dec. 24, 1895, of American parents; occupation, farmer; inducted at Fort Yates on March 4, 1918; sent to Camp Dodge, IA; served in Company A, 351st Infantry, to March 25, 1918; Headquarters, 43rd Engineers, to March 29, 1918; Company D, 42nd Engineers, to Nov. 1, 1918; 45th Company, 20th Engineers, Forestry, to discharge; overseas from May 10, 1918, to June 1, 1919. Discharged at Camp Dodge, IA, on June 9, 1919, as a Private.

In the Standing Rock Census Roll taken in 1908, Julius is listed with his father, Martin (Matowahacanka) and his mother, Scarlet Nation (Oyatelutawin) Bearshield. They are listed as Yanktonai. In the 1915 Census Roll, Julius was living with his wife, Lena, an enrolled member from Crow Creek. In the 1917 Census Roll, they have a daughter, Julie. They also had a son who died after Julius had left for his military training.

When Julius left the U.S., his unit sailed on the transport *Abraham Lincoln*. When they arrived in France, part of his unit, Company D, 42nd Engineers was sent to the forested region of Les Landes in southwest France, while the rest of Company D went to the Vosges in eastern France. The duty of the men was to cut trees and produce lumber in sawmills for the Army to use in construction, probably both buildings and coffins. After the war, the engineers sailed for Hoboken, NJ. Upon arrival, they hiked eight miles in full gear to Camp Merritt, NJ. Following his discharge, Julius arrived back in Fort Yates on June 11, 1919. Julius enjoyed playing baseball. The local newspaper noted that he played third base in a game against Selfridge.

In the Census Roll for the Standing Rock Sioux taken in 1926, Julius was living with his son, Joseph. In 1927, Julius re-enlisted in the Army. He was stationed with Troop A, 4th Cavalry at Fort Meade. The Army had sent him to their School for Bakers and Cooks at Fort Riley, KS. The article in the *Sioux County Pioneer* stated that the task of the cooks was to "take the regulation army ration and day after day convert the materials into dozens of palatable dishes, both appetizing and wholesome." In 1934, Julius married Pearl Grindstone. Julius passed away on June 19, 1936, in Little Eagle, SD. He is buried in Little Eagle.[3]

**Bears Tail, John.** Army number 2,704,319; registrant, McLean County; born, Elbowoods, ND, April 4, 1896, of American parents; occupation, horseman; inducted at Washburn on June 23, 1918; sent to Camp Dodge, IA; served in 163rd Depot Brigade, to July 13, 1918; Company L, 352nd Infantry, to July 29, 1918; 163rd Depot Brigade, to Aug. 14, 1918; Company B, 37th Battalion, US Guards, to Oct. 5, 1918; Company A, 38th Battalion, US Guards, to discharge. Grade: Bugler, Oct. 4, 1918. Discharged at Camp Lewis, WA, on Feb. 6, 1919, as a Bugler.

In the 1910 U.S. Census, John is listed as a student at the Wahpeton Boarding School. In the Census Roll for the Fort Berthold Reservation in 1912, John is listed as the stepson of Coffee and his wife, Weasel Woman. Coffee's daughter, Lucy, married Tom Rogers, a fellow veteran. When John registered for the draft in June 1917, he was farming with his father near Elbowoods.

During the war, John was also stationed for a short time at Camp Presidio, CA. After the war, John ranched. He married Emma Smith (1899-1969) in 1920. In the Census Roll for the Fort Berthold Reservation taken in 1939, the children of John and Emma include Vincent, Christine, Selina, Patrick, Susan, Clyde, Joyce, Saunders, and Thomas. Patrick served as a coxswain in the U.S. Navy during WWII. Clyde served in the U.S. Army and died in Korea. John was a charter member of the Joseph Young Hawk American Legion Post. John passed away in the Garrison Memorial Hospital on June 22, 1964. He is buried in the Memorial Congregational Cemetery near Parshall.[4]

**Bercier, Jerome.** Army number 4,726,334; registrant, Rolette County; born, Rolla, ND, Aug. 19, 1895, of American parents; occupation, farmer; inducted at Rolla on Sept. 26, 1918; sent to Camp Custer, MI; served in 160th Depot Brigade, to Oct. 30, 1918; 3rd Company, Labor Regiment, Camp Joseph E. Johnston, FL, to Nov. 29, 1918; Clothing and Bath Unit No. 327, to discharge. Discharged at Camp Dodge, IA, on Jan. 27, 1919, as a Private.

Jerome Bercier. *Chick LaRocque*

Jerome was the son of William and Magdaline Bercier. When Jerome registered for the draft before the war, he was working as a farm laborer for A.A. Munday of St. John. In the 1920 U.S. Census, Jerome lived with his father, William. He married Hannah Hanlan (1904-1974) on Oct. 19, 1921 in Belcourt. The family lived near St. John. In the 1930 U.S. Census, Jerome was listed as the teamster for the school hack. He also worked for the Great Northern Railway for 17 years. After that he worked as a farm laborer. He was a member of Carey-Dolan American Legion Post No. 125. Jerome died suddenly while working on a farm in Baxter Township southwest of St. John on Oct. 28, 1965. His wife, three daughters, and two sons survived him. They include Maxine Richard, Jean Stewart, Loretta James, Lyle, and Richard. Their son, Lyle, had served in WWII, and narrowly missed being captured by the Japanese. Jerome is buried in Holy Cross Cemetery near St. John.[5]

**Bercier, Joseph Lawrence.** Army number, none; not a registrant, under age; born, Turtle Mountains, ND, Feb. 15, 1893, of American parents; occupation, farmer; enlisted in Company G, 2nd Infantry, North Dakota National Guard, at Rolla, on July 23, 1917; served in Company G, 2nd

Infantry, North Dakota National Guard, to discharge. Discharged at Camp Greene, NC, on Oct. 9, 1917, as a Private, Surgeon's Certificate of Disability.

Lawrence was the son of Joseph and Franzine Bercier. Late in the war, Lawrence did register with the Selective Service. At that time he was working as a farm laborer for Charley Johnson of Perth. After the war, he married Seraphine Azure at Belcourt. In the 1930 U.S. Census, the family lived with Seraphine's parents. Lawrence worked as a construction laborer. He passed away at his home near Belcourt on March 1, 1958. His wife, four daughters, and four sons survived him. They were Eva Longie, Marion Zuck, Victoria, Violet, Norman, Gilbert, Prudent, and Leo. Lawrence is buried in St. Ann's Cemetery at Belcourt. The American Legion Post of Belcourt conducted military rites at the funeral.[6]

**Bercier, Louis.**  Army number 2,704,192; registrant, Rolette County; born, Rolla, ND, Jan. 2, 1896, of American-Canadian parents; occupation, farmer; inducted at Rolla on June 24, 1918; sent to Camp Dodge, IA; served in Company K, 352$^{nd}$ Infantry (Eighty-eighth Division), to discharge. Grades: Private 1$^{st}$ Class, Oct. 1, 1918; Cook, Dec. 4, 1918; overseas from Aug. 16, 1918, to June 1, 1919. Engagement: Defensive Sector: Center (Alsace). Discharged at Camp Dodge, IA, on June 14, 1919, as a Cook.

Louis Bercier in the 1930s. *Chick LaRocque*

Louis and his brother, Mike, were the sons of Corbert and Justine Bercier. Mike also served in the Army. Louis received his stateside training with the 352$^{nd}$ Infantry at Camp Dodge. There were over 430 men from North Dakota who served in the 352$^{nd}$ Infantry. Another man from Belcourt, Peter Wilke, also served in Company K, 352$^{nd}$ Infantry with Louis. Their unit packed all their gear on August 9, in preparation for going overseas. The 3$^{rd}$ Battalion of the 352$^{nd}$ sailed to England on the SS *Ulysses*. They saw active duty in the Alsace Sector from the middle of October to early November. After the Armistice, the 352$^{nd}$ Infantry was billcttcd at Lucey, west of Toul. After two weeks, the regiment was transferred to the villages of Bonnet and Ribeaucourt. Companies K and M remained at Lucey to police the area. The two companies completed their task and took off for Bonnet, completing the 32-mile march with full packs in one day. Much of the rest of the winter was spent in drill and maneuvers. Some time was allowed for entertainment and athletic competition. Each of the Companies formed a baseball team. Company K had a good pitcher, so they won quite a few games. The men from the 352nd won the division horse show. Some of the men also started a weekly paper called *The Tars and Tripes*. The 88th Division Headquarters also published a newspaper for the troops, entitled *The Camp Dodger*. The men were very glad to return home in the early summer of 1919.

In the 1920 U.S. Census, both Louis and Mike lived with their parents and worked as laborers. Louis married Ada May Jay at Rolla on Dec. 20, 1930. Louis worked as a farm laborer. He passed away in the Rolla Community Hospital on Aug. 6, 1960. His wife, seven daughters, and three sons survived him. They were Ada Elizabeth Desjarlais, Betty Justine Desjarlais, Joann Marie LaRocque, Mary Alice Dammen, Gertrude Ann Bartle, Margaret Helen, Rosalie Rae, Louis, John and Franklin. Louis is buried in Holy Cross Cemetery near St. John. Members of the Carey-Dolan American Legion Post of St. John conferred military honors.[7]

**Bercier, Mike.** Army number 4,037,100; registrant, Rolette County; born, Rolla, ND, May 8, 1890, of American-Canadian parents; occupation, farmer; inducted at Rolla on July 22, 1918; sent to Camp Custer, MI; served in 160th Depot Brigade, to Aug. 10, 1918; Company L, 77th Infantry, to discharge. Discharged at Camp Dodge, IA, Jan. 28, 1919, as a Private.

Mike was a brother to Louis. His unit, the 77th Infantry Regiment, was part of the 14th or Wolverine Division. Marcel Paul served with Mike in Company L, 77th Infantry at Camp Custer, MI. The Armistice was signed before they had completed their stateside training. After the war, Mike married Jane Vallie. They had several daughters, including Ernestine and Lillian. They were later divorced. In the 1930 U.S. Census, Mike was working as a farm laborer for James Keegan of Mount Pleasant. After he retired from farming, he lived for four years in a retirement home in Rolla. Mike passed away in the hospital at the Minot Air Base on Sept. 21, 1962. He is buried in St. Ann's Catholic Cemetery in Belcourt.[8]

**Bergie, Joseph.** Army number 3,681,522; registrant, Benson County; born, St. Peter Mission, MT, July 15, 1890, of American parents; occupation, laborer; inducted at Minnewaukan on June 27, 1918; sent to Camp Dodge, IA; served in 163rd Depot Brigade, to July 13, 1918; Battery D, 337th Field Artillery (Eighty-eighth Division), to discharge. Grades: Private 1st Class, Sept. 20, 1918; Private, Oct. 16, 1918; overseas from Aug. 17, 1918, to Jan. 20, 1919. Discharged at Camp Dodge, IA, on Jan. 31, 1919 as a Private.

In the Census Roll for the Fort Peck Reservation taken in 1896, Joseph and his brother, Martin, are listed with their parents, Bernard and Caroline Burshia, as well as their two sisters. Shortly after this, the family moved to the Fort Totten Reservation in North Dakota. Joseph's mother is buried in St. Michael's Cemetery in Mission Township. After attending the boarding school at Fort Totten, Joseph transferred to the Carlisle Boarding School on Feb. 6, 1910, to start a three-year enrollment.

As a student there, he learned the masonry trade, as well as the basic academics. In August 1910, he ran away from the school. After returning to the school that fall, he played football for the scrubs team. For the 1911 season, he joined the varsity team, where he played center. He was a stout man of medium height. His nickname was "Stonewall." His coach was Pop Warner, and Jim Thorpe was one of his teammates. The school newspaper reported that Bergie made more tackles than anyone else did on the team. During the summer, Joseph worked in Altoona, PA. The school at Carlisle had a program that located jobs for students in the surrounding communities. Joseph played again during the 1912 season, when Carlisle's team defeated many of the other powerful football teams from the eastern United States. One of the teams they played was West Point. Rumor has it that Bergie was rough on Dwight Eisenhower, who was a cadet at West Point.

After completing his schooling at Carlisle, he stayed in the Altoona area where he worked and also played football for several semi-pro independent teams. In 1916, he was the coach and played center for the local team sponsored by the Pennsylvania Railroad. They wore jerseys with the PRR logo on the back. The Pennsylvania Railroad had extensive repair and maintenance shops as well as their locomotive construction facility at Altoona. For more than a century, Altoona was one of the most important rail facilities in the U.S. Joseph likely worked in Altoona as a boilermaker for PRR, as he listed that as his occupation when he registered for the draft on June 4, 1917. In the summer of 1917, he worked as a farm laborer for August Carlson of Warwick. In the fall of 1917, Joseph returned to Pennsylvania where he played center and coached for the Pitcairn Quakers.

Joseph Bergie at Carlisle. *Cumberland County Historical Society, PA*

Joseph was fortunate to have served in France with his brother, Martin, in a field artillery unit that was part of the 88th Infantry Division. It was unusual for brothers to serve in the same unit. The Bergie brothers began their training at Camp Dodge, IA. On August 11, 1918, their regiment left Iowa for New York. On August 17, they boarded the H.M.T. *Bohemian* and arrived in Liverpool, England, on August 31. Upon arrival in France, the regiment was assigned billets near Clermont-Ferrand. The 337th occupied the villages of Blanzat, Gerzat, and Cobezat. The received training in the operation of the 155 mm, Grand Puissancs Filloux, motorized. These guns weighed nearly 15 tons. However, the Armistice was signed several days before their training was scheduled to be completed. After this, the men were eager to return home. Three weeks after the Armistice, the

337th left their billets near Clermont-Ferrand and headed toward the port of Bordeaux. The unit spent December turning in equipment, filling out paperwork, going through the delousing process, and receiving new uniforms. On Jan. 8, 1919, they boarded the USS *Sierra* and sailed for Hoboken, NJ. After about a week, they took the train to Camp Dodge, IA, where they were discharged. From there, it took about a day for the train to arrive back in North Dakota.

Following his service, Joseph returned to Pittsburgh, PA, where he coached football for several years, as well as taking up professional wrestling. After injuring his hand, he returned to North Dakota. He married Rosalie Bercier (1902-1965) at Minnewaukan on June 10, 1920. He worked on local farms until moving to Poplar, MT, in 1929. In 1940, Jim Thorpe came to stay with the Bergie family when the new football field was dedicated. Joseph, himself, was the guest of honor at the 1968 Athletic Award Banquet given by the Poplar Chamber of Commerce.

Joseph worked as a ventilation worker during WWII at a Vancouver shipyard. His son, Ronald, served in WWII. Joseph passed away in the Poplar Community Hospital on March 10, 1970. He was survived by his children, including four sons: Bernard, Ronald, Blaine and Franklin, and three daughters: Genevieve, June, and Helen. He is buried in the Poplar City Cemetery.[9]

**Bergie, Martin.** Army number 3,681,502; registrant, Benson County; born, Poplar, MT, Dec. 23, 1895, of American parents; occupation, carpenter; inducted at Minnewaukan on June 22, 1918; sent to Camp Dodge, IA; served in 163rd Depot Brigade, to July 13, 1918; Battery D, 337th Field Artillery (Eighty-eighth Division), to discharge. Grade: Private 1st Class, Nov. 1, 1918; overseas from Aug. 17, 1918, to Jan. 20, 1919. Discharged at Camp Dodge, IA, on Jan. 31, 1919, as a Private 1st Class.

After the family moved to North Dakota, Martin attended the boarding school at Fort Totten. When he registered for the draft on June 5, 1917, he was working as an assistant carpenter for the Indian Service at Fort Totten. During the war he served in France with his brother. After the war, he returned to Fort Totten, and married Mary Poitra on Nov. 4, 1919 in Devils Lake. Martin continued to work as a carpenter at Fort Totten. In the 1930 U.S. Census, he was living with his family at the Fort Peck Agency. He worked for the Department of Interior until retiring in 1956. He and his wife operated M & M Cabins at Flathead Lake for 18 years. In 1972, they moved to Havre, MT. Martin passed away in the Northern Montana Hospital in Havre on Nov. 4, 1976. His wife and daughters, Madeline LaRocque, and Irene Rowe survived him. He is buried in St. Louis Cemetery in Dunseith.[10]

**Bighorn Elk, Louis.** Army number 2,559,180; registrant, Sioux County; born, Fort Yates, ND, June 30, 1890, of American parents; occupation, farmer; inducted at McLaughlin, SD, on March 29, 1918; sent Camp Dodge, IA; served in 163rd Depot Brigade, to June 24, 1918; Company C, 350th Infantry (Eighty-eighth Division), to discharge; overseas from Aug. 11, 1918, to May 30, 1919. Engagement: Defensive Sector: Center (Alsace). Discharged at Camp Dodge, IA, June 5, 1919, as a Private.

Louis was the son of John and Mary Big Horn Elk. In the Census Roll taken at Standing Rock in 1903, Louis was living with his grandmother, Hold the Heart (Canteyuza). In the Census Roll for 1908, he is listed as an orphan. In the 1910 U.S. Census, he was a student at the boarding school in Bismarck. Louis was also a student for five years at the Carlisle Boarding School. When he registered for the draft on June 5, 1917, he was working for Tom Frosted. On March 29, 1918, Louis was one of a group of 18 men who were given a big farewell in Fort Yates, before being escorted to the train station in McLaughlin, SD. Each of the men received a comfort kit provided by the ladies of the Red Cross. In June 1918, *The Sioux County Pioneer* reported that Louis was able to come home on furlough before the 88th Division sailed for Europe.

Louis sailed to England with the rest of the 1st Battalion aboard the H.M.S. *Delta*. After passing through England, they arrived in Cherbourg, France, on August 29, 1918. In October, they spent some time in the front lines. Following the Armistice, one of his officers, Captain Minor S. Wasson stated that Private Bighorn Elk had "excellent character and exceptional ability as a soldier." The 350th Regiment was stationed near Gondrecourt, France. A photo of Private Big Horn Elk, with the rest of Company C, was included in a unit history published in 1919.

Louis married Bessie Blackplume (1891-1951). In 1919, they had twin daughters, Louisa and Mary. They also had a son, William, who died as a child. Their son, Francis, served in the Army during WWII. Louis later married Ida Red Hawk (1902-1965). Louis was a member of the American Legion Post at Fort Yates. Louis passed away in Fort Yates on Feb. 27, 1972. His son, Francis, survived him. Louis is buried in the Veteran's Plot in St. Peter's Cemetery in Fort Yates. Members of the American Legion Albert Grass Post 137 served as pallbearers.[11]

**Birds Bill, Frank.** Army number 2,858,166; registrant, McLean County; born, Fort Berthold, ND, March 1893, of American parents; occupation, farmer; inducted at Washburn on April 28, 1918; sent to Camp Dodge, IA; served in 163rd Depot Brigade, to Aug. 11, 1918; Battery C, 338th Field Artillery (Eighty-eighth Division), to discharge. Grade: Bugler, Aug. 5, 1918; overseas from Aug. 18, 1918, to Jan. 5, 1919. Discharged at Camp Dodge, IA, on Jan. 17, as a Bugler.

In the Census Roll taken on the Fort Berthold Reservation in 1906, Frank and his younger sisters are listed with his parents, Birds Bill (Tsa-ka-a-pash) and Plain House (A-ti-ia-tash). As a young man, Frank played baseball with a team at Elbowoods.

When Frank was stationed at Camp Dodge, he helped break riding horses for the Army. The day after he was transferred to the 338th Field Artillery, the unit departed from Camp Dodge for Camp Mills, NY. Shortly after this, the unit sailed for Europe and managed to dodge a submarine attack off the Irish coast. They spent four days in England, before taking steamer across to Cherbourg, France. While in France, his field artillery unit was stationed in training camps at Camp de Souge, near Bordeaux. The training course consisted of daily firing on the range, special and general courses in radio, telephone, reconnaissance, and material and liaison, lasting for six weeks. His artillery regiment was not sent to the front lines. The news of the signing of the armistice reached his unit two days after they had completed their training. While in the Army, Frank was known as "Birdie." His fellow soldiers knew him as an "all around athlete." They sailed aboard the S.S. *Pocahontas* from France on Dec. 24, 1918, and arrived at Newport News, VA. From there, they marched to Camp Stewart, VA, on Jan. 5, 1919, where they were deloused before taking the train back to Camp Dodge, IA.

After returning to North Dakota, he continued to be active in amateur baseball circles. Family stories indicate that he played some with Satchel Paige. He lived near Mandaree. He was a charter member and historian for the Joseph Young Hawk American Legion Post No. 253. Frank passed away in the Watford City Hospital on Jan. 1, 1968. He is buried in Holy Family Catholic Cemetery.[12]

**Blackbird, Charles George.** Army number 87,751; registrant, Benson County; born, Fort Totten, ND, Nov. 4, 1894, of American parents; occupation, mechanic; enlisted in Company D, 2nd Infantry, North Dakota National Guard, at Devils Lake, on June 30, 1917; called into federal service, World War, on July 15, 1917; served in Company D, 2nd Infantry, North Dakota National

Guard, to Oct. 13, 1917; Company L, 164th Infantry, to discharge. Grade: Corporal, Aug. 1, 1917; overseas from Dec. 15, 1917, to Oct. 26, 1918. Discharged at Denver, CO, on Aug. 27, 1919, as a Corporal, Surgeon's Certificate of Disability, 25 %.

Charles attended boarding schools at Fort Totten and Carlisle, PA. He was one of the first men in enlist at Devils Lake in June 1917. After the war, he married Florence Longie (1907-1976) on Dec. 6, 1920. They had two children, Solomon and Mary who died as infants. Their other children were Karen, Louise and Jerome. Charles worked for the Bureau of Indian Affairs and served as chairman for two years in the late 1940s. Charles was a member of the Devils Lake American Legion Post. He passed away in Mercy Hospital in Devils Lake on Oct. 29, 1968. His wife and daughters, Karen and Louise, and his son, Jerome, survived him. He is buried in St. Jerome's Cemetery.[13]

**Blackhoop, Joseph.** Joseph was born on March 12, 1899 on the Standing Rock Reservation. In the Census Roll for the reservation taken in 1915, Joseph is listed with his father, Martin Blackhoop (Zuyala), and his mother, Wapahaska, as well as his sister, Maggie, and his brothers, Barney, William, and Charles. His sister, Maggie, married John Buckley, a fellow veteran. When Joseph registered for the draft on Sept. 7, 1918, he was farming near Cannon Ball. Joseph enlisted after the war ended, as he was too young to be drafted. In March 1920, a pair of Army recruiters traveled to Cannon Ball from Bismarck. Joseph was one of seven men who enlisted in the Third Field Artillery. The others were Ambrose Eagle Boy, John Ironroad, George Redhorn, Jacob Douglas, George Two Bears and Edward Two Bears. Joseph served in Battery B, 3rd Field Artillery. He was a member of the American Legion Post at Cannon Ball. After the war he married Louise Red Tomahawk (1904-1986). In the Census Roll for 1940, Joseph and Louise had three children, Pearl, Robert, and Oliver. Joseph worked as a laborer for the railroad. He passed away on Dec. 1, 1966, in a Jamestown hospital and is buried in St. Elizabeth's Cemetery in Cannon Ball.[14]

**Blake, Charles.** Charles was born on May 17, 1896, on the Fort Berthold Reservation. He inducted and served about a week at Camp Grant, IL, before being discharged. When he registered for the draft on June 5, 1918, he lived at Elbowoods and listed Little Owl as his nearest relative. After the war he ranched. His first wife was Nellie Grace Montclair. In the Census Roll for the Mandans taken in June 1925, Charles lived with his wife, Grace, and their sons, Finley, Charles Jr. and Eric. Grace died of tuberculosis at the end of July 1925. In the 1930 U.S. Census, he is shown living with his wife, Nora, and their children, Finley, Charles Jr., Eric, Karman, and Loretta. Charles later married Margaret Baker. Their sons, Finley and Karmen, served in the Army during WWII, while Charles Jr. served in the Navy. Charles Sr. passed away from pneumonia at the hospital in Elbowoods on Nov. 25, 1937.[15]

**Blue Earth, Richard.** Army number 45,907; registrant, Sioux County; born, Cannon Ball, Oct. 30, 1893, of American parents; occupation, rancher; enlisted on Company I, 2nd Infantry, North Dakota National Guard, on Aug. 2, 1917, at Bismarck; served in Company I, 2nd Infantry, North Dakota National Guard, to Oct. 5, 1917; 161st Ambulance Company, 116th Sanitary Train, to Nov. 14, 1917; Company A, 164th Infantry, to Jan. 9, 1918; Company A, 18th Infantry (First Division), to death. Grade: Corporal, Sept. 4, 1918; overseas from Dec. 15, 1917, to death. Engagements: Defensive: Montdidier-Noyon. Offensives: Aisne-Marne; St. Mihiel; Meuse-Argonne. Defensive Sectors: Ansauville and Saizerais (Lorraine); Cantigny (Picardy). Killed in Action on Oct. 9, 1918, in Meuse-Argonne Offensive; buried, Grave No. 97, Section No. 97, Plot No. 2, Cemetery No. 1232, Argonne-American Cemetery, Romagne-sous-Montfaucon, Meuse, France; reburied at Cannon Ball, ND. Cited in General

Orders No. 1, Headquarters, 1st Division, Camp Zachary Taylor, KY, Jan. 1, 1920, for gallantry in action and especially meritorious services. Entitled to wear a silver star.

In the Census Roll for Standing Rock taken in 1903, Richard is listed with his mother, Mary, and his sister, Mabel, who later married Edward Two Bears, another veteran. When Richard registered for the draft in 1917, he was working as a section laborer for the NP Railway. Richard completed his basic military training with the other men from the ND National Guard. When they reached France, many of these North Dakota soldiers were transferred over to the regiments of the First Division, sometimes known as the Big Red One. Richard was assigned to Company A, 18th Infantry Regiment, where he had good companions. Other soldiers in Company A with him were Albert Grass and Joseph Jordan from Standing Rock, as well as Tom Rogers and Joe Young Hawk from Fort Berthold.

Richard Blue Earth. *Todd Hanson*

A regimental history of the 18th Regiment describes the situation on the day that Corporal Blue Earth was killed.

> When the morning of October 9 came, it brought a fog so dense that friend and foe were indistinguishable at ten yards. Under cover of the barrage laid down by the artillery the attack started as scheduled, at 7:30 o'clock....

> In this attack the Germans had concentrated the fire of artillery and machine guns in the zone assigned to the Eighteenth. In the ravine between Hills 272 and 176 the advance was conducted slowly and painfully. Officers and men flattened themselves on the ground and crawled along what depressions they could find from one point of vantage to another. In spite of these precautions there were heavy losses in all grades. It was the heaviest concentration of fire received during the whole campaign.

Richard received the French Fourragère, which is similar to a unit citation award. Richard Blue Earth's body was returned from France to Cannon Ball on Sept. 17, 1921. Burial services for him were held in Cannon Ball on Sept. 19, 1921. Legion members who came from the Albert Grass

Post of Fort Yates were Herbert Keeps Eagle, James Tattoo, Mike Halsey, George Halsey, and J.R. Harmon. The American Legion Post in Cannon Ball, ND, was named in his honor.[16]

**Brave Bull, John.** Army number 508,832; registrant, Sioux County; born, Cannon Ball, ND, March 15, 1897, of American parents; occupation, farmer; inducted at Fort Yates on May 10, 1918; sent to Fort Logan, CO; served in Company G, 8th Ammunition Train, to discharge. Grade: Private 1st Class, Aug. 19, 1918. Discharged at Camp Dodge, IA, on Feb. 1, 1919, as a Private 1st Class.

John was the son of Claude Brave Bull and Agatha Ireland. When he registered for the draft on June 5, 1917, he said he worked as a laborer in Cannon Ball. In August, he met with his local board to tell them he was claiming exemption on account of his being a non-citizen Indian.

After the war, John married Eva Kuntz. They had five children: Alice, Susan, Josephine, John Jr., and Frank. In the 1930 U.S. Census, they are shown as living with John's parents. John Jr. served with the U.S. Navy during WWII, while Frank served in the Army during the Korean War. John was a member of the American Legion Post at Cannon Ball. He passed away in the hospital in Fort Yates on Oct. 18, 1965. He is buried in St. James Cemetery in Cannon Ball.[17]

John Brave Bull. *Todd Hanson*

**Brien, Edward William.** Army number 5,125; registrant, Rolette County; born, Kalispell, MT, Sept. 22, 1896, of American parents; occupation, rancher; enlisted in Company G, 2nd Infantry, North Dakota National Guard at Rolla, on July 13, 1917; called into federal service, World War, on July 15, 1917; served in Company G, 2nd Infantry, North Dakota National Guard, to Oct. 5, 1917; 164th Field Hospital, 116th Sanitary Train, to March 16, 1918; Company B, 302nd Battalion,

Tank Corps, to Aug. 2, 1918; Company B, 301<sup>st</sup> Heavy Battalion, Tank Corps, to Nov. 29, 1918; Company A, 302<sup>nd</sup> Battalion, Tank Corps, to discharge. Grades: Corporal, Aug. 15, 1917; Private, May 14, 1918; overseas from Dec. 11, 1917, to July 13, 1919. Engagement: Offensive: Somme. Discharged at Camp Dodge, IA, on July 19, 1919, as a Private.

The 1910 U.S. Census noted that Edward spoke Cree. He was the son of Gregoire and Betsy (Cardinal) Brien. Betsy died in 1966 at the age of 102. Edward attended the boarding school at Carlisle, PA. When he registered for the draft on June 5, 1917, Edward listed his occupation as laborer. He was a tall man of slender build. Edward served much of his military career with Joseph Warren. They both received training at the AEF Tank Center commanded by Captain George Patton.

In the Census Roll for Turtle Mountain Reservation in 1921, Edward was shown living with his son, Joe. Around 1925, he married Lucy Gardner-Godon. Lucy was the sister of a fellow veteran, William Gardner. The Census Roll for 1930 shows Edward as living in Chicago. By this time, Lucy had left him to go live with her daughter in Phoenix. Sometime after this, Edward returned to Belcourt, where he married Rosina Herman in 1937. They had a son, Francis Willard. Edward worked as a carpenter. He passed away at his home on Feb. 12, 1940, and is buried in St. Ann's Catholic Cemetery at Belcourt. His widow, Rosina (1914-1977), married Clarence Sotendahl. Rosina died in a car accident near Belcourt.[18]

**Brought Plenty, August.** Army number 1,427,432; not a registrant, enlisted prior; born, Fort Yates, ND, May 9, 1899, of American parents; occupation, student; enlisted in Troop D, 1<sup>st</sup> Cavalry, South Dakota National Guard, at Flandreau, SD, on April 4, 1917; called into federal service, World War, on July 15, 1917; served in Troop D, 1<sup>st</sup> Cavalry, South Dakota National Guard, to Oct. 22, 1917; Company D, 136<sup>th</sup> Infantry, to July 15, 1918; Company A, 162<sup>nd</sup> Infantry, to July 31, 1918; Company A, 28<sup>th</sup> Infantry, to discharge. Grade: Private 1<sup>st</sup> Class, Feb. 19, 1919; overseas from June 28, 1918, to Aug. 30, 1919; wounded, severely, Oct 1, 1918. Engagements: Offensives: St. Mihiel; Meuse-Argonne. Defensive Sectors: Ansauville and Saizerais (Lorraine). Discharged at Camp Dodge, IA, on Sept. 24, 1919, as a Private 1<sup>st</sup> Class.

August and his brother, John, were the sons of Charles Brought Plenty and Annie Left Hand Bull. August and his brother were later adopted by Tom Frosted. August most likely was a student at the Flandreau Boarding School when he enlisted in the South Dakota National Guard two days after President Wilson declared war on Germany. On May 9, 1918, August sent a letter to the *Sioux County Pioneer*, thanking them for his subscription. He wrote that reading "the *Pioneer* is just like a letter written to me from my folks back home." At that time he was stationed at Camp Cody, NM, with the 136<sup>th</sup> Infantry, which was a National Guard unit from Minnesota. He added "I am certainly in a good company and the officers are all good to us, as we have an Indian Lieutenant and Sergeant." In the final offensive of the war, August was assigned to Company A, 28<sup>th</sup> Infantry Regiment. The 28<sup>th</sup> and the 26<sup>th</sup> Regiments formed the Second Brigade of the First Infantry Division. On Sept. 30, 1918, the First Division was ordered to replace the 35<sup>th</sup> Division, which had suffered many casualties in the opening days of the Meuse-Argonne Campaign. After a 16-kilometer forced march in a rainstorm, the Division moved into position to the southeast of Exermont. On October 1, the day that Private Brought Plenty was wounded, an officer with the 26<sup>th</sup> Infantry reported that the Germans "pounded the area with high explosives and drenched the ravines and woods with gas, and machine guns and snipers harassed constantly whenever movement was observed." After the Armistice, Joseph Dixon interviewed August, when he stated that "it was hell over there. Wounded in the left hip by a machine gun bullet. In the hospital two months. All right now." August received the French Fourragère and the Purple Heart. August was one of the charter members of the Albert Grass Legion Post at Fort Yates.

In the 1920 U.S. Census, August was living with Thomas and Susie Frosted. In the 1920s, August married Lulu End of Horn. In the 1930 U.S. Census, August and Lulu were living in Corson County with their daughter, Genevieve, as well as Lulu's father, William. Lulu died in 1934. August married Christine Red Horn in Selby, SD, on July 3, 1936. Christine was the widow of George Red Horn, a fellow veteran who had died in 1935. August passed away in the VA Hospital in Minot on Dec. 8, 1956. His son, Cyril, and daughters, Genevieve, Irene, and Rose survived him. He is buried in St. Peters Cemetery in Fort Yates.[19]

**Brought Plenty, John.** Army number 2,558,368; registrant, Sioux County; born, Fort Yates, ND, June 28, 1895, of American parents; occupation, farmer; inducted at Fort Yates on March 4, 1918; sent to Camp Dodge, IA; served in Company A, 351st Infantry, to April 4, 1918; Company F, 132nd Infantry (33rd Infantry Division), to discharge. Grade: Private 1st Class, May 1, 1918; overseas from May 16, 1918, to May 17, 1919. Engagements: Offensives: Somme; Meuse-Argonne. Defensive Sectors: Amiens (Picardy); Verdun-Fromereville and Troyon (Lorraine). Discharged at Camp Dodge, IA, on May 26, 1919, as a Private 1st Class.

Before Private 1st Class Brought Plenty was discharged, his commanding officers were interviewed. Speaking of John, they stated: "Senses very keen, and while acting as Bn. Runner was very efficient finding way through woods and paths, which he had never been over before; has always used good judgement in any task that has been given him; shown ability in reading maps; his work at night has been as good as in daylight. Able to transmit a complicated verbal message without error." John received the French Fourragère.

John was an older brother of August, who also served. In his youth, John was a student at the Indian boarding school in Carlisle, PA. In the Census Roll taken in Standing Rock Reservation in 1917, John and his wife, Emma, had a daughter, Mary Jane. When John registered for the draft on June 5, 1917, he was farming. He is described as a tall man of medium build. While John was in the service, he wrote several letters that were published in the *Sioux County Pioneer*. On Aug. 3, 1918, he wrote: "We just came back from the front line, and we are going to return in a few days. Shells have fallen within 100 ft. of me, and that's close enough. You can hear the shells whistling through the air, and it seems as though they are going to land right on your bean. It is a grand and glorius feeling when they explode and you feel that you are still whole." In 1919, John married Agnes Goodwood in McIntosh, SD. He later married Lucy LaFramboise (1887-1954). In the Census Roll taken at Standing Rock in 1940, John and Lucy had three children: Kenneth, Mary and Victoria. John passed away in the Fort Yates Hospital on Feb. 5, 1966, and is buried in St. Peter's Cemetery in Fort Yates.[20]

**Bruce, Fred.** Army number 186,035; registrant, (not given); born, Belcourt, ND, Aug. 27, 1890, of American parents; occupation, electrician; enlisted in Headquarters Company, 2nd Infantry, North Dakota National Guard, at Harvey, on July 9, 1917; called into federal service, World War, on July 15, 1917; served in Headquarters Company, 2nd Infantry, North Dakota National Guard (Company B, 116th Engineers), to Jan. 5, 1919; Headquarters Detachment, 116th Engineers, to discharge. Grades: Musician 2nd Class, July 28, 1917; Private, Oct. 9, 1917; Corporal, Oct. 10, 1917; Sergeant, May 24, 1918; Sergeant 1st Class, Sept. 17, 1918; overseas from Nov. 26, 1917, to Feb. 23, 1919. Discharged at Camp Dodge, IA, on March 11, 1919, as a Sergeant 1st Class, Surgeon's Certificate of Disability, 5%.

In the Census Roll for the Turtle Mountain Band of Chippewa taken in 1896, Fred and his brother, Robert, are listed with their parents, Joseph and Rosalie Bruce, at Devils Lake. In the 1900 U.S. Census, their parents lived at Leech Lake, MN, while Fred and Robert and their older brother, Lewis, were students at Fort Totten. Fred and Robert undoubtedly were members of the band at the school, as they both became interested in serving in the Army band. When Fred registered for the draft in June 1917, he was farming near Medicine Lake, MT. Fred was a tall man of stout build. In the 1920 U.S. Census, Fred was farming with his father in Sheridan County, MT. His parents later lived near Froid. In the 1930 U.S. Census, Fred was working as a plumber in Caliente, NV. Fred was living in Minnesota when his father died in Belcourt in 1933. When Fred applied for his Social Security number on Dec. 2, 1936, he was working for Montgomery Ward & Co. in Albuquerque, NM. In the 1940 U.S. Census, he was shown as working as a plumber on a construction project southeast of Phoenix, in Pinal County, AZ. Fred lived in Arizona when he passed away in June 1964.[21]

**Bruce, Robert Emil.** Army number 186,020; registrant, Benson County; born, Belcourt, ND, Sept. 15, 1893, of Canadian-American parents; occupation, tailor; enlisted in Headquarters Company, 2nd Infantry, North Dakota National Guard, at Harvey, on July 9, 1917; called into federal service, World War, on July 15, 1917; served in Headquarters Company, 2nd Infantry, North Dakota National Guard (Company B, 116th Engineers), to discharge. Grades: Musician 1st Class, July 28, 1917; Private, Oct. 9, 1917; Sergeant, Oct. 10, 1917; Sergeant 1st Class, May 24, 1918; Master Engineer, Junior Grade, Oct. 9, 1918; overseas from Nov. 26, 1917, to Feb. 23, 1919. Discharged at Camp Dodge, IA, on March 11, 1919, as a Master Engineer, Junior Grade.

Robert and his older brother, Fred, were students at the Fort Totten Boarding School in 1900. Robert later attended the boarding school at Carlisle, PA. He learned to play the cornet. In 1912, Robert was a member of the Shields Cornet Band at Shields, ND. He also ran a tailor shop over the Murphy Pool Hall. When the war broke out, he had a tailor's shop in Leeds, ND. He and his brother enlisted at Harvey on July 9, 1917.

Robert and Fred both served in the same unit during the war, enlisting as musicians. Shortly after they arrived in France, their band performed a musical program at Christmas of 1917. Gen. Hunter Liggett referred to their unit as "The Million Dollar Band," following their performance. After the war they moved to their parents' farm in Sheridan County, MT. In the 1920 U.S. Census, Robert was working as a traveling musician. He became a member of the concert band, also known as the "Million Dollar Band." Shortly after Robert's discharge from the Army, the band gave a performance in Lakota, ND. Martin Lafrombois also became a member of that civilian band. In the 1930 U.S. Census, Robert lived in Minot and worked as a musician and band instructor. Robert was living in Minnesota when his father died in Belcourt in 1933. As given in the Census Roll for the Turtle Mountain Reservation taken in 1937, Robert was married to Dorothy Neil and had a son, Robert. They lived in Lawrence, KS. In the 1940 U.S. Census, he is shown as living in Elkhart, IN, where he was a field supervisor for the salesmen of a musical instrument company. For many years, Elkhart was known as the "Band Instrument Capital of the World." In his later years, Robert moved back to Belcourt. He passed away on Nov. 25, 1968, in the VA Hospital at Hot Springs, SD, and is buried in Black Hills National Cemetery (Section C, Site 976).[22]

**Brunelle, Patrice Frank.** Army number, none; registrant, Rolette County; born, Belcourt, ND, May 26, 1897, of American parents; occupation, farmer; enlisted in Company G, 2nd Infantry, North Dakota National Guard, at Rolla, on July 14, 1917; called into federal service, World War, on July 15, 1917; served in Company G, 2nd Infantry, North Dakota National Guard, to discharge. Discharged at Camp Greene, NC, on Oct. 9, 1917, as a Private; Surgeon's Certificate of Disability.

Pat was the son of John and Julia Brunelle. In 1918, Pat married Mary J. Peronteau. They had ten children. Pat had worked as a laborer in road construction. Mary passed away on Sept. 17, 1936, with Pat passing away from tuberculosis on July 22, 1937. His children, Patrick Jr., Mary Rose, Emma, Helen Jane, and Philip Jerome survived him. Pat was buried in St. John's Catholic Cemetery. Members of the Fred C. Wagner American Legion Post conducted military rites.[23]

**Buckley, Charles T.** Army number 3,075,270; not a registrant, under age; born, Fort Rice, ND, August 1896, of American parents; occupation, rancher; enlisted at Bismarck on June 2, 1918; sent to Jefferson Barracks, MO; served in Troop K, 312th Cavalry, to Aug. 13, 1918; Battery F, 61st Field Artillery, to discharge. Discharged at Camp Dodge, IA, on Jan. 11, 1919, as a Private.

Charles had two brothers, James and John, who also served. Their father, John P. Buckley, had served in the 14th Iowa Infantry during the Civil War era. Their mother was Monica (Cankawastewin). Their older sister, Mandy, married Turkey Track Bill Molash. Charles enlisted shortly after his brother, James, died at Camp Dodge, IA. After the war, Charles married Hazel Wells. In the Census Roll for Standing Rock taken in 1930, Hazel and her children, Edwin, Beverly and Becky, were listed as living in Tacoma, WA. In the 1930 U.S. Census, Charles was listed as divorced and working as a miner near Missoula, MT. Charles later moved to Portland, OR. In the 1940 U.S. Census, he is shown as living with his wife, Philomena, and her daughters, Marcella and Mary. The census also showed that he had been living on the Standing Rock Reservation in 1935. Charles later married Elsie, who survived him, along with his three children, Edwin, Becky, and Beverly. He passed away in Portland on March 2, 1966 and is buried Williamette National Cemetery, (Section F, Site 5207).[24]

**Buckley, James Francis.** Army number 2,559,182; registrant, Sioux County; born, Fort Rice, ND, Sept. 2, 1892, of American parents; occupation, laborer; inducted at Fort Yates on March 29, 1918; sent to Camp Dodge, IA; served in Company A, 1st Battalion, 163rd Depot Brigade, to death. Died of pneumonia at Camp Dodge, IA, on April 15, 1918. Buried in family plot at Fort Rice Cemetery.
James came down with pneumonia a few days after he arrived at Camp Dodge.[25]

**Buckley, John J.** Army number 466,639; not a registrant, over age; born, Fort Rice, ND, Dec. 30, 1880, of American parents; occupation, rancher; enlisted at Bismarck on March 4, 1918; sent to Jefferson Barracks, MO; served in Company E, 5th Engineers (7th Division), to discharge. Grades: Private 1st Class, Aug. 22, 1918; Private, Oct. 4, 1918; overseas from July 31, 1918, to Jan. 6, 1919; wounded, slightly, Oct. 18, 1918. Engagement: Defensive Sector: Puvenelle (Lorraine). Discharged at Camp Grant, IL, on Feb. 24, 1919, as a Private.

In the Census Roll for Standing Rock taken in 1913, John is listed with his son, Henry. John was stationed at Corpus Christi, TX, when his brother died in April 1918. He received leave to return home for the funeral. In the 1930 U.S. Census, John lived near Raleigh, ND. In the Census Roll taken at Standing Rock in 1934, John is listed with Nellie (Maggie) Blackhoop (1897-1986), and her daughter, Helen. Maggie was the sister of Joseph Blackhoop, a fellow veteran. In the 1940 U.S. Census, John and Nellie were living with their children, Theresa and William. John passed away at his home on March 10, 1955. He is buried in the family plot at the Fort Rice Cemetery.[26]

**Burr, Oscar.** Army number 3,775,360; registrant, Dunn County; born, Fort Berthold, ND, Dec. 26, 1894, of American parents; occupation, stockman; inducted at Manning on Aug. 8, 1918; sent to Jefferson Barracks, MO; served in Company D, 10th Battalion, Infantry Replacement and Training Camp, Camp MacArthur, TX, to Aug. 30, 1918; Company B, 10th Battalion, Infantry Replacement and Training Camp, Camp MacArthur, TX, to Sept. 18, 1918; 38th Company,

Infantry, Camp MacArthur September Automatic Replacement Draft, to Feb. 6, 1919; 1<sup>st</sup> Replacement Depot, St. Aignan Convalescent Camp, Hospital Center, Army Post office No. 939, to March 6, 1919; Casual, in hospital, to April 4, 1919; Rest Camp Section, Registration Station A, Army Post Office No. 712, to June 1, 1919; Le Mans Casual Company No. 1251, to July 5, 1919; Casual Detachment No. 977, Demobilization Camp, Camp Dodge, IA, to discharge; overseas from Sept. 29, 1918, to July 5, 1919. Discharged at Camp Dodge, IA, on July 11, 1919, as a Private.

Oscar was also known on the census rolls as Oscar Horn. In the 1910 U.S. Census, Oscar was a student at the boarding school in Wahpeton. In the 1915 N.D. Census, he was still a student at Wahpeton. He first married Dora Smith, who was a sister to John Smith, a fellow veteran. Oscar's half sister, Pearl Burr, married Walter Young Bear, also a fellow veteran. When Oscar registered for the draft on June 8, 1917, he was raising livestock with his father near Elbowoods. On Oct. 26, 1925, he married Mary Wounded Face (1904-1977). In the Census Roll for Fort Berthold taken in 1939, Oscar and Mary are listed with four children, Christine, Newton, Violet, and Willard. Newton served with the U.S. Army during the Korean Conflict. Oscar ranched with his family near Mandaree, until moving to Watford City in 1969. He passed away in Watford City on Feb. 19, 1970. His wife and children, including Mary, Marilyn, Rachel, Christine, Newton, and Harold survived him. He was buried in Snow Bird Cemetery near New Town. Military rites were conducted by the Carl E. Rogen Post 29, American Legion, of Watford City.[27]

# C

**Carufel, Arthur Oliver.** Navy number 1,207,750; not a registrant, enlisted prior; born, Belcourt, ND, June 6, 1896, of Canadian-American parents; occupation, laborer; enlisted in the Navy at Minneapolis, MN, on May 25, 1917; home awaiting orders until Aug. 9, 1917; served at Naval Training Station, Great Lakes, IL, to Dec. 27, 1917; Naval Training Camp, Charleston, SC, to Feb. 21, 1918; Naval Air Station, Miami, FL, to Nov. 11, 1918. Grades: Apprentice Seaman, 99 days; Seaman 2nd Class, 212 days; Seaman, 224 days. Discharged at Minneapolis, MN, on June 30, 1919, as a Seaman.

In the 1910 U.S. Census, Arthur lived in Thorne, where his father operated a hotel. Arthur's brother, Adolph, was a student at Haskell Boarding School when he registered for the draft. After the war, Arthur moved to Spokane, WA. On March 8, 1922, he married Doris Gaskill. In the 1930 U.S. Census, Arthur is shown as living in Spokane with his wife, Jennie and her daughter, Vivian. Arthur was working as a truck driver for a lumber mill. He drowned in the Spokane River on Feb. 9, 1935. He is buried in Fairmount Memorial Park, near Spokane.[1]

**Chapman, Guy George.** Army number 2,143,707; registrant, Sioux County; born, Santee, NE, July 24, 1895, of American parents; occupation, farmer; inducted at Fort Yates on Sept. 18, 1917; sent to Camp Dodge, IA; served in Battery D, 338th Field Artillery, to April 1, 1918; Company K, 326th Infantry (82nd Division), to June 8, 1919. Grade: Corporal, Aug. 12, 1918; overseas from April 29, 1918, to May 29, 1919; wounded, slightly, Oct. 15, 1918. Engagements: Offensive: St. Mihiel; Meuse-Argonne. Defensive Sector: Marbache and Lucey (Lorraine). Discharged at Camp Dodge, IA, on June 8, 1919, as a Corporal.

When Guy registered for the draft on June 5, 1917, he was farming near McIntosh, SD. His brother, Joseph also registered with him. Guy returned to Fort Yates on June 12, 1919. The local paper reported that he had been wounded in the right wrist, as well as being gassed during the campaign in the Argonne Forest. The day that Corporal Chapman was wounded, the 326th Regiment was fighting around St. Juvin and helped drive back a German attack. The left flank of the 326th Infantry was supported by the 306th Infantry, in which Walter Young Bear served. By the end of the day, the 82nd Division had been reduced to one-third its original strength.

After the war, Guy married Mayme Silk in McIntosh on Dec. 5, 1919. They had four children, James, Mildred, Clement, and Rena. Mayme passed away on June 6, 1930. Their son, James, served with the US Marine Corps in the Pacific during WWII. Guy later married Mable Carrier (1910-1988). Guy was a member of the American Legion in Fort Yates. He passed away in a Bismarck hospital on June 20, 1972, and is buried at St. Luke's Episcopal Church cemetery in Fort Yates.[2]

**Chapman, Joseph.** Army number 2,141,749; registrant, Sioux County; born, Santee, NE, Nov. 26, 1888, of American parents; occupation, farmer; inducted at McLaughlin, SD, on March 30, 1918; sent to Camp Dodge, IA; served in 163rd Depot Brigade, to April 20, 1918; Company E, 139th Infantry (35th Division), to discharge; overseas from May 2, 1918, to April 24, 1919. Engagements: Offensive: Meuse-Argonne. Defensive Sectors: Gerardmer (Alsace); Grange-le-Comte (Lorraine). Discharged at Camp Dodge, IA, on May 2, 1919, as a Private.

In the Census Roll for the Santee Sioux (Nebraska) taken in 1895, Joseph and Guy were listed with their parents, Joseph and Sarah, along with three other siblings. Joseph's younger brother, Guy, was one of the first men to be drafted from Sioux County in September 1917. When Joseph registered for the draft on June 5, 1917, he was farming near McIntosh, SD.

While serving in France, Private Chapman was a company runner, his duties being to carry messages from company to company. Later he became a liaison, carrying messages from regiment to regiment. Finally he acted as battalion scout, which meant scouting at night and cutting through barbed wire entanglements in No Man's Land. After the Armistice, Joseph's commanding officer, Capt. George Klinkerfuss, was interviewed. In regard to Private Chapman, he stated "This man was under me as intelligence officer, 2nd Battalion, and proved himself individual in scouting. He was used as a runner on emergencies and proved himself doubly value (sic) in that capacity, as a trail once gone over was forever familiar."

In December 1918, Chapman sent a letter back to the *Sioux County Pioneer* describing his experiences in France. His regiment spent time in the towns of Muhlbach, Metxeral and Sondernach on the Alsace Front, before they became part of the drive through the Argonne Forest. He wrote that he was enjoying a happy life in France. Once the fighting was over, the men of the 139th Infantry spent the winter of 1918-1919 in rough, unheated billets in the vicinity of Commercy, France, not far from the Meuse River. On May 6, 1919, a reception, sponsored by his parents, was held in Fort Yates for Joseph and a few other returned soldiers. At that time, his brother, Guy, had not yet been discharged. Joseph indicated that he enjoyed serving as a scout in France. He had brought back a souvenir cup made from a French 75mm shell. In July 1919, he married Emma Cold Hand. They later were divorced. In the 1930 U.S. Census, he was living with a cousin on the Pine Ridge Reservation. In the 1930s he was admitted to the VA Hospital in Hot Springs for treatment of a back injury. In the 1940 U.S. Census, he was living in Fort Yates. Joseph passed away in the Fort Yates hospital on May 8, 1965. He is buried at St. Luke's Cemetery in Fort Yates.[3]

**Charlebois, Ernest Francis.** Army number 985,851; registrant, Rolette County; born, Belcourt, ND, Aug. 2, 1895, of Canadian-American parents; occupation, student; enlisted in the Medical Reserve Corps, at Fort Sheridan, IL, on Dec. 10, 1917; called into service on July 17, 1918; sent to Camp Grant, IL; served in Central Department Surgeon's Office, Chicago, IL, to July 17, 1918; Base Hospital No. 58, Medical Department, to Feb. 10, 1919; Headquarters, 4th Battalion, 22nd Engineers, to May 9, 1919; Medical Detachment, Company F, 2nd Battalion, 22nd Engineers, to discharge. Grade: Private 1st Class, July 26, 1918; overseas from Aug. 23, 1918, to July 12, 1919. Discharged at Camp Grant, IL, on July 22, 1919, as a Private 1st Class.

Ernest grew up on the Turtle Mountain Reservation and was the son of Alexander and Christine Charlebois. In the 1900 U.S. Census, his father's occupation is shown as "Indian trader." When Ernest registered for the draft on June 5, 1917, he was living in Belcourt, and listed his occupation as dental student. He had studied dentistry at Marquette University. The 22nd Engineers that Ernest served with was a light railroad outfit. In the 1920 U.S. Census, Ernest was working in Bottineau County as a dentist. In the 1925 North Dakota State Census, he was working in Wilton. He married Mary Elizabeth Duffy in St. Thomas, ND, on May 4, 1926. In the 1930 U.S. Census, Ernest and Mary lived in St. Maries, ID, where he worked as a dentist. That same year he applied for a license to practice dentistry in Washington State. He practiced dentistry in several cities in Washington. He was a member of the James J. Sexton Post No. 224, VFW. He last worked in Aberdeen, WA, for ten years, before passing away suddenly on Dec. 6, 1948. His wife and two sons, Gerald Michael and Robert survived him. Gerald changed his name to Michael Forest, and is known under that name as a very talented actor. Ernest is buried at Fern Hill, in Aberdeen, WA.[4]

**Chase, Daniel.** Army number 4,041,734; registrant, Mercer County; born, Elbowoods, ND, Jan. 23, 1894, of American parents; occupation, farmer; inducted at Stanton on July 24, 1918; sent to

Camp Custer, MI; served in 19th Company, 5th Battalion, 160th Depot Brigade, to Aug 16, 1918; Supply Company, 77th Infantry, to Sept. 14, 1918; Veterinary Corps, 40th Field Artillery, to death. Died of broncho pneumonia (sic), at Camp Custer, MI, Oct. 13, 1918; buried at Elbowoods, ND.

When Dan registered for the draft on June 5, 1917, he was farming and raising livestock. Shortly after this he married Mattie Hall. They had a son, Daniel Jr., who was born about two months before Dan was inducted. After Dan passed away, the local paper reported that his death was from a relapse of the Spanish Influenza. Dan's grave has been moved to the Chase Cemetery.[5]

Dan Chase was stationed at Camp Custer, MI. *Four Bears Museum*

**Cloud, Benjamin D.** Army number, none; registrant, Burleigh County; born, Fort Shaw, MT, Oct 21, 1888, of American parents; occupation, stenographer; enlisted in Headquarters Company, 1st Infantry, North Dakota National Guard, at Bismarck, on May 26, 1917; called into service, World War, on July 15, 1917; served in Headquarters Company, 1st Infantry, North Dakota National Guard (Headquarters Company, 164th Infantry), to discharge. Grade: Regimental Sergeant Major, July 10, 1917. Discharged at Camp Mills, NY, on Nov. 28, 1917, as a Regimental Sergeant Major, to accept commission. Commissioned 2nd Lieutenant, Nov. 30, 1917; assigned to 164th Infantry, to Feb. 6, 1919; 305th Company, Military Police Corps, to discharge; overseas from Dec. 15, 1917, to Sept. 15, 1919. Discharged at Camp Dix, NJ, on Sept. 19, 1919, as a 2nd Lieutenant. Previous military record: North Dakota National Guard from Feb. 2, 1914, to Feb. 15, 1917, including Mexican border duty.

In the Standing Rock Census Roll taken in 1904, Ben is listed with his mother as Benedict Dog Cloud. At Christmas of that year, Frank Fiske took a photo of Ben serving as an altar boy in the church at Fort Yates. In 1910 he became a student at the Carlisle Boarding School. He was given the opportunity to learn the telegraphy trade. He was a successful student. He also took a year of coursework at Dickinson College, which is adjacent to the boarding school. After graduating from Carlisle, he applied to attend Haskell Institute in Lawrence, KS. He may also have been a teacher at the Bismarck Boarding School.

Shortly after President Wilson declared war on Germany, Ben sent a letter to Captain T.S. Henry of the ND National Guard, stating "Have discussed the war situation frequently…with my wife and she has consented to let me go back in, so will reenlist at once." When he registered for the draft in 1917, he was working as a salesman for A.E. Jones in Bismarck. His registration indicates that he was a tall man of slender build. At that time, he used the name of Benjamin D. Cloud. Ben was considered one of the first Native Americans to receive an officer's commission in WWI. When he sailed to France, his wife was living in Minneapolis, MN.

In January 1919, Lt. Cloud was interviewed by Lt. Eddy, who then submitted the following report to Joseph Dixon. "When Lt. Cloud arrived in France with the 164th Infantry, he tried to get duty at the front, but owing to his knowledge of office work and the illness of the Adjutant in his organization, he was appointed adjutant and held that office throughout the different periods of his service. At the present time he is in charge of the Service Battalion at Langres and Dijon. During his service with the Supply Co., A.B.C., 1st Bn., 41st Division, he came in contact with quite a number of Indians, and endeavored to get them into his battalion, which at that time was a signal battalion. His idea was to show them how they could listen in and make use of their language in outwitting the enemy. In addition to being an attorney, Cloud was an expert telegraph operator (line), and while in charge of the signal battalion he conceived the idea of getting together as many Indians as possible for instruction in telegraphing and signaling. The idea of using Indian language as a code also occurred to him, but he was unable to put his plans into execution." A problem that needed to be overcome was the native language vocabularies lacked modern military terms. Many Indian languages were holophrastic, meaning that they expressed a whole phrase in a single word. The Navahos during WWII later overcame these problems.

After the war, Lt. Cloud was a member of the Officers Reserve Corps. In the Standing Rock Census Roll for 1922, Benedict Dog Cloud is listed with his wife, Doris, and their daughter, Donna Irene, who was born in 1920. In the 1930 U.S. Census, the family was living in Minneapolis, where Benjamin is listed as a physician/chiropractor. The Standing Rock Census Roll for 1936 shows the family still living in Minneapolis. Ben may have served during WWII also. Ben passed away at the VA Medical Center in Dayton, OH, on March 26, 1959. His daughter, Donna, of Indianapolis, IN, survived him. He is buried in Dayton National Cemetery, Section 10, Row 25, Site 34.[6]

**Court, Joseph.** Army number 3,681,398; registrant, Benson County; born, Fort Totten, ND, Dec. 23, 1896, of American parents; occupation, farmer; inducted at Minnewaukan on June 27, 1918; sent to Camp Dodge, IA; served in Headquarters Detachment, Motor Battalion, 313th Ammunition Train (88th Infantry Division), to discharge; overseas from Aug. 17, 1918, to May 29, 1919. Engagement: Defensive Sector: Center (Alsace). Discharged at Camp Dodge, IA, on June 11, 1919, as a Private.

In the Devils Lake Sioux Census Roll taken in 1906, Joseph lived with his mother and stepfather, Harriet and Simon Court. In the 1910 U.S. Census, he was a student at the Fort Totten boarding school. After the war Joseph married Julia Merrick, a sister to Joseph Merrick. Court and Merrick had served together in the 313th Ammo Train. Joseph and Julia had a daughter, Mary. After Julia passed away in 1930, Joseph married Mary Abraham. Joseph worked as a laborer. In the 1940 U.S. Census, he was living with his mother and sister in Benson County. He passed away at his home on Jan. 6, 1970, and is buried in St. Michael's Cemetery.[7]

**Crow Necklace, Thomas.** Army number 2,858,763; registrant, Sioux County; born, Fort Yates, ND, May 5, 1894, of American parents; occupation, car repairer; inducted at Fort Yates on April 20, 1918; sent to Camp Dodge, IA; served in Headquarters Detachment, 175th Infantry, to Sept. 12, 1918; Company B, 338th Machine Gun Battalion (88th Division), to discharge; overseas from Aug. 7, 1918, to June 4, 1919. Engagement: Defensive Sector: Center (Alsace). Discharged at Camp Dodge, IA, on June 15, 1919, as a Private.

In the Standing Rock Census Roll taken in 1896, Thomas, also known as Opijataska, lived with his father and mother, Frank Crow Necklace and Meets, as well as a brother, Louis. Thomas attended schools at both the Flandreau Boarding School and the Carlisle Boarding School. He played left halfback on the school's football team from 1911-13 alongside of Jim Thorpe.

During the war, Private Crow Necklace's commanding officer noted that Crow Necklace "demonstrated fitness for machine gun." While the soldiers waited for space on the transport ships back to the States, they took part in sports activities, as well as drill exercises. Thomas played football for the 88th Division's team, which was known as the Hunhuskers. According to the *Camp Dodger,* the in-country division newsletter, the football team for the 88th played some close games against other units. For uniforms, the men wore aviation caps for head guards, Red Cross sweaters for jerseys, padded blue denim fatigue trousers for pants, stockings bought in Paris and Nancy, and garrison cleats for shoes. The 88th Division had special medals designed by a Paris business. These medals, shaped like the unit insignia, were presented to winners in the various athletic contests held for the soldiers.

Thomas was one of the many young men who played baseball for the Fort Yates team after the war. He played the position of catcher. After the war he married Alice Has Horns. In the 1930 U.S. Census, Thomas and Alice were shown as living in Corson County with their children, Thamar, Thomas Jr., Christina, Viola, Andrew and Serena. Their son, Thomas Jr., served in WWII and died of his wounds in France in 1945, and is buried in the Black Hills National Cemetery. The family later moved to Lemmon, SD. Thomas passed away in Lemmon on March 1, 1962. He is buried in the Episcopal Cemetery at Bullhead, SD.[8]

**Crow Skin, Louis.** Louis was born in South Dakota on June 7, 1894. In the Census Roll for Standing Rock taken in 1896, Louis is listed with his father, Andrew (Kangihola), and his mother, Sophia (Appearing Day). In the 1900 U.S. Census, they are listed as living in North Dakota. Louis was inducted in South Dakota and sent to Camp Funston, KS, on June 24, 1918. Less than a month later, he was sent to Camp Dodge, IA, where the various regiments that formed the 88th Division were finishing their training. Louis was assigned to Company I, 352nd Infantry Regiment, which left the U.S. on Aug. 16, 1918. The 352nd Infantry remained in France until June 1, 1919. A photo of Louis in his uniform was published in *Memoirs of France and the Eighty-Eighth Division.*

Louis Crow Skin
Co. I, Kenel, S. D. (Taken in France)
*Memoirs of France and the Eighty-Eighth Division*

After the war, Louis returned to the Kenel area. He had a reputation as a "speedy baseball pitcher." Louis served as commander of the Martin Yellowfat American Legion Post in Kenel in 1927. In the 1930 U.S. Census, he worked as a farm laborer and lived with the Vermund Hand family. On Feb. 8, 1934, he married Philomine Sack. In the Census Roll taken in 1939, Louis and Philomine are listed with their three children, Henry, Ursula and Agatha. Philomine passed away on Dec. 12, 1941. Louis later moved to Fort Yates. He passed away in the hospital in Fort Yates on July 2, 1965, and is buried in the Catholic Cemetery in Kenel.[9]

# D

**Dancing Bull, Robert.** Army number 4,705,777; registrant, McLean County; born, Fort Berthold, ND, Sept. 30, 1897, of American parents; occupation, farmer; inducted at Washburn on Aug. 28, 1918; sent to Camp Lewis, WA; served in 44th Infantry, to discharge. Grade: Private 1st Class, Nov. 13, 1918. Discharged at Fort Lawton, WA, on April 4, 1919, as a Private 1st Class.

In the Gros Ventre (Hidatsa) Census Roll for 1909, Robert is listed with his parents, Dancing Bull (Kirapiwakilisi) and Bug Woman, and two brothers, Jackson and Joseph. Robert attended the Shell Creek School, as well as the Bismarck Boarding School. After four years at Bismarck, he transferred to Haskell Institute in Lawrence, KS. He returned to North Dakota when his father became ill, shortly before the start of the war. Robert served with Mark Necklace. Their regiment was part of the 13th Infantry Division, which completed its training around Nov. 1, 1918. They were not sent to France. Robert became a member of the Clarence Spotted Wolf-John Irwin, Jr., American Legion Post. After the war, he farmed and ranched south of Van Hook with his nephew. Robert was a member of the Shell Creek District Livestock Association. Their ranching operation was terminated in 1953 by the construction of the Garrison Reservoir. During the 1930s, Robert worked as an assistant leader at the CCC Camp located on the reservation. In the late 1940s, Robert changed his name to Robert Cherries. In 1953 he moved to New Town and became a deacon of the Shell Creek Congregational Church. In October 1961, he was elected pastor of the Shell Creek Congregation. He passed away at the New Town Nursing Home on Nov. 15, 1973. He is buried in the Holy Family Catholic Cemetery.[1]

**Dauphanais, Nicholas F.** Army number 2,704,195; registrant, Rolette County; born, Fargo, D. T., July 18, 1885, of American parents; occupation, farmer; inducted at Rolla on June 24, 1918; sent to Camp Dodge, IA; served in Company M, 352nd Infantry, to Oct. 1, 1918; Supply Company, 352nd Infantry (88th Infantry Division), to discharge; overseas from Aug. 16, 1918, to

June 1, 1919. Engagements: Defensive Sector: Center (Alsace). Discharged at Camp Dodge, IA, on June 14, 1919, as a Private.

In the 1900 U.S. Census, Nicholas was attending the Fort Totten Boarding School. Nicholas was living in Belcourt when he registered for the draft. He was working as a farm laborer for J.W. Noel. He was a man of medium height with a slender build. He indicated that he had "bad eyes" and needed to wear glasses. Nicholas traveled to Europe with Company M on the S.S. *City of Exeter*. The former English semi-freighter and passenger ship had sailed between Liverpool and Calcutta, and had a crew of men from India. Upon arriving in England, the ship continued up the Manchester canal to the inland port. The men reported that English youngsters ran for miles following the boat and picking up the coins that were thrown to them. Upon arrival in France, one of their more extended billets was at Vezelois, where they spent six weeks. They were issued steel helmets and gas masks and were required to wear them at all times. While their unit was in the trenches in the Alsace Sector, only one man from Company M was killed by enemy fire. Toward the end of November, the 352nd was billeted at Lucey, where the soldiers performed close order drill, and then "policed" the grounds with brooms. When it came time for the regiment to move to another town, Companies K and M were held back to do a final policing. Once completed, K and M companies marched with full packs to Bonnet, which was 32 miles away. "They made it by midnight. Their rolling kitchen was drawn by horses behind the company, but together with the distance, proved too much for the horses and was brought up the following day." The 352nd spent about five months in Bonnet. They got to know this 500-year-old town very well. It was not all hard work. Apparently, it was common for men to drop into the supply room for a game of poker. This was where Private Dauphanais was detailed. No doubt his knowledge of French was a great help to communicating with the local people. The men spent almost seven months at the peacetime activities. Company M sailed back on the USS *Pocahontas*. By June of 1919, they were very glad to be back in the United States. One of Dauphanais' fellow soldiers composed a poem entitled "Ode to be chanted as the *Pocahontas* pulls away from France and the band begins to play."

> Farewell, oh misty land,
> Oh hazy shore,
> Farewell, oh rainy hours,
> Wet to the corps-
> Goodbye billets dreary, dour,
> Perfumed with the fragrance
> Of valuable manure.
> Adieu, Bonnet and Vezelois
> And Gondrecourt.

After the war, he continued to farm for a number of years. In the 1920 Census he was working for Alphonse Tetrault in Towner County. Alphonse was also a veteran. In his later years Nicholas moved to Fargo, where he worked as a cook in a café. He never married. He passed away in the VA Hospital in Fargo on Jan. 18, 1956, and is buried in Fort Snelling National Cemetery, Section G, Site 3535.[2]

**Davis, Frank.** Army number 2,704,197; registrant, Rolette County; born, Belcourt, D.T., Sept. 11, 1886, of American parents; occupation, farmer; inducted at Rolla on June 24, 1918; sent to Camp Dodge, IA; served in Company L, 352nd Infantry (88th Division), to discharge; overseas from Aug. 16, 1918, to June 1, 1919. Engagement: Defensive Sector: Center (Alsace). Discharged at Camp Dodge, IA, on June 14, 1919, as a Private.

During the war, Frank served in the Company L, 352<sup>nd</sup> Infantry Regiment. He had received his stateside training at Camp Dodge. The 88<sup>th</sup> Division left the camp on August 9, heading for New York. Along the way, their Nickel Plate train stopped east of Cleveland. 500 men from Companies L and M went swimming in Lake Erie. By the time the men climbed back up the muddy bank to the train, many were dirtier than when they first went in the water. Many of the men in the 3<sup>rd</sup> Battalion of the 352<sup>nd</sup> Infantry sailed aboard the S.S. *Ulysses,* which had been an English cattle transport that had been repainted in camouflage colors. Some of the men saw a pod of whales following the ship for awhile. The 352<sup>nd</sup> Infantry saw active duty in the Alsace Sector from the middle of October to early November. Following the Armistice, the division was billeted in the villages of Bonnet and Ribeaucourt. Afterward, the men indicated that they would "never forget those two French towns. They policed and swept every square inch of them. They knew every turn, every house. They had walked post past its barns and houses, built one to the other, until they knew every window, every iron bar, every door." When the fighting was over, Private Davis' commanding officer reported that Davis was an "exceptional good soldier and willing worker, causing no trouble whatever. Lack of education his only drawback. Regarded as a very good man by whites."

In the 1920 U.S. Census, Frank was living with his parents, Joseph and Josephine Davis. Frank remained single. In the 1930 U.S. Census, Frank was living with Charles and Beatrice Poitra. Charles was also a veteran. Beatrice was Frank's cousin. He remained single. Frank worked as a laborer for the railroad. He passed away in Belcourt on Sept. 17, 1945. He is buried in St. Michael's Cemetery.[3]

William Deane. *Four Bears Museum*

**Deane, William J.** Army number 3,769,502; not a registrant, under age; born, Elbowoods, ND, July 11, 1897, of American parents; occupation, farmer; enlisted at Bismarck on July 22, 1918; sent to Jefferson Barracks, MO; served in Company L, 43<sup>rd</sup> Infantry, to discharge. Grade: Private 1<sup>st</sup> Class, Oct. 1, 1918. Discharged at Camp Dodge, IA, on May 31, 1919, as a Private 1<sup>st</sup> Class.

In the Arikara Census Roll taken in 1910, Bill is listed with his parents, William and Grace, as well as his sister, Mary, and brothers, Samuel and Michael. Bill attended school at Armstong and the Wahpeton Boarding School. He enlisted in Bismarck shortly after his 21st birthday. Bill was stationed with the 43rd Infantry Regiment, which was part of the 15th Infantry Division. The 15th Division was trained at Camp Logan, near Houston, TX. Three other men from the Fort Berthold Reservation were also part of the 43rd Regiment, but in different companies. They were Henry Perkins, Andrew Reed and Philip Star. After the war, Bill's sister, Mary, married Fred Wheeler, a fellow veteran from Elbowoods. In 1920 Bill married Leona Yellow Bird (1901-1971), who was a sister to Charles Yellow Bird, also a fellow veteran.

Bill, also known as Lone Chief, was the last remaining sub-chief of the Arikara. From 1913-1921 he was noted as an outstanding saddle bronc rider in many states. Throughout most of his life, he ranched and was the first rancher on the reservation to raise Herefords. He retired in 1960. He was involved in tribal government and served on the tribal council, holding the position of treasurer. He also held positions with the Bureau of Indian Affairs as relocation officer and credit officer. He was a life member of the American Legion and an active member of the Joseph Young Hawk Post No. 253 at Elbowoods, serving as commander several times. He later re-organized the post that became the Joseph Young Hawk-Elmer Bear Post No. 253 of Whiteshield.

Bill was a member of the Prairie Sod Village band, and spoke fluent Arikara and Hidatsa. He was recognized as a linguistic and cultural authority. Bill passed away on Jan. 23, 1982, in the Garrison Memorial Hospital. His children, Gerald, Marie, Marcella, Delores, Katherine and Kenneth survived him. His son Gerald served in the U.S. Navy during the Korean Conflict, and Kenneth was an officer in the Navy. Bill is buried in the Scout Cemetery near Whiteshield.[4]

**Decoteau, John B.** Army number, none; registrant, (not given); born, Belcourt, ND, April 27, 1893, of (nationality of parents not given); occupation, (not given); enlisted in Company G, 2nd Infantry, North Dakota National Guard, at Rolla, on July 16, 1917; served in Company G, 2nd Infantry, North Dakota National Guard, to discharge. Discharged on Aug. 15, 1917, as a Private, Surgeon's Certificate of Disability, 12 ½ %.

In the Census Roll for the Turtle Mountain Reservation taken in 1910, John is listed with his parents, Daniel and Judie. John married Mary Jane Vondal of Belcourt in 1916. He worked as a laborer. In the 1940 U.S. Census, John was living in rural Bismarck. He lived there for several years before returning to Belcourt. He passed away in the hospital in Belcourt on May 7, 1965. His wife and six sons, Joe, Johnny, Larry, Ernest, Roy, and Francis, as well as three daughters, Mary, Celia and Florence, survived him. His son, Ernest, served in the U.S. Navy during WWII. John is buried in St. Ann's Cemetery in Belcourt.[5]

**Decoteau, Napoleon.** Army number 465,355; not a registrant, under age; born, Belcourt, ND, April 13, 1899, of American parents; occupation, farmer; enlisted at Flandreau, SD, on April 13, 1918; sent to Jefferson Barracks, MO; served in Company L, 48th Infantry, to discharge. Grade: Private 1st Class, Dec. 20, 1918. Discharged at Camp Dodge, IA, on Feb. 27, 1919, as a Private.

In the Turtle Mountain Census Roll taken in 1899, Napoleon lived with his mother and father, La Rose and Norbert Decoteau, as well as several brothers and sisters. Napolean likely was attending the boarding school at Flandreau when he enlisted on his 19th birthday. During the war, the mission of the 48th Infantry Regiment was to perform guard duty at the port at Newport News, VA. Some notes from the National Archives show that Private Decoteau helped guard German prisoners at Brest, France. After the war, Napoleon married Emma Vallie. They had two daughters, Ann and Ruth. Napoleon worked as a farm laborer. He passed away on Dec. 11, 1922, and is buried in St. Michael's in Belcourt. Emma later married Telespore Renault.[6]

**Desjarlais, Patrick.** Army number, none; registrant, Rolette County; born, Minnesota, March 25, 1891, of (nationality of parents not given); occupation, farmer; enlisted in Company G, 2nd Infantry, North Dakota National Guard, at Rolla, on July 26, 1917; served in Company G, 2nd Infantry, North Dakota National Guard, to discharge. Discharged at Devils Lake, ND, on Aug. 31, 1917, as a Private, Surgeon's Certificate of Disability.

In the Census Rolls for the Turtle Mountain Chippewa, Pat's name is given as Patrice. In the Census Roll taken in 1893, he is listed with his parents, Andre and Adele, as well as his brothers and sisters. On Nov. 23, 1915, he married Rosalie St. Germain. Her brother, Philip, also served in WWI. Pat worked as a laborer. In the Census Roll taken in 1934, the Desjarlais family is shown as living in Elbowoods. In the 1940 U.S. Census, Pat was working on road construction. He died at the hospital in Belcourt the evening before Thanksgiving, Nov. 27, 1946. His wife and two sons, Andrew and Clifford, survived him. He is buried in St. Ann's Cemetery in Belcourt.[7]

**Desjarlais, Victor.** Army number 5,080; registrant, Rolette County; born, Buffalo Lodge, ND, March 27, 1894, of American parents; occupation, laborer; enlisted in Company G, 1st Infantry, North Dakota National Guard, at Rolla, on July 23, 1917; served in Company G, 1st Infantry, North Dakota National Guard, to July 23, 1917; Medical Department, 164th Field Hospital Company, Army Post Office No. 722, to Oct. 3, 1918; Base Hospital No. 65, to July 13, 1919; Medical Detachment, Segregation Camp No. 5, to discharge. Grades: Private 1st Class, June 27, 1918; Cook, March 1, 1919. Discharged at Camp Dodge, IA, on Nov. 6, 1919, as a Cook.

In the 1910 U.S. Census, Victor was living with his parents, Frank and Rachel, on Graham's Island near Devils Lake, ND. When he registered for the draft on June 5, 1917, he had worked as a farm laborer and had two children. Victor received training in the U.S. at Camp Greene, North Carolina and Camp Mills, NY, before being transported to Liverpool, England. Then he went to Le Havre, France, and finally to Base Hospital No. 65 at the port city of Brest, France. Most of the ships transporting soldiers back home to the U.S. sailed from Brest. Victor spent 21 months in France. After the war, Victor listed Elbowoods as his home. He later moved to Dunseith.

Victor married Rose Peltier (1895-1934) before the war. They had a son, Joseph, and a daughter, Maggie, and lived in Dunseith. Victor worked as a farm laborer after the war. Victor died in a farm accident near Dunseith on Sept. 11, 1953. Victor was hauling bundles for a grain threshing crew on a farm that was 8 miles to the northwest of Dunseith, when the rack he was riding on tipped over. His son and daughter survived him. He is buried in St. Mary's Cemetery at Dunseith.[8]

**Dickens, Edward W.** Army number 2,560,094; registrant, McLean County; born, Elbowoods, ND, Sept. 21, 1893, of American parents; occupation, farmer; inducted at Washburn on March 28, 1918; sent to Camp Dodge, IA; served in 163rd Depot Brigade, to discharge. Discharged on May 23, 1918, as a Private, Surgeon's Certificate of Disability, 50%.

In the Gros Ventre (Hidatsa) Census Roll for 1905, Edward was listed with his mother, Two Teeth (Irupash), and his three sisters. His father, George, was a white man who had served in the 11th New Jersey Infantry during the Civil War. In the 1910 U.S. Census, George was the postmaster at Elbowoods. When Edward registered for the draft on June 4, 1917, he was farming his mother's land. He stated that he was in poor health. In the 1920 U.S. Census, he was living with his sister, Margaret, and her husband, Stanley Deane. Edward died later that summer, on

Sept 17, 1920. He was buried in the Catholic Cemetery at Elbowoods. His grave was moved to St. Anthony's Catholic Cemetery.[9]

**Douglas, Jacob.** Army number 1,335,502; not a registrant, under age; born, Cannon Ball, ND, July 25, 1898, of American parents; occupation, farmer; enlisted at Rapid City, SD, on Feb. 1, 1918; sent to Jefferson Barracks, MO; served in Aviation Mobilization Depot, Camp Sevier, SC, to March 8, 1918; 499th Aero Squadron, to discharge. Grade: Private 1st Class, Dec. 1, 1918; overseas from Oct. 21, 1918, to March 6, 1919. Discharged at Camp Dodge, IA, on March 22, 1919, as a Private 1st Class.

In the Census Roll for Standing Rock taken in 1907, Jacob is listed with his parents, Stephen (Hana) and Bobduwin. Jacob was a student at the Bismarck Boarding School in the 1910 U.S. Census. He was 19 years old when he enlisted. The 499th Aero Squadron did construction work in France. After the war, he married and lived in Cannon Ball. Jacob re-enlisted in the Army in March 1920 with a group of men from Cannon Ball. He served in the 3rd Field Artillery at Camp Grant, IL.

In the Census Roll taken in the summer of 1927, he and his wife, Louisa, are shown with their two children, Cecelia and Gene. Jacob passed away on Oct. 21, 1927. The local newspaper reported that about 500 people attended his funeral services. Among those attending were Legion members from the posts in Kenel, Cannon Ball, Fort Yates, and Shields. Some older warriors in attendance were Shoot Holy, Iron Road, Lean Warrior and Grey Bull. Jacob was laid to rest next to Richard Blue Earth in the Cannon Ball Cemetery. The *Sioux County Pioneer* described how the long procession of mourners proceeded, as the women sang the death song. The military evolutions of the line of veterans was directed by Frank Zahn.[10]

**Drags Wolf, Louis.** Louis was born on May 30, 1896, in the Shell Creek area of the Fort Berthold Reservation. The Census Roll taken at Fort Berthold Reservation in 1899 lists Louis with his parents, Drags Wolf and Prairie Dog Woman, as well as two brothers and a sister. When Louis registered for the draft on June 5, 1917, he indicated that he was married and was farming for a living. He was a tall man of slender build. His first wife was Sally Sitting Crow. Louis was inducted in Washburn on May 24, 1918, and sent to Camp Lewis, WA. (Records do not indicate how long he served, but the *Washburn Leader* lists him as one who served.) Louis and Sally had several sons, including Kenneth and Calvin, who both served in the military during WWII. Kenneth married a daughter of Mark Necklace. Louis married Alice Bad Gun (1899-1973) on June 4, 1928, in Stanley. In the 1940 U.S. Census, he was working as a laborer with the CCC program. He and his wife farmed in the Shell Creek area until moving into New Town in 1953. Louis passed away in a Minot hospital on Aug. 5, 1968. His wife and son, Hugh, as well as three daughters, Ernestine, Allison, and Germaine survived him. He is buried in Shell Creek Congregational Cemetery.[11]

E

**Eagle Boy, Ambrose.** Ambrose was born at Cannon Ball on Feb. 15, 1899. He was the son of Samuel (Hoksina Wanbli) and Elizabeth Eagle Boy. He registered for the draft in 1918, but was too young to be called up. In March 1920, he enlisted with a group of other men from Cannon Ball. Two Army recruiters from Bismarck came to Cannon Ball to encourage men to enlist for service in the 3rd Field Artillery for duty at Camp Grant, IL. After his return to civilian life, Ambrose became a member of the Richard Blue Earth American Legion Post at Cannon Ball. In the 1930 U.S. Census, he was single and living with Robert Red Bow. Shortly after this, he married Edith Blackcloud (1897-1968). In the Census Roll taken in 1934, Ambrose and Edith are listed with their children, Serena and Emmerine. He worked in Cannon Ball for many years as a laborer. He passed away at Fort Yates on March 23, 1976. His daughters, Serena, Emmerine, Jane, Connie, Elaine, as well as his son, Ivan, survived him. He is buried in St. Elizabeth's Cemetery in Cannon Ball.[1]

D COMPANY

John Elk (back row, center) with Company D, 139th Infantry in France
(*Kenamore*, 38) (see also photo p. 100)

**Elk, John .** Army number 2,559,179; registrant, Sioux County; born, Cannon Ball, ND, March 15, 1896, of American parents; occupation, farmer; inducted at Fort Yates on March 29, 1918; sent to Camp Dodge, IA; served in Company D, 139th Infantry (35th Division), to discharge. Grade: Private 1st Class, Nov. 14, 1918; overseas from May 2, 1918, to April 28, 1919. Engagements: Offensive: Meuse-Argonne. Defensive Sectors: Gerardmer (Alsace); Grange-le Comte (Lorraine). Discharged at Camp Dodge, IA, on May 7, 1919, as a Private 1st Class.

John was the son of Jerome Elk and Kate Bighead. When John registered for the draft on June 5, 1917, he was farming with his father at Cannon Ball. He was a tall man of medium build. While John was on his way to Europe, he connected up with John Red Bean, who was in a different unit but headed in the same direction. The two sent a letter to the *Sioux County Pioneer* telling how much fun they had while visiting Niagara Falls. While these two men were in Camp Dodge, they had their picture taken together (see p. 100). Once Private Elk reached Europe, he had some familiar faces in his same unit, Company D, 139th Infantry Regiment. They included Thomas Grey Bull and James Murphy, as well as Fred Wheeler of Elbowoods. The 35th Division took very heavy casualties in the opening days of the Meuse-Argonne offensive. In the first four days, the division suffered 8,023 casualties. After the fighting was over, Private 1st Class Elk's commanding officer was interviewed. His evaluation read: "good runner and night worker. Exceptionally good scout, was very cool and calm but very quiet." After his discharge, John traveled back to Cannon Ball with Thomas Grey Bull, arriving on May 9, 1919.

John married Catherine Thunder (also known as Mary Streaked Eye) on May 6, 1926. They had several children. In the early 1930s, they moved to Poplar, MT. John and Catherine were later divorced. In the 1940 U.S. Census, he is shown as still living in Montana with his wife, Lucy, and their children, John worked as a farm laborer. He passed away in the VA Hospital in Fargo on Feb. 18, 1976. He is buried in Big Lake Cemetery in Cannon Ball, ND.[2]

**Ellis, Charles.** Army number 54,193; not a registrant, enlisted prior; born, Onigum, MN, May 20, 1898, of American parents; occupation, student; enlisted in Company I, 1st Infantry, North Dakota National Guard, at Wahpeton, on April 9, 1917; called into federal service, World War, on July 15, 1917; served in Company I, 1st Infantry, North Dakota National Guard (Company I, 164th Infantry), to Jan. 13, 1918; Company H, 26th Infantry (1st Infantry Division), to discharge. Grades: Corporal, Feb. 27, 1918; Sergeant, Aug. 1, 1918; overseas from Dec. 15, 1917, to March 6, 1919; wounded, severely, Sept. 12, 1918. Engagements: Offensives: Aisne-Marne; St. Mihiel. Defensive: Montdidier-Noyon. Defensive Sectors: Ansauville and Saizerais (Lorraine); Cantigny (Picardy). Discharged at Fort Sheridan, IL, on June 4, 1919, as a Sergeant, Surgeon's Certificate of Disability, 10 %.

In the Census Roll for the Leech Lake Pillager Chippewa taken in 1909, Charles is listed with his mother, Mary Bedeau, and a sister, Celestine. Charles was a student at the Wahpeton boarding school. On April 9, 1917, he was one of a group of students from the boarding school who enlisted in the 1st ND Regiment at Wahpeton. The six men who enlisted were mostly Chippewa from Leech Lake. The day that Charles was wounded, the 26th Infantry Regiment occupied a 600-meter front in the attack of the St. Mihiel salient. According to the regimental history, the regiment's objectives were accomplished, with relatively light casualties. There were six killed, 96 men wounded, while 350 prisoners, and including one officer were captured. Charles was still in the hospital during the Meuse-Argonne Offensive. After the war, a photo of Charles in uniform was published in a roster of Richland County veterans.

Charles Ellis, *Richland County Roster*.

Once discharged, Charles returned to the Leech Lake Reservation, where he farmed north of Leech Lake near Cass Lake, MN. He married Julia Cloud. In the Census Roll for the Leech Lake Pillagers taken in 1927, he is listed with his wife, Julia (1898-1977), and two sons, Charles and Lawrence. In the 1930 U.S. Census, The family lived on a farm in Wilkinson Township, south of Cass Lake, MN. In the Census Roll taken on the reservation in 1937, their family included Edna, Phillip, Alice and Morris. They later had one more son, Matthew. Charles passed away on July

17, 1973 in St Mary's Hospital in Duluth. His wife and three sons, Charles Jr., Phillip and Morris, survived him, as well as two daughters, Edna and Alice. Charles is buried in their family burial plot in Wilkinson Township, south of Cass Lake, MN.[3]

# F

**Feather, Jerome.** Army number 1,028,358; not a registrant, enlisted prior; born, Fort Totten, Oct. 5, 1895, of American parents; occupation, student; enlisted at Harrisburg, PA, on June 2, 1917; sent to Columbus Barracks, OH; served in Company K, 35th Infantry, to discharge. Grades: Private 1st Class, Aug. 1, 1917; Corporal, May 22, 1918; Sergeant, Sept. 17, 1918. Discharged at Camp Meade, MD, on Jan. 31, 1919, as a Sergeant.

Jerome was the son of Charles Feather and Adimaniwin. Jerome also was known as Mazakahomni. In the 1910 Census, he was a student at the Fort Totten Boarding School. He had previously attended the Sister's School at Fort Totten. Early in 1916, Jerome received a job working with the dairy operation at the Fort Totten School. On Nov. 25, 1916, Jerome started at the Carlisle Boarding School. When he registered for the draft on June 4, 1917, he was still a student at Carlisle. He had enlisted in the U.S. Army two days before. Once Jerome had completed his training, he was stationed at Yuma, AZ. The 35th Infantry Regiment was responsible for guarding the border. On Aug. 27, 1918, three men from the regiment were killed by some Mexicans. While Sgt. Feather was stationed in Arizona, he received a subscription to *The Arrow*, which was published at Carlisle. He sent a photo of himself in uniform back to the school at Carlisle.

Jerome Feather sent his photo to the staff at Carlisle.
*NARA Folder 4725*

After his discharge, he returned to Tokio, ND, where he married Maggie Ringing Cloud. He worked as a laborer. In the 1925 North Dakota State Census, Jerome and Maggie were living in Mission Township, north of Tokio, with two of their children, Mary and Archie. They had two other girls, Frances and Marguerite, who died as infants. Maggie passed away on April 8, 1933. Jerome passed away on Sept. 27, 1937. He is buried in St. Michael's Cemetery in Mission Township.[1]

**Fiddler, Moses.** Army number 2,352,764; registrant, Rolette County; born, St. Johns, D.T., Dec. 9, 1886, of Canadian-American parents; occupation, farmer; enlisted in Company G, 2$^{nd}$ Infantry, North Dakota National Guard at Rolla, on July 13, 1917; called into federal service, World War, on July 15, 1917; served in Company G, 2$^{nd}$ North Dakota National Guard, to Oct. 5, 1917; Headquarters, Field Hospital Company No. 164, 116$^{th}$ Sanitary Train, to Aug. 11, 1918; Battery C, 119$^{th}$ Field Artillery (32$^{nd}$ Infantry Division), to discharge; overseas from April 17, 1918, to April 23, 1919. Engagements: Offensives: Oise-Aisne; Meuse-Argonne. Defensive Sector: Fismes (Champagne). Discharged at Camp Dodge, IA, on May 7, 1919, as a Private.

In the Census Roll for the Turtle Mountain Chippewa taken in 1889, Moses and his brother, Joseph, are listed with their mother, Mrs. Frank Fiddler. In the Census Roll taken in 1902, Moses is listed as an orphan. When Moses registered for the draft on June 5, 1917, he was working in Rolla and supporting his wife and child. During the war, he served with the 119$^{th}$ Field Artillery of the 32$^{nd}$ Division, which was also known as the Red Arrow Division. He was gassed while in France. This likely affected his health after he returned. James R. Jollie of Belcourt also served with him in the 119$^{th}$ Field Artillery. Moses had married Louise Jeanotte on Nov. 27, 1909, but she passed away in 1919. He married Florence Azure (1899-1998) on July 24, 1919. Moses passed away in the Belcourt hospital on Oct. 14, 1932. His wife and seven children survived him. They were John, Mary, Cecelia, Francis, Joseph, Angeline, and Moses Jr., who was born the day before his father died. Moses had been sick for several weeks. Of their children, John and Francis served in the U.S. Navy during WWII, while Moses Jr. served with the Marine Corps during the Korean Conflict. Military rites for Moses were performed in the Belcourt Catholic Cemetery. The firing squad consisted of Mike Coghlan, James R. Jollie, Mike Bercier, William Azure, Warren Elliott, and O.J. Charbonneau, who also sounded taps. Moses' widow lived to be 99 years old.[2]

Frank Fiske. *Richard Birklid*

**Fiske, Frank Bennett.** Army number 3,088,921; not a registrant, over age; born, Fort Bennett, D.T., June 11, 1883, of American parents; occupation, photographer; enlisted at St. Louis, MO, on July 11, 1918; sent to Jefferson Barracks, MO; served in Company D, 10$^{th}$ Infantry, to Oct. 22,

1918; Company A, 41<sup>st</sup> Machine Gun Battalion, to discharge. Grades: Corporal, Dec. 5, 1918; Sergeant, Jan. 21, 1919. Discharged at Camp Dodge, IA, on Feb. 11, 1919, as a Sergeant.

Frank moved to the Fort Yates area with his parents in 1889. Frank's father, who had served as a soldier at Fort Bennett, worked as a civilian wagon master at Fort Yates. Frank attended the post's school until transferring to a government boarding school where most of his classmates were Indians. He soon developed an affinity for the people and their culture. Frank also worked as a cabin boy on a steamboat and learned the photography trade from S.T. Fansler, the operator of the post studio. After Fansler abandoned the studio in 1900, Frank took it over, though he was still in his teens. When the military post closed in 1903, there was less demand for photos. Frank spent some time in Bismarck, where he had his own shop and later worked for Butler Studio. For several years in the 1920s, he ran a shop in McLaughlin, SD. After these interludes away from Fort Yates, he continued to operate his photography business in Fort Yates until his death in 1952. He also worked for a time before the war as an assistant riverboat pilot along the Missouri, as well as Sioux County Auditor and Treasurer. He was the publisher of the *Sioux County Pioneer-Arrow* from 1929-1939. He wrote two books, *Taming of the Sioux* (1917) and *Life and Death of Sitting Bull* (1933).

After Frank was discharged, he married Angeline (Angela) Cournoyer (1883-1974) on June 11, 1919, in St. George's Church in Armour, SD. Angela was a piano teacher, playwright, and the great-granddaughter of the Yanktonai chief, Forked Horn. Frank and Angela had a daughter, Francine. In the Census Roll of the Yankton in 1934, Angeline is listed with her daughter.

Frank was best known for his Indian portraits, for which he received the North Dakota Art Award in 1950. His portraits of the Standing Rock people and activities provided his main livelihood, as well as receiving recognition for their artistic merit. He produced almost 8000 photos, dating back to a time when photography was still in its infancy. His photos are recognized for their high quality. Following his death, his photos remained in the possession of his family until 1970, when they were acquired by the State Historical Society of North Dakota. Frank passed away in a Bismarck hospital on July 18, 1952. His wife, daughter, and five grandchildren survived him. Frank and Angela are buried in St. Peter's Cemetery in Fort Yates.[3]

**Fox, Charles.** Army number 2,787,554; registrant, McLean County; born, Fort Berthold, ND, Sept. 15, 1895, of American parents; occupation, farmer; inducted at Washburn on May 24, 1918; sent to Camp Lewis, WA; served in 14<sup>th</sup> Company, 4<sup>th</sup> Battalion, 166<sup>th</sup> Depot Brigade, to June 16, 1918; Company A, 158<sup>th</sup> Infantry, to Sept. 11, 1918; Company D, 128<sup>th</sup> Infantry (32<sup>nd</sup> Division), to discharge; overseas from Aug. 11, 1918, to March 30, 1919; wounded, severely, Oct. 8, 1918. Engagement: Offensive: Meuse-Argonne. Discharged at Camp Dodge, IA, on April 14, 1919, as a Private.

Charles was a student at the Wahpeton boarding school in the 1910 U.S. Census. On March 1, 1916, he married Emily Grady. When he registered for the draft on June 5, 1917, he was farming for himself near Van Hook. He was a short man of slender build. Charles took part of his training at Camp Kearny, CA, when he was assigned to the 158<sup>th</sup> Infantry Regiment. During the war, he served with the Red Arrow Division (32<sup>nd</sup>). On Oct. 8, 1918, he was hit in the neck by a bullet and spent about six months in a French hospital before he was ready to return home.

After the war, he farmed and ranched near Elbowoods and Shell Creek. Charles was a charter member of the Joseph Young Hawk American Legion Post. In the 1940 U.S. Census, he was serving as a tribal policeman at Elbowoods. His son, Burt, served in the U.S. Army during WWII. Charles and his wife moved to New Town in 1960. After his first wife died, he married Lucy

Spotted Wolf, in May 1973. Charles passed away in a Fargo hospital on March 31, 1980. His wife, son, Burt, and daughters, Martha, Sophie, and Carrie, survived him. He is buried in the Shell Creek Congregational Cemetery. The Shell Creek Legion Post No. 300 conducted military rites.[4]

**Frederick, Robert.** Army number 4,576,309; registrant, Rolette County; born, Belcourt, ND, Dec. 17, 1896, of American parents; occupation, laborer; enlisted in Company G, 2nd Infantry, North Dakota National Guard, at Rolla, on July 13, 1917; called into federal service, World War, on July 15, 1917; served in Company G, 2nd Infantry, North Dakota National Guard, to discharge. Discharged at Camp Greene, NC, on Oct. 9, 1917, as a Private; Surgeon's Certificate of Disability.

After the war, he married Clemence Houle (1908-1948). They lived in Belcourt, where Robert worked as a farm laborer. Robert passed away in Belcourt on Dec. 8, 1964. His daughter, Nora, and son, Dennis, survived him. He is buried in St. Ann's Cemetery in Belcourt.[5]

**G**

**Gardner, William Jenning.** Army number, none; not a registrant, over age; born, Towner, D.T., Jan. 25, 1885, of American parents; occupation, lawyer; enrolled in the First Officers Training Camp, Fort Sheridan, IL, on May 12, 1917; commissioned and called into active service as a Captain, on Aug. 15, 1917; assigned to 338th Infantry (85th Infantry Division), to discharge. Principal stations: Fort Sheridan, IL; Camp Custer, MI; France; Camp Zachary Taylor, KY; overseas from July 13, 1918, to March 28, 1919. Discharged at Fort Sheridan, IL, on Oct. 11, 1919, as a Captain, Surgeon's Certificate of Disability, 10%.

Wedding Day for Bill Gardner and Alene French. *Diane Garrard*

In the Turtle Mountain Census Roll taken in 1893, Bill is listed with his parents and brothers and sisters. Shortly after this, his father died. His mother then married Joseph Rolette. In the 1900 U.S. Census, Bill was a student at the Fort Totten Boarding School. That same year, his sister, Lucy, was a student at a boarding school in Wakarusa, KS. Lucy was married to Ed Brien for awhile in the 1920s. On Sept. 4, 1904, Bill started school at the Carlisle Boarding School. Bill's size (six feet tall and 172 lbs.) made him a candidate for the Carlisle football team. He played for their championship team for 3-4 years. He was also on Carlisle's track team as well as basketball and baseball. After completing his studies at Carlisle, he was admitted to Dickinson School of Law, which was within walking distance of the Carlisle campus. He received his law degree on June 9, 1909. At that time, he was also coaching football for the high school in Louisville, KY. In 1912, he was athletic director at Oberlin College. In the 1930s, Knut Rockne named Gardner to his All-Time All-American Team for *Colliers* magazine. Gardner undoubtedly was one of the players who helped the growth of professional football in America.

After Gardner received his commission, he was given a 10-day furlough, during which he returned to Belcourt to visit his mother. Once Gardner was in the army, he was chosen captain of the football team at Camp Custer. During the war, the 338th Infantry was held in reserve in the Lorraine area of France. They were never in the front line. After he returned to the U.S., he married Alene French on July 19, 1919. Her father owned French Paper Mill in Niles, MI. Bill and Alene had a son, Frank, and two daughters, Jacqueline and Alene. In the 1920 Census, Bill had a law office in Devils Lake, ND. In the 1920s, the family moved to Texas, and later to Florida. In 1929, he accepted a position with Eliot Ness and went to work for the U.S. Revenue Service. He became one of the "Untouchables." Bill and Alene were divorced. One reason for this was that Eliot Ness preferred that his agents be single. In Bill's later years, he lived with his son for a while before finally moving to the Veterans Hospital in Prescott, AZ. He passed away there on June 15, 1965. He is buried in the nearby Prescott National Cemetery (Section 2, Row E, Site 86). [1]

**Garfield, John Gabriel.** Army number 2,858,938; registrant, Benson County; born, Fort Totten, ND, Nov. 18, 1896, of American parents; occupation, farmer; inducted at Minnewaukan on April 29, 1918; sent to Camp Dodge, IA; served in 163rd Depot Brigade, to April 30, 1918; 313th Trench Mortar Battery (88th Division), to discharge. Grades: Bugler, Oct. 1, 1918; overseas from Aug. 23, 1918, to Jan. 5, 1919. Discharged at Camp Dodge, IA, on Jan. 18, 1919, as a Bugler.

In the Census Roll for the Devils Lake Sioux taken in 1908, John (Kininanpina) is listed with his father (Tatankaciqana). In the 1910 Census, he was a student at the Fort Totten Boarding School. He also was a student at the boarding school in Carlisle, PA. When he registered for the draft in June 1917, he wrote that he was farming for Iron Cloud of Fort Totten. John had a wife and two children. He was a short man of medium build. After the war, he was farming in Mission Township, Benson County. His wife's name was Mary. They had several children who died as infants. John passed away from tuberculosis in St. Luke's Hospital in Fargo on Sept. 21, 1925. His wife and daughter, Julia, survived him. He is buried in St. Jerome's Catholic Cemetery, in Lallie Township on the Spirit Lake Reservation. [2]

John Garfield (not in photo) was a bugler with a Trench Mortar Battery (88th Division).
*Postcard, author's collection.*

**Gladue, Ellis Andrew.** Army number 1,072,644; not a registrant, under age; born, Dunseith, ND, Oct 10, 1895, of Canadian parents; occupation, farmer; enlisted at Culbertson, MT, on Nov. 16, 1917; sent to Fort George Wright, WA; served in 621st Aero Squadron, to March 20, 1918; 672nd Aero Supply Squadron, to July 8, 1918; 674th Aero Supply Squadron, to Aug. 25, 1918; 58th Balloon Company, to discharge; overseas from Oct. 21, 1918, to June 27, 1919. Discharged at Camp Lee, VA, on July 1, 1919, as a Private.

In the Census Roll on the Turtle Mountain Reservation for 1907, Andrew is listed as the stepson of Laron Duchain. His mother's name was Julia. In the 1910 U.S. Census, Andrew lived with his uncle, Frank Gladue, at Wolf Creek. When the 1920 U.S. Census (January 23) was taken, Private Gladue was still stationed at Camp Lee, VA. He likely had re-enlisted when his first tour was completed. After he was discharged, he moved to Montana, where he worked as a farm hand. In the 1930 U.S. Census, he was working for Edward Luebke in Roosevelt County, MT. The Census Roll for the Turtle Mountain Reservation taken in 1932 lists him as living near Froid. He never married. After he retired, he moved into Friendship Villa in Miles City, MT. He passed away in

45

the VA Hospital in Miles City on Sept. 8, 1978, and is buried in the veteran's section of the Custer County Cemetery in Miles City.[3]

**Goodiron, Paul.** Army number 461,858; not a registrant, under age; born, Shields, ND, Dec. 5, 1897, of American parents; occupation, rancher; enlisted at Bismarck on April 5, 1918; sent to Jefferson Barracks, MO; served in Headquarters Company, 66th Regiment, Coast Artillery Corps, to May 3, 1918; 6th Company, Narragansett Bay Coast Artillery Corps, to discharge. Discharged at Camp Dodge, IA, on March 31, 1919, as a Private, Surgeon's Certificate of Disability, 10%.

In the Census Roll for the Standing Rock Reservation taken in 1903, Paul is listed with his parents, Jerome (Wagi) and Annie Good Iron. Paul had attended the boarding school at Carlisle, PA. Shortly before the war, he married Mary Walker. When Paul enlisted in Bismarck, he requested to be in the band with the Coast Artillery. Paul had likely played in the band while a student at Carlisle. Band members were assigned to the Headquarters Company in each regiment. After the war, he was a charter member of the Shields American Legion Post #190. In the Census Roll taken at Standing Rock Reservation in 1926, Paul and his wife are listed with three children, Hermine, Joseph, and Gilbert. Gilbert served in the U.S. Army during WWII. Paul passed away from tuberculosis in Sioux Falls, SD, on July 3, 1927. When his body arrived back at the reservation, 35 ex-servicemen met the train. He is buried in St. James Cemetery in Porcupine, ND.[4]

**Grady, Charles.** Army number 2,704,365; registrant, McLean County; born, Fort Berthold, ND, June 1, 1895, of American parents; occupation, farmer; inducted at Washburn on June 23, 1918; sent to Camp Dodge, IA; served in Company A, 352nd Infantry, to discharge. Discharged at Camp Cody, NM, on Nov. 27, 1918, as a Private; Surgeon's Certificate of Disability, 12 ½ %.

In the 1910 U.S. Census, Charles was a student at the Bismarck boarding school. When he registered for the draft before the war, he indicated that he had a wife to support. When Charles arrived in Camp Dodge, he was assigned to the 352nd Infantry Regiment, which was part of the 88th Infantry Division. However, he must have had some health problems, because he did not travel to France with the rest of the 88th Division.

His first wife was Jessie. They farmed on the Fort Berthold Reservation. Jessie died on July 14, 1932. On Sept. 23, 1932, Charles married Mary Catherine Vondall (1914-1970) at Van Hook. Charles was a member of the Little Shell American Legion Post No. 300 for 50 years. Charles' son, Harry, served in the U.S. Navy during WWII. In 1970, Charles moved into New Town, where he passed away on April 22, 1973. Catherine had passed away in 1970. He had five sons, Harry, Roger, Edwin, William, and Kenny, and six daughters, Regina, Mary, Loretta, Marilyn, Marie, and Judy. Grady is buried in Shell Creek Cemetery.[5]

**Grandbois, Fred.** Army number, none; not a registrant, under age; born, Belcourt, ND, Feb. 1, 1897, of American parents; occupation, farmer; enlisted in Company G, 2nd Infantry, North Dakota National Guard, at Rolla, on July 13, 1917; called into federal service, World War, on July 15, 1917; served in Company G, 2nd Infantry, North Dakota National Guard, to discharge. Discharged on Aug. 15, 1917, as a Private, Surgeon's Certificate of Disability.

In the 1910 U.S. Census, Fred was listed as Joseph, along with his parents, Isidore and Sarah Granbois. Fred, also known as Joseph Alfred, married Mary Celine Gourneau. In the Census Roll of the Turtle Mountain Reservation taken in 1934, the couple is listed with three children, Rosalie, Francis, and Shirley. In the 1940 U.S. Census, Joseph was living in Belcourt and working as a tractor and truck driver with the CCC program. Later, they likely moved out of North Dakota.

**Grass, Albert.** Army number 45,935; born, Fort Yates, ND, Feb. 7, 1896, of American parents; occupation, farmer; enlisted in Company I, 2nd Infantry, North Dakota National Guard, July 22, 1917; served in Company I, 2nd Infantry, North Dakota National Guard, to Oct. 5, 1917; 161st Ambulance Company, 116th Sanitary Train, to Nov. 14, 1917; 164th Infantry, to Jan. 9, 1918; Company A, 18th Infantry (1st Division), to death; overseas from Dec. 15, 1917, to death. Engagements: Offensive: Aisne-Marne. Defensive: Montdidier-Noyon. Defensive Sectors: Ansauville (Lorraine); Cantigny (Picardy). Killed in action at Soissons-Paris Road, July 18, 1918. Buried in Romagne Cemetery, France. Reburied at Cannon Ball, ND. Cited in General Orders No. 1, Headquarters, 1st Division, Camp Zachary Taylor, KY, Jan. 1, 1920, for gallantry in action and especially meritorious services. Entitled to wear a silver star.

Albert Grass. *State Historical Society of North Dakota, 1952-1248*

Albert was the grandson of Chief John Grass. His parents were John Grass Jr. (Gleskayuha) and his wife Annie. After his father, John, died, his mother married Basil Two Bears, an uncle of Joseph Two Bears. Albert had been a student at the boarding school in Bismarck. In July 1917, Captain A.B. Welch met with John Grass and other elders on the Standing Rock Reservation. Chief Grass stated, "Go, my son, and do thy duty by the Great White Father in Washington." With Chief Grass' approval, Albert Grass and Joseph Jordan were the first men from the Standing Rock Reservation to volunteer in Company I, 2nd Infantry, North Dakota National Guard. Once Albert reached France and was transferred to Company A, 18th Infantry, four men from Company I were still in his unit. They included Joe Young Hawk and Tom Rogers from Fort Berthold, and Joe Jordan and Richard Blue Earth from Standing Rock. Private Grass was killed when he volunteered to try to get some water for his fellow soldiers. The 18th Infantry received heavy fire from the German troops along the Soissons-Paris road in July 1918. The First and Second

Battalions of the 18th Infantry were so depleted that combined they hardly represented half a battalion. The regimental history for the 18th describes a similar situation:

> Here, as elsewhere, the greatest difficulty was met in bringing up rations and water from the rear. Due to the continuous bombardment only one meal was brought up each day and this invariably was cold. A half canteen of water had to last through an entire day for most of the men. On several occasions ration carts coming up from the rear were destroyed by shells and the men went hungry.

In May 1921, the body of Albert Grass was returned to Cannon Ball. On May 18, a detail of American Legion members, including Tom Gray Bull, Alphonse Bear Ghost, and Frank Zahn, met the body at the Mandan station. Once his body arrived in Cannon Ball, the White Cavaliers (Sunk'ska akan'yanka), under the leadership of Thomas Mentz, took charge and managed the occasion of the last tribute and honor to the dead hero. Once the religious ceremonies were over, Major A.B. Welch, Rev. A.T. Tibbets, and Claude Kill Spotted were each scheduled to give an address. The local newspapers estimated that at least 3000 Standing Rock members, as well as many whites, were in attendance. Grass was buried on Holy Hill in Cannon Ball. The American Legion Post in Fort Yates is named in his honor.[6]

Joseph Grey Day. *Four Bears Museum*

**Grey Day, Joseph.** Army number 474,477; not a registrant, under age; born, Shields, ND, Feb. 28, 1898, of American parents; occupation, farmer; enlisted at Fort Yates on April 20, 1918; sent to Jefferson Barracks, MO; served in 29th Company, Coast Artillery Corps, Puget Sound, Fort Casey, WA, to Sept. 20, 1918; Battery F, 39th Artillery, Coast Artillery Corps, to discharge. Discharged at Camp Dodge, IA, on Dec. 19, 1918, as a Private.

In the Census Roll for Standing Rock taken in 1899, Joseph is listed with his parents, Hawk (Cetan) and Ida Grey Day. Later, he was adopted by Barney and Margaret Trackhider, and was known by some as Joseph Trackhider. Eventually, he was known as Joseph G. Day. He attended the boarding school at Standing Rock, where he was recognized as an outstanding pitcher on their baseball team.

While he was in the service, he received training at Fort Casey and Fort Worden in Washington before transferring to Camp Upton, NY. In a letter home, he described his training in the firing of 12-inch mortars, as well as the use of gas masks and signals. Apparently, his unit never made it to Europe. While he was at Camp Worden, WA, he had a photo taken of himself in his uniform, holding his rifle with bayonet. He sent a copy of the photo to the editor of the *Sioux County Pioneer*. It seems likely that photographers were present in the training camps, giving soldiers a chance to get a photo to send back home. On Nov. 22, 1918, Joseph sent a letter to the local paper stating that he would be home by Christmas.

After the war, Joseph (now known as Joe) returned to Shields. In August 1919, he accepted a job with the agency in Fort Yates. He carried on a correspondence with Joseph Dixon, who was interested in documenting the military service of all Indian men. Joe was one of the charter members of Shields American Legion Post #190. He became very involved in the great American pastime of that era, baseball. In a game between Shields and Carson, he struck out 19 batters. In 1923, he was playing for the Plano Indians, a semi-pro team from northern Illinois. He was known as "Mighty Smoke Ball Choker."

Joe married Dorothy Christian from Barnesville, MN in 1926. They had five children: Gladys, Joseph Jr., Michael, Adelaide and Loretta. Joseph Jr. served in the Air Force during the Korean Conflict, and Michael was a member of the Navy.

Dorothy and Joseph divorced in 1945, and he married Daisy See Walker / Iron Shield (1906-1954). They had two children, Richard and Catherine. In the 1930 U.S. Census, Joe lived near Shields with his wife and two children, Gladys and Joseph Jr.. Joe's wife died in a car accident near Shields in 1954. In September 1969, Joe moved into the Veterans Hospital in Fargo, where he died on Oct. 4, 1969. Military graveside rites were conducted at his grave next to St. James Catholic Church in Porcupine, ND.[7]

**Greybull, Thomas.** Army number 2,559,179; registrant, Sioux County; born, Cannon Ball, ND, June 15, 1896, of American parents; occupation, farmer; inducted at Fort Yates on March 29, 1918; sent to Camp Dodge, IA; served in Company A, 1st Battalion, 163rd Depot Brigade, to April 20, 1918; Company D, 139th Infantry (35th Division), to discharge. Grades: Private 1st Class, Oct. 31, 1918; Corporal, Nov. 10, 1918; overseas from May 3, 1918, to April 28, 1919. Engagements: Offensive: Meuse-Argonne. Defensive Sectors: Gerardmer (Alsace); Grange-le Comte (Lorraine). Discharged at Camp Dodge, IA, on May 7, 1919, as a Corporal.

Thomas was the son of Charles (Tatankarota) and Isabelle Greybull (Sisakewin). He attended boarding schools in Fort Yates and Wahpeton. In July 1917, he married Gertrude Hairychin at Fort Yates.

Shortly after Thomas arrived for training at Camp Dodge, he was one of the men from Standing Rock who were selected as riding instructors. The horsemen from Standing Rock desired these positions. Thomas served in France with Company D, 139th Infantry Regiment with John Elk, James Murphy, as well as Fred Wheeler from Fort Berthold. On July 16, 1918, Private Greybull sent a letter from "Somewhere in France" to the editor of the paper:

Dear Friend,

Thought of the *Sioux County Pioneer* today, so I will write a few lines. It certainly does a fellow good to know he is not forgotten by his friends at home. Did you get any card from me lately? I wrote one before we left New York. Landed right side up and was transferred to Co. D 139th Infantry. I and James Murphy are in the same company, and we are sure getting on first rate.

We sure enjoyed the trip coming over and saw many interesting things, and expect to see more yet before we go back. We are having fine weather so far. The people here are wearing wooden shoes, and sure have Standing Rock reservation beat for good roads. Saw in a Minneapolis paper the other day the news of Chief John Grass' death. The paper was about two months old. The country here is sure good looking, but is way behind in everything.

Well, Chris, we are making pretty good soldiers. This will be all for this time. So will close sending kind handclasp and good luck to you and the rest also. From your Sioux friend in France.

On Dec. 17, 1918, Thomas and James sent another letter back to the editor of the *Sioux County Pioneer*. They described how they were doing in France, and stated that if they "had a copy of the *Sioux County Pioneer*, they'd feel right at home." Later, Corporal Greybull's commanding officer, Captain Gus Gehlbach was interviewed. He stated that Greybull was "very cool & calm and at all times has the qualities of a natural born leader. Good judgement, leader and scout." Once he was discharged, he traveled back to Fort Yates with John Elk, arriving on May 9, 1919.

In the Census Roll taken at Standing Rock in 1929, Thomas was listed with his wife, Josephine, along with three sons, Thomas Jr., Edgar and Elmer. In 1932 the family moved to Poplar, MT. Thomas worked in construction and did some farming. On Nov. 24, 1937, he married Annie Kill Spotted. He was a member of the Nathan Crazy Bull American Legion Post #54. His son, Thomas, Jr., served in the U.S. Army during WWII. Thomas, Sr. passed away on Dec. 10, 1982, at the VA Hospital in Miles City, MT. His wife and sons, Matt, Miles, and Melvin, as well as two daughters, June and Mary Ann survived him. He was buried in St. Ann's Cemetery in Poplar, MT. Military rites were performed at graveside by members of the Poplar Legion Post and the visiting Cannon Ball, ND, members.[8]

**Greyhawk, Benjamin.** Army number 2,559,192; registrant, Sioux County; born, Poplar, MT, Aug. 5, 1891, of American parents; occupation, farmer; inducted at Fort Yates on March 29, 1918; sent to Camp Dodge, IA; served in Veterinary Corps, Auxiliary Remount Depot No. 322, to discharge. Discharged at Camp Dodge, IA, on Feb. 24, 1919, as a Private.

In the Census Roll of the Yanktonai at Fort Peck taken in 1905, Benjamin is listed with his parents, Gray Hawk (Cetanhota) and Good Cloud Woman (Mahpiyawastewin), as well as his sister. Benjamin married Josephine Kidder in Fort Yates on Jan. 21, 1917. When he registered for the draft on June 5, 1917, he was farming near Fort Yates. He is described as a tall man of medium build. Shortly after he arrived at Camp Dodge, IA, he was one of a number of men from the Standing Rock Reservation who were selected as riding instructors. He was photographed with Harry Lean Elk at Camp Dodge. Sometime after the war, Benjamin moved his family back to Poplar, on the Fort Peck Reservation, where he was enrolled. He worked as a laborer. He passed away in the Poplar Community Hospital on Feb. 21, 1964. His wife, Josephine, and three sons, Stephen, Benjamin Jr., and Melvin, as well as a daughter, Mary Louise, survived him. He is buried in the Poplar City Cemetery.[9]

**Halsey, George Jacob.** Army number 2,787,764; registrant, Sioux County; born, Fort Yates, ND, Aug. 21, 1893, of American parents; occupation, clerk; inducted at Fort Yates on May 25, 1918; Sent to Camp Lewis, WA; served in 166th Depot Brigade, to June 20, 1918; Company B, 361st Infantry (91st Infantry Division), to discharge. Grades: Private 1st Class, Aug. 6, 1918; Corporal, Oct. 21, 1918; overseas from July 6, 1918, to April 15, 1919. Engagements: Offensives: Meuse-Argonne; Ypres-Lys. Defensive Sector: Aubreville (Lorraine). Discharged at Camp Dodge, IA, on April 26, 1919, as a Corporal. Previous military record: Three years in Battery E, 1st Minnesota Field Artillery, Minnesota National Guard.

George and his younger brother, Mike, were the sons of William and Sophie Halsey. William worked as an interpreter at the agency. Sophie died in 1949 at the age of 96. At Christmas in 1904, Frank Fiske took a photo of George and Mike serving as altar boys at the church in Fort Yates. George attended school at Fort Yates, Columbus College in Chamberlain, SD, and the Minnesota Business College. He worked in Minneapolis for awhile before taking a job as clerk with the Indian Service in Fort Yates. Shortly before entering the service, George married Cecelia Cottonware who was from near Tacoma, WA. While George was overseas with the 91st Division, his wife stayed with relatives in Washington State. George and his brother, Mike, who also was in Company B, 361st Infantry Regiment, saw quite a lot of action. After taking part in the opening attacks on the Meuse-Argonne front, the 91st Division was transferred to the Belgian Front in mid-October. George was not wounded, but he likely was exposed to gas attacks, which undoubtedly affected his health. The 91st Division suffered 1,702 casualties, while capturing 2,412 prisoners.

After the war, George worked as an accountant for the Indian Service. He was the first adjutant for the Legion Post in Fort Yates, and also served a term as commander. However, his health was not good, due to his heart. His brother said he had been in good health before entering the service, but following a physical exam prior to discharge, a physician noticed some heart trouble. George and Cecelia did not have any children. George passed away on Dec. 2, 1923 at the agency hospital. He is buried in St. Peter's Cemetery in Fort Yates. Several hundred mourners attended the service, including ten American Legion members from the Cannon Ball Post.[1]

**Halsey, Michael.** Army number 2,787,772; registrant, Sioux County; born, Fort Yates, ND, April 6, 1896, of American parents; occupation, farmer; inducted at Fort Yates on May 25, 1918; sent to Camp Lewis, WA; served in 166th Depot Brigade, to June 20, 1918; Company B, 361st Infantry (91st Infantry), to discharge; overseas from July 6, 1918, to April 15, 1919; wounded, severely, Sept. 30, 1918. Engagements: Offensives: Meuse-Argonne; Ypres-Lys. Defensive Sector: Aubreville (Lorraine). Discharged at Camp Dodge, IA, on April 26, 1919, as a Private.

When Mike registered for the draft, he was farming near Fort Yates. Mike served with his brother in the 91st Infantry Division, also known as the Wild West Division. The division's battle cry was "Powder River! Let'er Buck!" Mike sent a number of letters back to his hometown newspaper. Once they arrived in France, he wrote that Ben Cloud was stationed in a town near them. On Sept. 30, 1918, the day that Mike was wounded, the 361st Regiment was in the front line east of Exermont, near Bois de Cierges. The divisional history states, "When they found that wooded area full of gas, they moved forward to the ridge north of Bois de Cierges and occupied shell holes made by the German counter barrage on September 29. They continued to be shelled by the German artillery."

After the Armistice on November 11, the 361st Regiment was stationed in Belgium. On Dec. 23, 1918, Mike sent a letter from Crombeke, Belgium, to the editor of the *Sioux County Pioneer*. He indicated that he was fine, and enjoyed reading the weekly paper, but was ready to return to Fort Yates. He wrote: "I've seen all of the world that I wanted to see and now I'd like to see the U.S. again." The regimental history indicates that they spent three weeks in Crombeke, during which it rained most of the time. The soldiers appreciated that because it kept them inside, as opposed to being outside for drill and road marches. Some of their activities included physical exercise, bayonet work, guard duty, first aid, rifle range practice, and live grenade practice. Men were also given passes to visit some of the nearby Belgian towns. In Belgium, they were separated from the main Army supply units. Apparently, some of the men did not have a good pair of shoes. Their isolation also protected them from the flu epidemic that swept through some units. However, the 361st Regiment did not return to the U.S. until April 1919. The First Battalion of the 361st sailed from St. Nazaire, France, aboard the *Edward Luckenbach* on April 3, 1919. On May 15, 1919, a dance was held in the agency hall to honor George and Mike Halsey.

In January 1922, Mike went to Kansas City to attend the Sweeny Auto School. While there, he married Bessie Tallbear of Geary, OK. Bessie had worked several years at the Standing Rock agency. In the 1930 U.S. Census, Mike was farming in Sioux County. Mike and Bessie lived about five miles south of Fort Yates. They had two children; Gladys and Michael, Jr. Bessie passed away in the agency hospital on May 21, 1933, from a severe cold. On March 2, 1935, he married Effie Gayton. In the Census Roll for 1937, Mike and Effie are listed with one more son, Wesley. In the 1940 U.S. Census, Mike was working as a truck driver for the road department. Mike later moved to Rapid City, SD, where he worked in construction. He passed away at his home in Rapid City on Dec. 16, 1970. Effie had died about ten years previously. Two daughters, Mrs. Woodrow Perry and Mrs. Josephine Webster, as well as three sons, Raymond, Wesley, and Victor survived Mike. Mike is buried in the Black Hills National Cemetery, Section C, Site 1455.[2]

J.R. Harmon and horn spoon. *State Historical Society of North Dakota, A1103*

**Harmon, Joseph Richard.** Army number 3,832,203; registrant, Sioux County; born, Bismarck, D.T., May 17, 1882, of American parents; occupation, stockman; enlisted at Camp Pike, AR, on Sept. 10, 1918; served in Central Officers Training School, Camp Pike, AR, to discharge. Discharged at Camp Pike, AR, on Nov. 30, 1918, as a Private.

In the Census Roll for Standing Rock taken in 1890, Richard (Dick) is listed with his mother, Lulu, and two older brothers. Lulu, a half sister to Alma Parkin, had married Lieutenant William Harmon. Dick attended high school in Miles City, MT, and Menominee, MI. He was also a graduate of the commercial course offered by Notre Dame University at South Bend, IN. When he registered for the draft on Sept. 7, 1918, Dick was living in Selfridge and working as a stockman for his brother, Leo. In the 1920 U.S. Census, Dick was working as an accountant for the county treasurer. He was active in the American Legion Post, and served a term as commander. Around that time, he married Frieda Gimble. In September 1921, their first son, Leo, was born at the agency hospital. The local paper reported that several minutes after the birth, Dick was already walking around passing out cigars. In the 1930 U.S. Census, Dick was working as county auditor. In the 1940 U.S. Census, Dick was living in Fort Yates. Sometime later the family moved to Portland, OR. Dick passed away on Dec. 19, 1964, in Portland and is buried in Mt. Calvary Cemetery. His wife and sons, Leo and William, survived him. Frieda passed away in Portland on July 1, 2008, at the age of 106. Their son, Leo, served as a fighter pilot with the U.S. Marine Corps (VMFA-321) in the Pacific, and retired as a Major, before going to work for Lockheed Aircraft.[3]

Tom & Susie Hawk, *Denver Museum of Nature and Science*

**Hawk, Thomas.** Army number 502,070; registrant, Dunn County; born, Elbowoods, ND, April 1, 1894, of American parents; occupation, rancher; inducted at Manning on March 6, 1918; sent to Fort Logan, CO; served in Battery B, 2nd Battalion, Trench Artillery, Coast Artillery Corps, to discharge; overseas from May 29, 1918, to July 5, 1919. Engagements: Defensive Sector: Lorraine. Discharged at Mitchel Field, NY, on July 12, 1919, as a Private.

In the Census Roll for Fort Berthold taken in 1896, Thomas is listed with his father, Hawk (Ihtataki), and his mother, Buffalo Woman, as well as two sisters and Hawk's mother, Blossom. In the Census Roll for 1900, Thomas and his sister, Bertha, are listed as orphans. In the 1910

Census Roll, he is listed as the adopted son of Joseph Ward and his wife, Mink. In 1910, Thomas was enrolled as a student at the Wahpeton Boarding School. After this, he attended the boarding school at Carlisle, where he was an outstanding athlete. He participated in football, wrestling and boxing. He was still a Carlisle student when he registered for the draft in June 1917.

Thomas received some training with trench mortars at Fort Caswell, NC, before sailing for France. Thomas' unit, the 2nd Trench Mortar Battalion, traveled overseas on the HMS *Cardiganshire*. They were sent to the Trench Mortar School at Fort de la Bonnete near Langres, France. Thomas served as a wagoner. His unit provided artillery support at Chateau-Thierry, Soissons, and was in front of Metz when the Armistice was signed.

After returning to North Dakota, he married Cora Chase, a sister of Dan Chase, who had died while in the service. They had several daughters before their divorce. Sometime in the late 1920s, Thomas moved to Eagle City, OK, where he married Susie Bringing Good, an Arapaho. They had several children. Thomas was a member of the Joseph Young Hawk American Legion Post at Elbowoods. Thomas last lived in Durham, OK. He passed away on July 16, 1965, and is buried at Fort Logan National Cemetery in Denver (Section Q, Site 344).[4] Susie (1910-1990) is buried with Tom.

**Hayes, John Wilson.** Army number, none; not a registrant, under age; born, Devils Lake, ND, June 30, 1897, of American parents; occupation, laborer; enlisted in Company A, 1st Infantry, North Dakota National Guard, at Bismarck, on Aug. 30, 1917; served in Company A, 1st Infantry, North Dakota National Guard (Company A, 164th Infantry), to discharge. Discharged at Camp Greene, NC, on Jan. 25, 1918, as a Private, Surgeon's Certificate of Disability, 12 ½ %.

In the Census Roll for the Turtle Mountain Reservation taken in 1906, John is listed with his parents, John and Veronica Hayes, as well as three sisters, Margaret, Mary, and Elvina. While John was in the Army, he was detailed as orderly to the chaplain. He likely had some health problems that kept him from traveling to France with the other members of the 164th Infantry Regiment. After his discharge, John returned to North Dakota. In the Census Rolls taken from 1934 to 1937, John is listed as living in Washington, DC. His wife's name was Marie. He passed away on Aug. 23, 1940, at the VA Hospital in Washington, DC, and is buried in Arlington Cemetery, Section Col. E, Site 1338.[5]

**Hoksina, Jesse.** Army number 572,663; registrant, Benson County; born, Standing Rock, ND, January 1891, (nationality of parents not given); occupation, laborer; inducted at Minnewaukan on March 17, 1918; served in Company B, 58th Infantry, to discharge. Discharged on June 15, 1918, as a Private, Surgeon's Certificate of Disability, 50 %.

Jesse (Sutapi) was born at Cannon Ball. His parents were from Fort Peck. In the Census Roll for the Fort Totten Devils Lake Sioux taken in 1907, Jesse is listed with his mother, Winona, and several other siblings. When Jesse registered for the draft before the war, he was married to Agnes (Tatiyopasnawin) and was working for his uncle, Mazawanapeya, in the Crow Hill area near Fort Totten. Jesse and Agnes had a son, Stephen. Jesse was divorced in December 1917. While he was in military training, he came down with tuberculosis, and was discharged three months after his induction. There were other soldiers from Fort Totten who were also in Company B, 58th Infantry at Camp Greene, NC. So it is likely that Jesse contracted the disease at that camp. He died on Jan. 2, 1919, and is buried in the cemetery in Lallie Township, Benson County.[6]

**Hopkins, Daniel.** Army number 3,769,455; not a registrant; born, Elbowoods, ND, Aug. 26, 1899, of American parents; occupation, farmer; enlisted at Bismarck on July 22, 1918; sent to Jefferson Barracks, MO; served in Headquarters Company, 33rd Infantry, to April 4, 1918; Supply Company, 33rd Infantry, to discharge. Discharged at Camp Dodge, IA, on May 18, 1919, as a Private.

In the Census Roll for Fort Berthold taken in 1906, Dan (Rabbit Goes in the Middle) and his brother, Harvey, are listed with their parents, Ernest and Ida Hopkins, along with their other siblings. Their younger sister was Kate. Their father, Ernest, had been the first native Congregational minister on the Fort Berthold Reservation. In the 1910 U.S. Census, Dan was a student at the Bismarck Boarding School. During the war, Dan may have spent some time in the Canal Zone, as that is where the 33rd Infantry Regiment had its permanent station. After the war, Dan married Agnes Gillette, who died in December 1924. He married Ruth Eagle in 1944. Ruth died in a car accident in June 1960. His sister, Kate, married Philip Star, a fellow veteran. His brother, Harvey, also served in the Army in France. Dan farmed and ranched all his life on the Reservation. He was known as a singer, and had been a member of the Nishu singers. He had learned the ritual for the death feast and conducted it on a few occasions before his own death. In late fall of 1982, he moved to Havre, MT, to spend the winter with his daughter, Ernestine Belcourt. He passed away in the Havre hospital on Nov. 26, 1982. He is buried in the Scouts Cemetery near White Shield, ND.[7]

**Hopkins, Harvey.** Army number 2,704,364; registrant, McLean County; born, Elbowoods, ND, Feb. 23, 1895, of American parents; occupation, farmer; inducted at Washburn on June 23, 1918; sent to Camp Dodge, IA; served in 163rd Depot Brigade, to July 13, 1918; Company D, 352nd Infantry (88th Division), to discharge. Grade: Private 1st Class, Sept. 3, 1918; overseas from Aug. 15, 1918, to June 3, 1919. Discharged at Camp Dodge, IA, on June 13, 1919, as a Private 1st Class.

Harvey was an older brother of Dan. He married Susie Enemy (1893-1962) before the war. Their oldest son, Harvey, Jr., was born in 1915. During the war, Harvey's regiment served in a number of towns in France, but not in the front line. Harvey was in Company D, 352nd Infantry, along with John Jordan from the Standing Rock Reservation, as well as Arthur Lezotte from Belcourt. Harvey spent six weeks in a French hospital after catching the flu. His unit sailed from France to Newport News, VA. The unit was stationed at Camp Morrison, VA, for a short time before taking the train to Camp Dodge, IA. A photo of Harvey in his uniform was published in *Memoirs of France and the Eighty-Eighth Division.*

After the war, Harvey returned home and farmed near Nishu. He was very active in community affairs, and served as an associate minister in the Congregational Church. He was also one of the Nishu singers. He was a charter member and chaplain in the Joseph Young Hawk American Legion Post No. 253 at Elbowoods. His son, Harvey, Jr., served in the U.S. Army during WWII. Harvey, Sr. passed away in the Good Samaritan Hospital in Rugby on Feb. 27, 1952. His wife and son, Harvey, Jr., as well as three daughters: Winona Zotti, Mary Louise Fool Bear, and Mildred, survived him. He is buried in the Scout Cemetery near White Shield.[8]

*Memoirs of France and the
Eighty-Eighth Division.*

Pvt 1st Cl. Harvey Hopkins with Pvt. Colsh, Company D, 352nd Infantry, Camp Morrison, VA, June 1919. (*Michael Rempfer*)

**Houle, Philip.** Army number, none; not a registrant, under age; born, Williston, ND, October 1896, of (nationality of parents not given); occupation, (not given); enlisted in Company G, 2nd Infantry, North Dakota National Guard, at Rolla, on July 17, 1917; served in Company G, 2nd Infantry, North Dakota National Guard, to discharge. Discharged on Oct. 9, 1917, as a Private, Surgeon's Certificate of Disability.

In the 1900 U.S. Census, Philip lived with his parents, Abraham and Margaret Houle, on the Turtle Mountain Reservation. In the 1910 Census, he was a student at the Fort Totten boarding school. After Philip enlisted in the ND National Guard, he spent several months in training in North Dakota, before arriving in Charlotte, NC, on Oct. 5, 1917. Four days later, he received a medical discharge. Sometime after the war, he married Eliza Peltier. They moved to Yorkton, Saskatchewan. In the Census Roll for the Turtle Mountain Chippewa taken in 1934, they are listed as living in Yorkton. In 1936, he married Stella DeLong. In the 1940 U.S. Census, the family lived near Belcourt while Philip worked as a building construction laborer. The Houles lived in Belcourt and New Town before moving to Billings, MT, in 1972. Philip had worked also as a farm laborer. In 1975, he moved into the Yellowstone County Nursing Home. He passed away there on April 30, 1985. His daughters: June, Pat, Phyllis, Thelma, and a stepdaughter, Elsie, as well as two sons, Frank and Richard, survived him. He is buried in Mountview Cemetery in Billings.[9]

**I**

**Irish, William.** Army number, none; registrant, Benson County; born, Fort Totten, ND, June 23, 1887, of American parents; occupation, farmer; enlisted in Company B, 2nd Infantry, North Dakota National Guard, at New Rockford, on Sept. 3, 1917; served in Company B, 2nd Infantry, North Dakota National Guard (Company B, 164th Infantry), to Oct. 26, 1917; Company H, 164th Infantry, to discharge. Discharged at Camp Greene, NC, on Nov. 28, 1917, as a Private, Surgeon's Certificate of Disability, 12 ½ %.

In the Census Roll of the Devils Lake Sioux taken in 1896, William (Wicibdeza) is listed with his parents, Irish Mike (Wasicupazi) and Shadow (Tohanzina), as well as another brother and sister. After William enlisted in the 2nd ND Regiment, he spent about a month in training in North Dakota before arriving at Camp Greene, NC. After the war, he married Annie Bear. She passed away in 1923. In the early 1930s he moved to Sisseton. He passed away at Fort Totten on Oct. 25, 1933. He is buried in St. Jerome's Catholic Cemetery in Lallie Township, Benson County.[1]

**Ironroad, John Samuel.** John was born on April 7, 1900, in Cannon Ball, ND. In the Census Roll taken 1906, he is listed with his parents, Daniel and Helen, as well as a sister, Annie. John also had a younger sister, Nellie, who married fellow veteran, Joseph Jordan, after the war. John registered for the draft on Sept. 7, 1918, but was too young to be inducted. In March 1920, he enlisted at Cannon Ball with a group of other young men from the community. They served with the 3rd Field Artillery at Camp Grant, IL, in Uncle Sam's peace-time army. John later returned to Cannon Ball, where he married Estella Rachel Many Horses (1903-1977). They had five children, Gertrude, Charlie, Leon, Lyman, and Daniel. Lyman served in Korea with an Engineering Construction Battalion. John passed away from diabetes on April 26, 1954, shortly after returning home from a fishing trip along the Missouri River. He is buried in St. Elizabeth's Cemetery in Cannon Ball.[2]

## J

**Jeannotte, George William.** Army number 2,858,009; registrant, Rolette County; born, St. John, ND, Dec. 25, 1891, of Canadian parents; occupation, laborer; inducted at Rolla on April 29, 1918; sent to Camp Dodge, IA; served in 163rd Depot Brigade, to (date not given); Company L, 350th Infantry, to May 16, 1918; Company L, 357th Infantry, to June 8, 1918; Company C, 315th Supply Train, to Sept. 6, 1918; Company G, 360th Infantry (90th Division), to discharge; overseas from June 29, 1918, to Feb. 2, 1919; wounded, severely, Nov. 1, 1918. Engagements: Offensives: St. Mihiel; Meuse Argonne. Defensive Sectors: Villers-en-Haye, and Puvenelle (Lorraine). Discharged at Camp Grant, IL, on Feb. 20, 1919, as a Private, Surgeon's Certificate of Disability, 10 %.

George was the son of Gaspard and Melanie Jeannotte. His parents were not enrolled. George is listed as living with them in St. John up through the 1920 U.S. Census. When George registered for the draft on June 5, 1917, he was working as a farm laborer for John Coughlan in St. John.

On the day that George was wounded, the 90th Division was in position to attack the German position known as "Freya Stellung" near Andevanne. Early in the war, the Germans had created three, strong defensive positions which they named after the witches in Richard Wagner's operas. George received shrapnel wounds in both shoulders, right hip and index finger of right hand.

After the war, he married Eliza Aiken. They lived in St. John. In the 1930 U.S. Census, George was working as a section hand for the Great Northern Railway. In the Census Roll for the Turtle Mountain Reservation taken in 1932, George (not enrolled) and Eliza are listed with their children, Josephine, Hubert, Mary Mae, Olive and Elmer. Elmer served in the US Navy during the Korean Conflict. In 1951, the family moved to Horton, KS. George passed away in a Horton nursing home on Aug. 26, 1977. Two sons, Elmer and James, as well as four daughters: Evelyn, Frances, Mary Mae, and Bernice, survived him. He is buried in St. Leo's Cemetery.[1]

Ernest Jeanotte was the last
surviving WWI veteran in
Belcourt.
*Chick LaRocque*

**Jeanotte, Ernest.** Army number, none; registrant, Rolette County; born, St. John, ND, Aug. 9, 1899, of Canadian parents; occupation, farmer; enlisted in Company G, 2nd Infantry, North Dakota National Guard, at Rolla, on July 13, 1917; called into service, World War, on July 15, 1917; served in Company G, 2nd Infantry, North Dakota National Guard, to discharge. Discharged at Camp Greene, NC, on Oct. 9, 1917, as a Private; Surgeon's Certificate of Disability.

Ernest was the son of John and Domitilde Jeanotte. In the 1910 U.S. Census, he was a student at the Fort Totten Boarding School. After Ernest enlisted in the 2nd ND Regiment, he participated in training in North Dakota until arriving at Camp Greene, NC, on Oct.5, 1917. After returning to Belcourt, he married Clara Schindler (1906-1987) on Nov. 22, 1922. Ernest worked as a laborer on WPA projects and the Garrison Dam. In the 1940 U.S. Census, he was working as a teamster on a road construction project. He also had worked for the railroad and Fagerlund Implement in Rolla. Several of their sons were also in the military. Vincent served in the U.S. Air Force during the Korean Conflict, while Melvin served as a helicopter gunner in Vietnam. Ernest had been a member of the Lilley-Dionne American Legion Post No. 262 in Belcourt. He passed away in the Belcourt hospital on May 21, 1993. He was survived by seven daughters: Leona, Sandra, Nora, Marlene, Gail, Geraldine, Carol, and four sons: Lyman, Melvin, Gerald, and Darrell. His wife and son, Vincent, had preceded him in death. Ernest is buried in St. Ann's Cemetery in Belcourt. The Legion Post of Belcourt conducted military rites. Ernest was one of the last surviving WWI veterans from the Turtle Mountain Reservation. Albert Tetrault died at the age of 101 in Florida on March 2, 1994.[2]

**Jeanotte, Patrick.** Army number, none; registrant, Rolette County; born, Rolla, ND, Feb. 10, 1899, of Canadian-American parents; occupation, farmer; enlisted in Company G, 2nd Infantry, North Dakota National Guard, to discharge. Discharged at Camp Greene, NC, on Oct. 9, 1917, as a Private, Surgeon's Certificate of Disability.

Patrick was the son of Frederick and Rose Jeanotte. In the Census Rolls for the Turtle Mountain Reservation, his name is listed as Patrice. When Patrick registered for the draft on Sept. 12, 1918, he was working as a farm laborer for Joe Carlson of Rolla. Patrick had been discharged four days after he arrived with his fellow ND National Guard soldiers at Camp Greene, NC. Presumably, the Army had a large team of medical people who screened the volunteer soldiers more closely. In the 1920 U.S. Census, Patrick roomed at Annie Smith's home in Mt. Pleasant, ND. In the Census Roll for the Turtle Mountain Reservation taken in 1923, Patrice is listed with his father, Frederick, and sister, Mary Louise. Patrick passed away at the VA Hospital in Minneapolis on Feb. 27, 1929, from pneumonia. He is buried in St. Ann's Catholic Cemetery in Belcourt.[3]

**Jerome, Frederick L.** Army number, none; registrant, (not given); born, Belcourt, ND, 1895, of (nationality of parents not given); occupation, (not given); enlisted in Company G, 2nd Infantry, North Dakota National Guard, at Rolla, on July 13, 1917; called into service, World War, on July 15, 1917; served in Company G, 2nd Infantry, North Dakota National Guard, to discharge. Discharged on Oct. 9, 1917, as a Private, Surgeon's Certificate of Disability.

Fred Louis was the son of Marc (St. Matthew) Jerome. In the 1910 U.S. Census, he lived with his grandparents, Marie and Archibold Aiken. When he registered for the draft on June 5, 1917, he was working as a farm laborer near Medicine Lake, MT. Fred enlisted in Rolla in the summer of 1917, but was another of the ND National Guard soldiers who was discharged four days after arriving at Camp Greene, NC. He passed away about a year later on Nov. 14, 1918, in Devils Lake. He is buried in St. Ann's Cemetery in Belcourt.[4]

**Jerome, Joseph A.** Army number 131,599; registrant, (not given); born, Belcourt, ND, January 1893, of (nationality of parents not given); occupation, (not given); enlisted at Jefferson Barracks, MO, on Nov. 9, 1917; served in Battery A, 17th Field Artillery (2nd Division), to discharge. Grade: Saddler, Feb. 15, 1918; overseas from Dec. 14, 1917, to June 2, 1919. Engagements: Offensives: Aisne-Marne; St. Mihiel; Meuse-Argonne. Defensive: Aisne. Defensive Sectors: Toulon, Troyon, Limey, and Marbache (Lorraine); Chateau-Thierry (Ile-de-France). Discharged on June 6, 1919, as a Saddler.

Joseph was the son of Marc (St Matthew) and Mary (Aikins) Jerome. He was a student at the Fort Totten Boarding School. Before the war, he lived near White Earth with his wife, Mary Kaplin, who was an enrolled member at White Earth. They had a son, John. When he registered for the draft, Joseph was working in a sawmill owned by J. Neils Lumber Co. at Cass Lake. Joseph arrived in France with the 17th Field Artillery on Dec. 31, 1917. After taking part in many campaigns as part of the 2nd Division, his unit was stationed near Ehrenbreitstein, Germany, after the Armistice. After the war, he returned to Minnesota. In the 1920 U.S. Census, he was working in a cordwood camp in Clearwater County, MN. He later took up the trade of painter and lived in Mahnomen. His wife, Mary, died in April 1933 of tuberculosis. Joseph passed away in the Mahnomen County Hospital from pneumonia on May 3, 1934. Joseph had been exposed to gas in France numerous times with the 2nd Division. This had affected his health after he returned, but he continued to work as a painter. Four children survived him. He is buried in St. Michael's Cemetery in Mahnomen.[5]

**Jettie, Alfred.** Army number, none; registrant, (not given); born, Dunseith, ND, January 1894, of (nationality of parents not given); occupation, (not given); enlisted in Company D, 2nd Infantry, North Dakota National Guard, at Devils Lake, on June 30, 1917; called into federal service, World War, on July 15, 1917; served in Company D, 2nd Infantry, North Dakota National Guard, to discharge. Discharged on Oct. 11, 1917, as a Private, Surgeon's Certificate of Disability.

In the Census Rolls for the Devils Lake Sioux, Fred's name is spelled "Jetty." Fred attended the boarding school at Fort Totten. When Fred registered for the draft on June 5, 1917, he was farming with his father in Mission Township of Benson County. He was discharged from the Army about a week after his arrival with the 2nd Infantry in Camp Greene, NC. In the 1920 U.S. Census, he was living with his parents, Frank and Julia, in Mission Township. Shortly after this, he married Angelique (Angeline) Morin. They farmed near St. Michael. They had 11 children including a daughter who died as an infant. They also raised five foster children. One of their daughters, Nora Cecelia, served in the US Navy as a Storekeeper. Fred passed away June 3, 1979, in Mercy Hospital in Devils Lake. Angeline passed away two months later on Aug. 6, 1979. Their surviving children included Oliver, Alfred, Cecelia, Sarah, Eleanor, Inez, Vivian, Marianne, Jean, Julie, as well as their foster children, Chris, Kenneth, Nita, Roland, and Jacob. Fred and Angeline are buried in St. Michael's Cemetery.[6]

**Jollie, David Pleasant.** Army number 5,056; registrant, Rolette County; born, St. John, ND, Jan. 31, 1893, of Irish-American parents; occupation, farmer; enlisted in Company G, 2nd Infantry, North Dakota National Guard, at Rolla, on July 13, 1917; called into federal service, World War, on July 15, 1917; served in Company G, 2nd Infantry, North Dakota National Guard (164th Field Hospital Company, 116th Sanitary Train), to Aug. 6, 1918; 104th Infantry (26th Division), Medical Department, to discharge. Grade: Sergeant, Aug. 15, 1917; overseas from Dec. 11, 1917, to April 4, 1919. Engagements: Offensive: St. Mihiel. Defensive Sectors: Rupt and Troyon (Lorraine). Discharged at Camp Dodge, IA, on April 17, 1919, as a Sergeant.

David's parents were James J. Jollie and Mary Belgarde. James had served in the U.S. Army, stationed at Fort Totten. He met Mary who also worked at the fort, before they moved up to the Turtle Mountain Reservation. In the 1910 U.S. Census, David was a student at the Carlisle Boarding School. His sister, Blanche, also attended that school. When David registered for the draft before the war, he was working as a farm laborer for William McDonald of Rolla.

David had two brothers who also served in the military. Following the Armistice, Sgt. Jollie's commanding officer, Major Sydney Hardwick, stated that Jollie "always performed his duties with dispatch and efficiency."

In the 1920 U.S. Census, David was living with his parents. On Feb. 14, 1922, he married Pholomene Warren (1902-1994). Philomene was the sister of Joseph Warren, who also was a vet. Joseph, in turn, married David's sister, Nora. David worked for the U.S. Government Roads Department at Belcourt until 1941. He then was employed on the Alcan Highway. In 1945, he moved to Portland, OR, to work in the shipyards. A year or so before that, his brother-in-law, Joseph Warren, had moved to California to work in the shipyards at Mare Island. David returned to Belcourt in 1950. He passed away on Dec. 29, 1977, in the Belcourt Hospital. His wife and two daughters, Doris and Peggy, as well as three sons, George, William, and Edward, survived him. His son, George, had served in the U.S. Army during WWII, reaching the rank of Staff Sergeant. David is buried in St. Ann's Cemetery. The Lilley-Dionne Post No. 262, American Legion of Belcourt, conducted military rites.[7]

**Jollie, James Richard.** Army number 626,532; not a registrant, over age; born, Leavenworth, KS, May 31, 1885, of Irish-American parents; occupation, painter; enlisted at Wahpeton on Nov. 21, 1917; sent to Jefferson Barracks, MO; served in Battery C, 57th Artillery, Coast Artillery Corps, to Aug. 19, 1918; Battery D, 119th Field Artillery (32nd Division), to discharge; overseas from June 30, 1918, to May 3, 1919. Engagements: Offensives: Oise-Aisne; Meuse-Argonne. Discharged at Camp Dodge, IA, on May 16, 1919, as a Private. Cited in General Orders No. 3, for gallantry in action near Montfaucon, France, Sept. 29, 1918, in carrying wounded comrades to the first aid station under heavy shellfire. Entitled to wear a Silver Star. Cited in General Orders No. 44, Headquarters, 32nd Division, Camp Upton, NY, May 8, 1919. The Division Commander takes pleasure in citing Private James R. Jollie, for acts of gallantry in action. Entitled to wear a silver star. Authorized to wear the French Fourragère in the colors of the French Croix de Guerre, as an individual decoration.

James was the older brother of John and David Jollie, who also served in the military during WWI. James was born while his father was stationed in Kansas with the U.S. Army. James never married. After the war, he spent a lot of time in Montana, though he often came back to Belcourt for funerals of his fellow veterans. In 1929, James was admitted to the VA Hospital at Leavenworth, KS. He had some health problems which likely date back to his war service. In the U.S. Census taken in April 1930, James was living in Phillips County, MT, where he was working as a shepherd for Joseph Hartman. James also worked as a painter. In 1932, he was in Belcourt, where he was part of the honor guard for the funeral of Moses Fiddler, who had served with him in the same regiment. Another time, he served as a pallbearer for Pat Sayers. In the 1940 U.S. Census, he was living at home with his mother and working as a painter. In his later years, James lived in Dixon, MT. He passed away at the Holy Family Hospital in St. Ignatius, MT, on Dec. 8, 1958. He is buried in St. Ann's Cemetery in Belcourt. The Belcourt American Legion Post conducted the military rites. Robert Bruce served as bugler.[8]

**Jollie, John Joseph.** Navy number 1,144,635; registrant, Rolette County; born, St. John, D.T., July 19, 1888, of Irish-American parents; occupation, farmer; enlisted in the Navy at Minneapolis, MN, on Feb. 9, 1918; served at Naval Aeronautic Station, Pensacola, FL, to Nov. 11, 1918. Grades: Landsman Quartermaster, Aviation, 81 days; Quartermaster 2nd Class, Aviation, 92 days; Quartermaster 1st Class, Aviation, 102 days. Released from active duty at Pensacola, FL, on Feb. 1, 1919, as a Quartermaster 1st Class, Aviation. Died at Naval Hospital, San Diego, CA, on Feb. 20, 1920.

John married Edith Didday. They lived in San Diego where he came down with pneumonia. He is buried in St. Ann's Catholic Cemetery in Belcourt.[9]

**Jones, Morgan.** Morgan (I-cit-ta) was born in Elbowoods around July 1886. His parents were Crow Ghost and Last Born Child. Morgan had been a student at the boarding school at Carlisle, PA, from 1901 to 1908. In the Census Roll for the Arikara taken in 1912, he is listed with his wife, Anna. When he registered for the draft before the war, he was farming near Elbowoods, and providing support for his father, wife and one child, Claudia. He was a tall man of slender build. Morgan was inducted at Washburn, ND on June 24, 1918. He went by train to Camp Dodge, IA. The *Washburn Leader* lists Morgan as one of the soldiers from McLean County. It is not known when he was discharged. In the 1920 U.S. Census, Morgan was living with Stephen Price near Elbowoods. In the late 1920s, he married Clara Bellanger. In the Census Roll for Fort Berthold taken in 1930, Morgan is listed with his young daughter, Corine Ethel. Morgan passed away in a Bismarck Hospital from appendicitis on April 16, 1931. His wife and daughter survived him. Another daughter, Evangene, was born to Clara less than four months after Morgan died. Morgan was buried at Nishu. He is now buried in the Old Scout Cemetery near White Shield. Clara later married Helmuth Krueger.[10]

**Jordan, John.** Army number 2,703,735; registrant, (place not given); born, Mound City, SD, Nov. 15, 1894, of (nationality of parents not given); occupation (not given); inducted at McLaughlin, SD, on June 23, 1918; served in Company D, 352nd Infantry (88th Division), to discharge. Grades: Private 1st Class, Sept. 23, 1918; Corporal, Oct. 19, 1918; overseas from Aug.

15, 1918, to June 3, 1919. Engagement: Defensive Sector; Center (Alsace). Discharged on June 13, 1919, as a Corporal.

John was the son of Arnold Jordan and his wife, Annie (Tatuye). Arnold Jordan had been a soldier in the U.S. Army. He was discharged at Fort Yates. John's younger brother, Joseph also served in the Army. In the 1910 U.S. Census, John and Joseph lived in Wakpala with their mother, as well as their brother, Jacob. John was first sent to Camp Funston, KS. About a month later, he was transferred to Camp Dodge, IA. During the war, he served in Company D, 352nd Infantry in France with Harvey Hopkins from Fort Berthold and Arthur Lezotte from the Turtle Mountain Reservation. When the Armistice was signed, the 88th Division members were assigned to billets around the city of Gondrecourt, France. After sailing from France in June 1919 on the USS *Connecticut*, they arrived at Newport News, VA. John reported that the return trip was a stormy voyage. A floating mine was sighted and sunk by sharpshooters on board. The 352nd Infantry was quartered a short time at Camp Morrison, before traveling by train to Camp Dodge, IA. John brought back a German watch as a souvenir.

After the war, John married Susan Defender (1896-1974). They ranched in Corson County, South Dakota. In the 1930 U.S. Census, John and Susie shared their home with John's mother, Annie, as well as her husband, Albert Young Eagle. In the Census Roll for Standing Rock taken in 1937, John and Susie are listed with their children, Walter, Delores, Elsie, and Irlene. John passed away in the McLaughlin Community Hospital on Feb. 20, 1976. He is buried in Assumption Catholic Cemetery in Kenel, SD.[11]

**Jordan, Joseph.** Army number 45,947; not a registrant; born, Mound City, SD, Jan. 25, 1896, of German-American parents; occupation, farmer; enlisted in Company I, 2nd Infantry, North Dakota National Guard, at Bismarck, on July 22, 1917; served in Company I, 2nd Infantry, North Dakota National Guard (161st Ambulance Company, 116th Sanitary Train), to Nov. 14, 1917; Company A, 164th Infantry, to Jan. 9, 1918; Company A, 18th Infantry (1st Division), to discharge. Grade: Private 1st Class, May 9, 1919; overseas from Dec. 15, 1917, to Sept. 3, 1919; wounded, slightly, Oct. 4, 1918. Engagement: Defensive: Montdidier-Noyon. Offensives: Aisne-Marne; St. Mihiel; Meuse-Argonne. Defensive Sectors: Ansauville and Saizerais (Lorraine); Cantigny (Picardy). Discharged at Camp Dodge, IA, on Sept. 24, 1919, as a Private 1st Class. Cited in General Orders No. 5, Headquarters, 1st Infantry Brigade, AEF, Selters, Germany, June 1, 1919, for gallant conduct and self-sacrificing spirit displayed during the battles of Montdidier-Noyon defensive; Aisne-Marne offensive; St. Mihiel offensive; Meuse-Argonne offensive. The success of these engagements was due to the efforts and spirit of the officers and enlisted men engaged. Entitled to wear a silver star.

Joseph was the younger brother of John. In the 1910 U.S. Census, Joseph was a student at the boarding school in Bismarck. Draft registration records from 1917 show that Joseph was working in an auto livery for Frank Halverson in Kenel, SD. On July 22, 1917, Albert Grass and Joseph Jordan enlisted in Bismarck. Around that time, Joseph married Sarah Turcott, whose parents were from the Fort Belknap Reservation. Sarah's sister, Rebecca, was married to Frank Halverson, with whom Joseph worked. Joseph was scheduled to leave for Camp Greene, NC, on Oct. 1, 1917. His wife, Sarah, upset that she could not travel with Joseph, took her own life. Jordan reported the information to his commanding officer, Captain A. B. Welch. Captain Welch's wife helped make burial arrangements for Sarah Jordan, as the soldiers were about to leave town on the train.

When Joseph arrived in France in January 1918, he was still serving in Company A, 18th Infantry Regiment with Albert Grass, Richard Blue Earth, Joe Young Hawk and Tom Rogers. As part of the First Division, they were soon serving in the front line trenches. Joe Young Hawk was severely wounded in early May near Cantigny. Albert Grass died in July at Soissons. In early October 1918, the 18th Infantry was advancing on the German lines south of Exermont, crossing a series of abrupt hills and deep ravines. On the night of Oct. 4, the day Joseph was wounded, their unit was camped at Exermont. Joseph received numerous shrapnel wounds to his face and body. He was the hospital for about four weeks. Richard Blue Earth was killed five days after Joseph was wounded. The First Division was one of the last units to return to the United States. They began sailing from Brest, France on Aug. 23, 1919, with the First Battalion sailing on the USS *Mobile*. Captain A. B. Welch's unpublished notes indicate that Jordan received the Croix de Guerre from the French Government. He also received the French Fourragère, similar to a unit citation given by the American military.

Joseph was a very talented athlete. While in the Army, he received a prize as athletic divisional runner. He also won a silver medal and a cup and a bronze medal. After the war, the *Sioux County Pioneer* reported on area sports activities. In the Standing Rock fair of September 1921, Joseph took first place in the relay foot race and the 220-yard dash. Earlier in September, Joseph and John Jordan had attended the fair at Timber Lake, SD, where Joseph took first place in the 100-yard dash. In 1922, he was a pitcher for the Kenel, SD, baseball team.

In the 1920 U.S. Census, Joseph lived with his brother, Jacob, and worked as a motor mechanic. During the 1920s, he had some health problems and was admitted at the VA Hospital in Hot Springs, SD. On July 15, 1932, he married Nellie Ironroad (1906-1993) in Selby, SD. Nellie was a sister to John Ironroad who enlisted in the U.S. Army in 1920. The Census Roll taken in 1939 lists their children as Grace and Joan. In the 1940 U.S. Census, Joseph was working as a truck driver and Nellie was a clerk in a general store on the Standing Rock Reservation. Joseph later served as a deputy sheriff for Sioux County. He passed away at his home in Cannon Ball on Sept. 24, 1949. He is buried in St. Elizabeth's Cemetery in Cannon Ball.[12]

# K

**Keeps Eagle, Herbert.** Herbert was born on Standing Rock Reservation on Dec. 5, 1884, the son of George Keeps Eagle and Mary Sage. Herbert was inducted at Fort Yates on March 29, 1918. He traveled to Camp Dodge, IA, with a group of men from the Standing Rock Reservation. The April 11, 1918, issue of the *Sioux County Pioneer* wrote that Herbert Keeps Eagle had been assigned to the 157th Brigade as a riding instructor. On April 22, 1918, friends of Herbert wrote back to the local paper that Herbert had been rejected due to weak eyes by the medical board. On May 2, 1918, the *Sioux County Pioneer* reported that Herbert had returned to Fort Yates earlier in the week. They quoted him as saying "he liked army life fine," and added that he made a splendid appearance in his uniform. It seems he was permitted to wear his uniform home from Camp Dodge.

The Census Roll for Standing Rock taken in 1926 listed Herbert with his brothers, Paul and Joe, as being single. Paul Keeps Eagle (1894-1965) had served in the U.S. Army in the early 1920s and was discharged from Fort Benjamin Harrison in April 1923. Paul had registered for the draft on June 5, 1918, and enlisted sometime after that. Herbert ranched near Fort Yates. In the late 1930s, Herbert married Martina Magpie Eagle. In the Census Roll taken in 1939, they are listed with their children, Vivian and Jean. They had a third daughter, Mary Ellen. Martina passed away in 1942. Herbert passed away at his home on Dec. 31, 1967. He is buried in St. Peter's Cemetery in Fort Yates.[1]

Herbert Keeps Eagle (front seat) before leaving to join the U.S. Army on March 29, 1918.
*State Historical Society of North Dakota, 1952-0358*

# L

**Laderoute, Ludger Benjamin.** Army number 5,058; not a registrant, over age; born, St. Boniface, Manitoba, March 26, 1885; naturalized citizen; occupation, mechanic; enlisted in Field Hospital, 2nd Infantry, North Dakota National Guard, at Rolla, on July 13, 1917; called into federal service, World War, on July 15, 1917; served in Field Hospital, 2nd Infantry, North Dakota National Guard (164th Field Hospital, 116th Sanitary Train), to discharge. Grade: Mechanic, Aug. 12, 1918; overseas from Dec. 11, 1917, to Feb. 11, 1919. Discharged at Camp Grant, IL, on March 6, 1919, as a Mechanic.

In the 1915 N.D. State Census, Ludger lived with his parents, John and Marguerite, in Olga, ND. He likely lived in Rolla when he enlisted in 1917. He was photographed with Edward Brien, Joe Warren, and Dave Jollie. In 1922, he moved to Long Beach, CA. In 1926, he was working there as a carpenter. He worked 50 years as a carpenter. He was never married. After he retired, he moved to La Puente, a suburb of Los Angeles. He passed away in Hacienda Convalescent Hospital in Long Beach on Aug. 13, 1973, and is buried in All Souls Cemetery in Long Beach.[1]

**Lafontaine, Moses.** Army number, none; not a registrant; born, Belcourt, ND, March 6, 1893, of American parents; occupation, farmer; enlisted in Company G, 2nd Infantry, North Dakota National Guard, at Rolla, on July 14, 1917; called into federal service, World War, on July 15, 1917; served in Company G, 2nd Infantry, North Dakota National Guard, to discharge. Discharged at Devils Lake, ND, on Aug. 15, 1917, as a Private; Surgeon's Certificate of Disability.

When Moses registered for the draft on June 5, 1917, he was working as a farm laborer for James Plant of Belcourt. At that time he was married to Mary St. Ann Grant, with a son, Joseph. About a month-and-one-half later he enlisted in the ND National Guard at Rolla. He was discharged a month later, due to some health issues. According to the Census Roll taken in 1924, Moses and Mary had three more children, Sylvio, Louis M., and Marie. Mary passed away on March 9, 1925. Moses married Rosalie Belgarde on Nov. 28, 1928. Moses passed away in the hospital at the Minot Air Base on May 2, 1964. His wife and three sons, Joseph, Silvio and Martin, survived him. Moses is buried in St. Ann's Catholic Cemetery in Belcourt. In 1915, Moses' sister, Mary, had married John Vallie, who had also enlisted with Moses at Rolla in 1917.[2]

**Lafrombois, Martin A.** Army number 85,532; registrant, Cass County; born, Williston, ND, May 7, 1897, of American parents; occupation, farmer; enlisted in Company B, 1st Infantry, North Dakota National Guard, at Fargo, on July 27, 1917; served in Company B, 1st Infantry, North Dakota National Guard (Company B, 164th Infantry), to Oct. 26, 1918; Headquarters Company, 164th Infantry, to discharge. Grades: Bugler, Nov. 5, 1917; Private, Aug. 1, 1918; Private 1st Class, Aug. 1, 1918; Bugler, Oct. 3, 1918; Private, Dec. 26, 1918; overseas from Dec. 15, 1917, to Feb. 26, 1919. Discharged at Camp Dodge, IA, on March 11, 1919, as a Private.

In the Census Roll for the Turtle Mountain Reservation taken in 1906, Martin is listed with his parents, Gabriel and Cecil, as well as a brother and a sister. In the 1910 U.S. Census, Martin was a student at the Fort Totten Boarding School. While there, he likely played in the band, as he developed an interest in music. When Martin registered for the draft on June 4, 1917, he was working as a bellhop at the Powers Hotel in Fargo. While he was serving in France, he played with the National Guard band, which Gen. Hunter Liggett called the "Million Dollar Band." The band leader was Howard Bachman. After the war, Bachman organized a concert band in Chicago known as Bachman's Million Dollar Band, which performed at American Legion conventions.

65

After the war, Martin moved to Chicago. In the 1930 U.S. Census, he was a musician in a dance orchestra. On Jan. 23, 1937, He married Agnes Margaret Coglan (1893-1961) in Chicago. Agnes worked as an office clerk. In the Census Roll taken in 1937, Martin is still listed on the Census Rolls with his father, Gabriel. In the 1940 U.S. Census, Martin is shown as an orchestra musician and Agnes was working as a bookkeeper for a retail coal company. They also had five renters living in their household. When Martin registered for the Selective Service in 1942, he and Agnes lived on Fulton Street in Chicago and rented rooms. Martin passed away on Oct. 17, 1959, and is buried in Calvary Cemetery in Evanston, IL. Agnes passed away on Nov. 18, 1961, and is also buried in Calvary Cemetery.[3]

Martin LaFromboise played in Million Dollar Band.

*State Historical Society of North Dakota*

**Landry, John.** Army number 4,707,156; registrant, Benson County; born, Belcourt, ND, Oct. 11, 1895, of American parents; occupation, laborer; inducted at Minnewaukan on Aug. 28, 1918; sent to Camp Lewis, WA: served in 166th Depot Brigade, to Sept. 5, 1918; Company F, 13th Ammunition Train, to discharge. Discharged at Camp Lewis, WA, on Feb. 20, 1919, as a Private.

When John registered for the draft before the war, he was working as an assistant at the Fort Totten Boarding School. After the war, John married Clara Monette (1889-1972). Clara had been married to Patrice Vandal, who died in 1920. Clara and Patrice were the parents of four children. In the 1930 U.S. Census, John worked in a butcher shop in Rolla. In the Census Roll for the Turtle Mountain Reservation taken in 1937, John and Clara (NE) are listed with their children, John Jr., Cecelia, Auralia, and Juanita. Their son, John, Jr, served with the US Army in Europe during WWII. John, Sr, continued to work as a meat cutter. He died at the hospital on the Minot

Air Base on Feb. 8, 1965. He is buried in St. Michael's Cemetery in Rolla. The Fred Wagner American Legion Post of Rolla were in charge of the military rites conducted at his gravesite.[4]

**Langer, Joseph.** Army number, none; registrant, (not given); born, Belcourt, ND, Dec. 11, 1895, (nationality of parents not given); occupation, (not given); enlisted in Company G, 2nd Infantry, North Dakota National Guard, at Rolla, on July 13, 1917; served in Company G, 2nd Infantry, North Dakota National Guard, to discharge. Discharged on Aug. 15, 1917, as a Private; Surgeon's Certificate of Disability.

Joseph's family name was spelled Longie in the *Official Roster of North Dakota Soldiers, Sailors and Marines*. The spelling of the family name seemed to depend on how non-French speaking people understood the French pronunciation. Joseph's brother, Frank, spelled his name Langie. In the Census Roll for the Turtle Mountain Reservation taken in 1904, Joseph was listed with his parents, his brother Frank (François), and three sisters. Their father, Frank, Sr., had been a member of the Indian Police. Joseph registered for the draft on June 5, 1917, and listed himself as an "Indian ward of USA." He was of short stature with stout build. He was discharged for medical reasons from the service while his unit was still in North Dakota. Around 1920, Joseph accepted a job as maintenance supervisor at the Indian School at Fort Totten. In the 1940 U.S. Census, he is listed as a sub-foreman with the Indian Service. In the late 1920s, he married Gertrude Page. They had two sons, Joseph, Jr., and Donald. Joseph, Jr. served with the Army in the Pacific during WWII. Donald served in the US Air Force during the Korean Conflict. In 1951, Joseph retired from his position at Fort Totten. He and his wife moved to Renton, WA. Gertrude passed away in Renton in 1964. Joseph passed away in Valley General Hospital in Renton on Dec. 3, 1972. He is buried in Greenwood Memorial Park Cemetery, in Renton, WA.[5]

**Langie, Frank.** Army number, none; not a registrant; born, Belcourt, ND, Sept. 29, 1889, of American parents; occupation, farmer; enlisted in Company G, 2nd Infantry, North Dakota National Guard, at Rolla, on July 15, 1917; served in Company G, 2nd Infantry, North Dakota National Guard, to discharge. Discharged at Camp Greene, NC, on Oct. 11, 1917, as a Private; Surgeon's Certificate of Disability.

In the Census Roll for the Turtle Mountain Reservation taken in 1904, Frank is listed as Francois Langer, the son of Frank and Caroline Langer. Frank's brother, Joseph, as well as his sisters are listed. In July 1917, Frank and his brother, Joseph, enlisted in the National Guard at Rolla. They both received early discharges for medical reasons. Frank was discharged about a week after the ND National Guard arrived in North Carolina. Frank married Anne Decoteau (1894-1983) in Belcourt on Nov. 15, 1910. They lived in Belcourt their whole life. In the 1940 U.S. Census, Frank was working as a log house construction laborer. For a number of years, Anne worked as a cook for the prisoners in the Belcourt jail. Their son, Patrick, served in the U.S. Navy during WWII and the Korean Conflict. Frank passed away in the hospital in Belcourt on April 5, 1970. His wife and two sons, Patrick and George, survived him. He is buried in St. Ann's Cemetery in Belcourt. The Lilley-Dionne American Legion Post of Belcourt conducted military rites.[6]

**Latrail, Louis Napoleon.** Army number, 55,192; registrant, Williams County; born, Belcourt, ND, July 27, 1896, of American parents; occupation, tailor; enlisted in Company E, 1st Infantry, North Dakota National Guard, at Williston, on July 20, 1917; served in Company E, 1st Infantry, North Dakota National Guard (Company E, 164th Infantry), to Jan. 18, 1918; Company M, 26th Infantry, to discharge. Grades: Private 1st Class, May 28, 1918; Corporal, Sept. 23, 1918; overseas from Dec. 15, 1917, to Sept. 2, 1919; wounded, severely, July 20, 1918. Engagements: Offensives: Aisne-Marne; St. Mihiel; Meuse-Argonne. Defensive: Montdidier-Noyon. Defensive Sectors: Ansauville (Lorraine); Cantigny (Picardy). Discharged at Camp Dodge, IA, on Sept. 24,

1919, as a Corporal; Surgeon's Certificate of Disability, 10 %. Cited in General Orders No. 6, Headquarters, 2nd Infantry Brigade, AEF, Montabaur, Germany, July 12, 1919, for gallantry in action and devotion to duty during the operations of 2nd Infantry Brigade, AEF, France, 1917-1918. A soldier with splendid qualities of courage and bravery. During the Meuse-Argonne operation, Oct. 4-12, 1918 displayed great gallantry and devotion to duty. Entitled to wear a silver star.

In the Census Roll for the Turtle Mountain Reservation taken in 1904, Louis is listed with his mother, Margaret, as well as three siblings. In the 1910 U.S. Census, he was a student at the boarding school at Fort Totten.

During the war, Louis served in Company M, 26th Infantry with John Smith from Fort Berthold and Alphonse Bear Ghost from Standing Rock. All three of them were cited for gallantry and were eligible to receive the Silver Star Medal, which actually was not created until 1932. A statement from Corporal Latrail's commanding officer indicated that "he was used as a company and battalion runner, and was very good at same." Latrail was severely wounded on July 20, 1918, during the Soissons Offensive. The regimental history states that "on July 20th orders were received that on account of the difficulties encountered by the French Division on our left, its progress had been delayed, and Berzy-le-Sec, the taking of which had been assigned to them, was placed in our sector and the 1st Division was ordered to take it…. It involved desperate work, and that day we failed. The fighting was intense, often at close quarters, when the bayonet was used with telling effect. We swayed to and fro with the balance slightly in our favor. But by nightfall, Berzy was still uncaptured."

Not long after Louis was discharged, he was married in Pipestone, MN, to Inga King, an Oneida from Wisconsin. In the 1920 U.S. Census, Inga was an assistant clerk at the Pipestone boarding school. After the wedding, they lived in North Dakota for a short time. Sometime in the 1920s, they moved to Green Bay, WI. In the 1930 U.S. Census, Louis was working as a laborer in a paper mill in Green Bay. Inga's sister, Irene, also lived with Louis and Inga and their children. Around 1935, he took a job with the Green Bay Park Dept. In the *Green Bay City Directory* for 1953, Louis was listed as a driver for the City Park Dept. He retired from the Park Dept. in 1965. Inga had passed away in 1961. Louis was a member of the Sullivan Wallen American Legion Post, VFW Post No. 2037, Veterans of World War I Barracks No. 1199, and the Russell Leicht Chapter No. 3 DAV. Louis passed away in Bellin Memorial Hospital in Green Bay on April 5, 1986. Three daughters, Jeanne, JoAnn, and Maxine, as well as his son, Louis, Jr., survived him. He is buried in Holy Apostles Cemetery in Oneida, WI.[7]

**LaValle, Roy.** Roy was born in Jamestown, ND, on Feb. 20, 1894. His father's name was Philip. Records of Native Americans in the service collected by Joseph Dixon list Roy as Cree/French descent. Roy enlisted in the U.S. Marine Corps in Jamestown on Dec. 10, 1916. In April 1917, Roy was transferred to Norfolk, VA. In May 1917, he served with a Marine detachment on the USS *Montana*. In August 1918, he had shore duty as an orderly at the rifle range at Wakefield, MA. For much of the rest of his career, he was stationed on the USS *Utah*. While stationed on board the *Utah*, Roy was interviewed by Joseph Dixon. Roy acted as an interpreter, as he spoke French and Spanish. Roy stated that "the service is just what you make of it. There are hard times and good times. You can make it hard for yourself if you want to. I have had a good time. I enjoy the devil dog part of the service. The Mexican trouble brought me into the service. I went down to get Villa. Didn't get him, so I set out to get a few Huns." In the 1920 U.S. Census, he was stationed on the USS *Utah* in Guantanamo Bay. He listed Chicago as his home. At various times he served as mail orderly; and in 1920 he was Assistant Navy Mail Clerk. He also qualified as a gun pointer 1st class on the 6-inch battery. On Dec. 9, 1920, he received a Good Conduct Medal

(#12582), as well as a Victory Medal with the Atlantic Fleet clasp and Maltese Cross. Roy was discharged in December 1921 as a Private 1st Class, after a five-year tour.

Roy married Ann Girard (1897-1982) of Westbrook, ME, in Portsmouth, NH, on Oct. 6, 1923. In 1925, Roy and Ann lived in Westbrook, near Portland, where Ann worked as a telegraph operator for the Western Union Co. After this, they moved to New York City, where Ann continued to work for Western Union. In 1931, Roy was working as a salesman for Emp-Electro Products of Toronto. During WWII, Roy may have served as a seaman. Customs Records (Ancestry.com) show that Roy returned to the U.S. on Jan. 25, 1946. When he arrived in Baltimore with seven other seamen, the customs form was stamped "The above named passengers are repatriated seamen possessing only hand baggage." In 1962, Roy and Ann returned to Portland, ME. In 1964, Roy was staying at the Sun Rest Nursing Home. Roy passed away on March 27, 1964, in Portland, ME. He is buried in Calvary Cemetery in Portland, ME.[8]

Corporal Roy LaValle, USMC, on board the USS *Utah* in New York City on April 29, 1919. Joseph Dixon, photographer. *William Hammond Mathers Museum, Wanamaker Collection, Indiana University*

**Laviolette, Joseph Noil.** Army number 2,704,191; registrant, Rolette County; born, St. John, ND, Sept. 23, 1891, of Canadian parents; occupation, railroad section foreman; inducted at Rolla on June 24, 1918; sent to Camp Dodge, IA; served in Company I, 352nd Infantry (88th Division), to discharge; overseas from Aug. 16, 1918, to June 1, 1919. Engagement: Defensive Sector: Center (Alsace). Discharged at Camp Dodge, IA, on June 14, 1919, as a Private.

Joseph was the son of Albert and Florestine LaViolette. When Joseph registered for the draft on June 5, 1917, he was working for the Great Northern Railway and providing support for his parents in St. John. He was a short man of medium build. Joseph served with the 88th Division in France. Louis Crowskin from the Standing Rock Reservation served in Company I, 352nd Infantry with Joseph. After the Armistice, they were billeted near Gondrecourt, France. Shortly after he returned from France, Joseph married Mary Rose Allard (1903-1975). In both the 1930 and 1940 U.S. Censuses, the family was farming in Couture Township. Around 1949, the family moved to Portland, OR. Joseph was a member of the American Legion, World War I Veterans, and the Eagles. He passed away in the VA Hospital in Vancouver, WA, on July 31, 1972. His wife and two sons, John and Jerrold, as well as four daughters, Irene Bushman, Marie Flores, Joanne Raivo, and Mabel Addington survived him. He is buried in Mt. Calvary Cemetery in Portland.[9]

**Lean Elk, Harry E.** Army number 2,559,194; registrant, Sioux County; born, Porcupine, ND, Feb. 10, 1895, of American parents; occupation, farmer; inducted at Fort Yates on March 29, 1918; sent to Camp Dodge, IA; served in Company A, 1st Battalion, 163rd Depot Brigade, to April 20, 1918; Company No. 2, 138th Infantry, to death; overseas from May 3, 1918, to death. Died of broncho pneumonia in England on June 17, 1918; buried in England; reburied in St James Cemetery in Porcupine, Sioux County, ND, on Sept. 25, 1920.

In the Census Roll for Standing Rock taken in 1903, Harry is listed with his father, Nicholas (Herakatamaheca), and his mother, Bessie, as well as his siblings, Lucille and Robert. When he registered for the draft on June 5, 1917, he was farming near Shields. After Harry arrived in Camp Dodge, he was selected to be a riding instructor for the 157th Brigade. While at Camp Dodge, he was photographed with Ben Grey Hawk.

Harry Lean Elk (left)
and Ben Grey Hawk
at Camp Dodge, IA.
*Todd Hanson*

**Lenoir, William Edward.** Army number 2,147,842; registrant, Benson County; born, Belcourt, ND, March 3, 1893, of American parents; occupation, farmer; inducted at Minnewaukan on April 1, 1918; sent to Camp Dodge, IA; served in Company K, 137th Infantry (35th Division), to March 26, 1919; 250th Military Police, to discharge. Grade: Private 1st Class, April 19, 1919; overseas from May 2, 1918, to June 28, 1919. Engagements: Offensive: Meuse-Argonne. Defensive Sectors: Gerardmer (Alsace); Grange-le-Comte (Lorraine). Discharged at Camp Dodge, IA, on July 8, 1919, as a Private 1st Class.

In the Census Roll for the Turtle Mountain Reservation taken in 1905, William is listed with his father, Joseph (Akichita), and mother, Adelle, as well as other siblings. When William registered for the draft before the war, he was working as a farm laborer for his father in the Graham Island area. After the war, he married Ella Olga Michels (1900-1933). In the Census Roll taken in 1933, he lived at Minnewaukan with his wife and son, John, and daughter, Edith. Ella passed away in 1933. In the 1940 U.S. Census, William lodged with the Mike Medved family and worked as a farm laborer. His son, John, enlisted in the Army during WWII and served in the Pacific.

**Lequier, Francis William.** Frank was born on March 13, 1896, in White Earth, MN. In the Census Roll for the White Earth Reservation taken in 1903, Frank is listed with Mah-je-ge-shig and his mother, Mary, as well as two brothers. Frank had attended the boarding school at Carlisle, PA. In 1917, Frank was a student at the boarding school at Wahpeton. He enlisted with a number of other students in Company I, 1st Infantry, North Dakota National Guard in July 1917. He was transferred to Camp Greene, NC, in October 1917. When he arrived in France, he was transferred to the 26th Infantry Regiment (1st Division). He was severely wounded by machine gun fire while attacking a German pillbox. Frank's brother, Louis, died while in the service. A photo of Frank in his uniform was published in a roster of WWI veterans from Richland County, ND.

Francis Lequier
*Richland County Roster*

After the war, Frank returned to Minnesota, where he married Pearl Royce (1899-1973) in Itasca County on March 15, 1920. They lived in Duluth for many years. In the 1930 U.S. Census, Frank was working as a laborer. At that time they had four children, Morna, Francis, Jr., Betty, and Olive. By the 1940s, he was working as an accountant for Works Progress Administration (WPA). Their son, Francis, Jr., served in the Army Air Corps, and was killed in 1944. He is buried at Fort Snelling. Pearl had served as national chaplain of the Military Order of the Purple Heart Auxiliary. After this, Frank separated from Pearl, and in 1951, he moved to Tacoma, WA, where he worked as an accountant at McChord Air Force Base. He married Ina Smith (1908-1994). Frank passed away at his home in Tacoma on June 22, 1986. His wife, Ina, and daughters,

Morna, Betty, and Olive, survived him. He is buried in Mountain View Memorial Park in Tacoma.[10]

**Levings, Martin.** Army number 2,560,057; registrant, McLean County; born, Fort Berthold, ND, Oct. 14, 1895, of American parents; inducted at Washburn on March 28, 1918; sent to Camp Dodge, IA; served in 1st Company, 4th Battalion, 163rd Depot Brigade, to April 20, 1918; Company L, 138th Infantry (35th Division), to discharge; overseas from May 3, 1918, to April 28, 1919; wounded, gassed, Oct. 3, 1918. Engagements: Offensive: Meuse-Argonne. Defensive Sectors: Gerardmer (Alsace); Grange-le-Comte (Lorraine). Discharged at Camp Dodge, IA, on May 12, 1919, as a Private.

In the Census Roll for Fort Berthold Reservation taken in 1897, Martin (Ah-pa-hi-si-pi-sa) was listed with his father, Hard Horn ((Asitsoki), and his mother, Looking for Medicine (Hupatikikili), as well as his siblings. His oldest sister, Hannah (Nak-tsu-a) (1878-1943), served as the model for the sculptor of the statue of Sakakawea that is north of the North Dakota Heritage Center on the Capitol Grounds in Bismarck. Hannah was the granddaughter of Sakakawea. In the 1910 U.S. Census, Martin was a student at the Bismarck Boarding School. When he registered for the draft on June 4, 1917, he was farming near Van Hook.

Martin served with the 35th Division which took heavy casualties in the opening days of the Meuse-Argonne Offensive. After the Armistice, his commanding officer evaluated him, stating that he was an "expert scout, and was in all engagements." After Martin returned home from the war in France, he summarized his feelings about his service. "Was glad to have fought for the land of my forefathers, glad that the world was at peace and that I was home with my old father and mother again."

William Langer (center) with Martin Cross, John Smith, Peter Beauchamp,
Martin Levings, and Ralph Case. *Four Bears Museum*

Martin married Vincentia Ring (1892-1960) and farmed and ranched in the Shell Creek area. Vincentia taught on the reservation for a few years. Martin had been a charter member and commander of the Joseph Young Hawk Legion Post No. 253. He also was a past commander of the Little Shell Legion Post No. 300, and a member of the VFW at Mandaree. He served as tribal chairman from September 1938 to August 1940. Their son, Martin, Jr., served in the U.S. Army during WWII. Martin's grandson, Sgt. James Levings, died in Vietnam in 1968. For a number of years, Martin and Vincentia lived in Wibaux and Livingston, MT, where Vincentia passed away in 1960. Martin moved back to New Town in 1960. He passed away in the New Town Nursing Home on Oct. 27, 1974. His son, Martin Jr., survived him. Martin Sr. is buried in St. Anthony's Catholic Cemetery in Mandaree.[11]

**Lezotte, Arthur.** Army number 2,704,205; registrant, Rolette County; born, St. John, ND, June 7, 1893, of Canadian parents; inducted at Rolla on June 24, 1918; sent to Camp Dodge, IA; served in Company D, 352nd Infantry (88th Division), to discharge; overseas from Aug. 15, 1918, to June 3, 1919. Engagement: Defensive Sector: Center (Alsace). Discharged at Camp Dodge, IA, on June 13, 1919, as a Private.

Arthur was the son of Louis and Veronica Lezotte. When he registered for the draft on June 5, 1917, he was farming near Rolette. When Arthur served in France, there were two other men from Indian Country in his company. They were Harvey Hopkins from Fort Berthold and John Jordan from Standing Rock. After the war, they sailed from France to Newport News, VA. They were stationed a short time in Camp Morrison before traveling on to Camp Dodge, IA. Upon arriving back in North Dakota, Arthur farmed. In the 1920 U.S. Census, he was living with his parents. On March 14, 1941, he married Pearl Halliday (1914-1998) at Rolla. He passed away in the VA Hospital in Fargo, and is buried in St. Ann's Cemetery in Belcourt.[12]

**Linnley, Thomas.** Army number 46,199; registrant, Ward County; born, Seattle, WA, Aug. 28, 1890, of American parents; occupation, auto mechanic; enlisted in Company A, 2nd Infantry, North Dakota National Guard, at Minot, on July 14, 1917; called in federal service, World War, on July 15, 1917; served in Company A, 2nd Infantry, North Dakota National Guard (Company A, 164th Infantry), to Jan. 9, 1918; Company B, 18th Infantry (First Division), to May 22, 1918; Company D, 1st Supply Train, 1st Division, to discharge; overseas from Dec. 15, 1917, to discharge; wounded, slightly, Feb. 8, 1918. Engagements: Offensives: Aisne-Marne; St. Mihiel; Meuse-Argonne. Defensive: Montdidier-Noyon. Defensive Sectors: Ansauville ans Saizerais (Lorraine); Cantigny (Picardy). Discharged at Camp Dix, NJ, on July 17, 1919, as a Private. Awarded the Polish Commemorative Cross.

Thomas was identified by his fellow soldiers as Native American. He was working in Minot as an auto mechanic when he registered for the draft on June 5, 1917. Thomas' commanding officer stated that "this man has natural scouting qualifications." After the war, he re-enlisted in the Army, serving from 1920-1923. When he registered for the Selective Service during WWII, he was working as a mechanic for Riverview Garage in New York City. He passed away on May 3, 1961, and is buried in Long Island National Cemetery (Section 2K, Site 308). His wife, Margaret (1900-1990), is buried with him.[13]

**Little Chief, Charles.** Army number 471,934; not a registrant, under age; born, Solen, ND, July 23, 1896, of American parents; occupation, farmer; enlisted at Bismarck on March 21, 1918; sent to Jefferson Barracks, MO; served in Company I, 48th Infantry, to discharge. Grades: Private 1st Class, Aug. 1, 1918; Corporal, May 29, 1919. Discharged at Camp Jackson, SC, on June 6, 1919, as a Corporal.

In the Census Roll for Standing Rock taken in 1904, Charles is listed with his mother, Canku, and sister, Alma. He attended school at Fort Yates and at the boarding school in Bismarck. After this, he was a student at the Carlisle Boarding School, where he played football with Jim Thorpe. Alex Traversie from Fort Yates was a fellow student with Charles, shortly before the war. Charles served with the 48th Infantry Regiment, which performed guard duty at a number of the major ports on the East Coast. He wrote about his military service, saying "my war experience wasn't very much as I didn't get over there, although I rendered splendid service to my country for I voluntarily enlisted and was very anxious to get a shot at one of those Jerries but I'm sorry I didn't get there." He added, "I'm glad I was in the army for I learned good many things which I wouldn't have learned if I stayed home."

Charles Little Chief. *Todd Hanson*

On Oct. 18, 1921, he married Eva Redfish (1894-1966). In the 1930 U.S. Census, Charles was farming in Sioux County, while Eva worked as a sales lady. They lived with their daughter, Germaine, and stepdaughter, Mary Rattlingtail. In the 1940 U.S. Census, Charles was working as a laborer for the WPA. During WWII, Charles moved to Bismarck in 1942, and enlisted in the Navy in 1943. In the 1945 Bismarck *City Directory*, Charles is listed as a defense worker. In the 1948 directory, Eva was working as a cook at the New Sweet Shop. Eva also had worked at the GP Restaurant in Bismarck. Charles worked as a carpenter. He was a member of the American Legion Post in Cannon Ball. Eva helped organize the Auxiliary of the Richard Blue Earth Post at Cannon Ball. Charles passed away in Bismarck on March 18, 1956. He is buried in St. Elizabeth's Cemetery in Cannonball.[14]

Albert Little Owl. *Four Bears Museum*

**Little Owl, Albert.** Army number 4,045,663; registrant, Mercer County; born, Elbowoods, ND, Dec. 28, 1893, of American parents; occupation, farmer; inducted at Stanton on July 24, 1918; sent to Camp Custer, MI; served in 160th Depot Brigade, to Aug. 31, 1918; Company G, 13th Ammunition Train, to discharge. Grade: Corporal, Oct. 1, 1918. Discharged at Camp Dodge, IA, on Feb. 7, 1919, as a Corporal.

Albert was the son of William Little Owl and Assiniboine Woman. He attended school at Elbowoods and the boarding school at Wahpeton. While he was stationed at Camp Custer, he came down with the flu and spent about a month in the hospital. In the Census Roll for the Mandans at Fort Berthold taken in 1920, he was married to Alice Old Dog. He had a son, Donald, with Alice. In the Census Roll taken in 1925, he was married to May Hunts Along. In 1933, he married Josephine Iron Bull (1908-1971). He farmed and ranched in the Twin Buttes area. Albert passed away at the home of his son, Ronald, on Feb. 27, 1975. His sons, Ronald, Orville, and Albert, Jr., as well as three daughters, Christine, Lorraine, and Elizabeth survived him. He is buried in Twin Buttes Community Cemetery. The Levi Lincoln Twin Buttes American Legion Post No. 303 conducted military rites at the cemetery.[15]

**Lizotte, Patrick.** Army number 2,259,190. Patrick was born at St. Johns, ND, on Jan. 17, 1895. In the Census Roll for the Ojibwe at the Devils Lake Agency taken in 1909, Patrick is listed with his mother, Julia, and his stepfather, J.B. Martell. When Patrick registered for the draft on June 5, 1917, he was farming near Medicine Lake, MT. He was a tall man of slender build. He was inducted on Sept. 18, 1917, at Sheridan, MT, and served in Headquarters Company, 362nd Infantry Regiment (91st Division), to discharge. He was promoted to Private 1st Class on Oct. 25,

1918. He served overseas from July 6, 1918, to April 14, 1919, and was discharged on May 1, 1919. In the 1920 U.S. Census, he lived with his parents in Rolette County. In the 1930 U.S. Census, he was working as a hired man for Henry Leiffring in Sheridan County, MT. In the Census Roll for the Turtle Mountain Reservation taken in 1937, Patrick was listed as living in Williston, ND.[16] According to FindaGrave, at the time of his death he was a farmer in Fort Peck, MT. Patrick died at the Veterans Hospital in Walla Walla, WA, on March 5, 1936, and is buried in Mountain View Cemetery, Walla Walla, Washington, plot Walla-VE-85-s2-111. He was survived by his wife and stepson, both of Fort Peck.

**Lockwood, Joseph.** Army number 54,133; not a registrant, enlisted prior; born, Verndale, MN, Nov. 26, 1898, of American parents; occupation, student; enlisted in Company I, 1st Infantry, North Dakota National Guard, at Wahpeton, on April 9, 1917; called into federal service, World War, on July 15, 1917; served in Company I, 1st Infantry, North Dakota National Guard (Company I, 164th Infantry), to Jan. 13, 1918; Company H, 26th Infantry (1st Division), to July 19, 1918; Casual, to discharge. Grade: Private 1st Class, Nov. 22, 1917; overseas from Dec. 15, 1917, to Sept. 28, 1918; wounded, severely, July 19, 1918. Engagements: Defensive: Montdidier-Noyon. Offensives: Aisne-Marne. Defensive Sectors: Ansauville (Lorraine); Cantigny (Picardy). Discharged at Walter Reed Hospital, D.C., on June 30, 1921, as a Private 1st Class; Surgeon's Certificate of Disability, 15%.

In the Census Roll for the Turtle Mountain Reservation taken in 1914, Joseph is listed with his mother, sister, and two brothers. His mother, Emily, was the daughter of Joseph Rolette. In the 1915 North Dakota State Census, Joseph was living in Wahpeton. In April 1917, he was one of a group of six students from the Wahpeton boarding school who enlisted in the North Dakota National Guard. When Joseph entered the service, his mother was a seamstress at the Standing Rock Boarding School in Fort Yates.

Joseph Lockwood. *Richland County Roster*

In France, Joseph served in Company H (2nd Battalion) with two other classmates from Wahpeton, Charles Ellis and James Munnell. According to the regimental history for the 26th

Infantry, on the morning of July 19, the day that Joseph was wounded, the "2nd and 3rd Battalions jumped off at 4:30 am behind a rolling barrage. Heavy machine gun fire was again encountered and there were many casualties." Private 1st Class Lockwood had been serving as a runner. At the time, it was not known what had happened to Joseph. In September, the Fort Yates paper reported that Mrs. Lockwood had received a letter from the War Department that her son was missing in action. Finally, on Oct. 4, 1918, the Red Cross sent her a letter saying that her son had just arrived from overseas and admitted to the hospital at Camp Dodge, IA. The Red Cross wrote that "the government has fully equipped this hospital with everything that money can buy, that it is believed will help the patients, and some of the best physicians and surgeons in the country are here, doing all in their power to bring the soldier back to the best possible health so you need not worry." Joseph was later transferred to Walter Reed Hospital in Washington D.C. After the war, a photo of Joseph in his uniform was published in a roster of soldiers from Richland County, ND.

Joseph was a patient at Walter Reed Hospital from Sept. 24, 1920, to Aug. 16, 1922. He received therapy for his wounds and vocational training. His wounds restricted the type of work he could perform. While in rehab, he worked for a while for the *Washington Post*, but his injured leg affected his efforts. He also employed as a student in the manufacturing and design of jewelry at the Washington Jewelry School. On July 1, 1924, he accepted a position as a clerk with the Finger Print Section of the Federal Bureau of Investigation. While employed there, one of his supervisors, Clarence D. McLean, wrote, "Mr. Lockwood is probably the hardest working man in this office. He is one of the first to arrive in the morning and last to leave at the close of the day. Although his education has been more or less limited he will, I feel sure, develop into a very efficient clerk. He is an enthusiastic worker." After a year with the Bureau, he was let go due to a reduction in force. After this he took a job with the Government Services Administration (GSA). He worked in their Washington, D.C., office until his retirement. He married Greta Coffman (1907-1971). After retiring, he moved to Ronceverte, WV, the hometown of his wife. Joseph passed away in his home on Aug. 22, 1966. He is buried in Coffman Hill Chapel Cemetery.[17]

**Lyon, Raphael.** Army number 4,366; not a registrant, under age; born, Fort Yates, ND, Oct 24, 1896, (nationality of parents not given); occupation rancher; enlisted in Company I, 2nd Infantry, North Dakota National Guard, at Bismarck, on July 25, 1917; served in Company I, 2nd Infantry, North Dakota National Guard, to Oct. 5, 1917; 161st Ambulance Company, to discharge; overseas from Dec. 12, 1917, to May 9, 1919. Engagements: Offensives: Aisne-Marne; Meuse-Argonne. Defensive Sectors: Champagne; Lorraine. Discharged at Camp Dodge, IA, on May 22, 1919, as a Private.

Ray was the son Frank Lyon and Imelda McLaughlin. Imelda, the daughter of James McLaughlin, died in 1899. In the Census Roll for Standing Rock taken in 1901, Ray was listed with his grandmother, Louisa McLaughlin. He was still listed with her in the Census Roll for 1913. Ray was among the first people to enlist in the ND National Guard in July 1917. He was awarded the French Fourragère, similar to a unit citation.

In the 1930 U.S. Census, Ray lived with his wife in Selfridge and worked as a laborer. In the 1940 U.S. Census, he was still living in Selfridge, ND. He later moved to Spokane, WA, where he worked as an auto mechanic. He was a member of American Legion Post No. 9 in Spokane. He married Eunice Ashley (1896-1987). He passed away in the VA Hospital in Spokane on Feb. 15, 1968. His wife and his son, Ray, Jr., as well as two daughters, Ramona and Joan, survived him. He is buried in Greenwood Memorial Terrace.[18]

# M

**Mahto, Ted.** Army number 4,045,748; registrant, Sioux County; born, Cartersville, MT, March 22, 1892, of American parents; occupation, stockman; inducted in Fort Yates on July 26, 1918; sent to Camp Custer, MI; served in 808th Pioneer Infantry, to July 21, 1919; Medical Detachment, 803rd Pioneer Infantry, to discharge. Grades: Sergeant, Nov. 22, 1918; Sergeant 1st Class, June 12, 1919; overseas from Sept. 17, 1918, to July 18, 1919. Discharged at Camp Dodge, IA, on July 26, 1919, as a Sergeant 1st Class.

Ted was the son of Frank and Martha Mahto. When he registered for the draft on June 5, 1917, he was working for a farmer near Fort Yates. While Ted was still in training at Camp Custer, he sent a letter back to the Fort Yates paper:

> Hello Chris,
> Just dropping you a few lines to let you hear from me. Getting along fine now, drilling every day and like the drills fine. Plenty to eat, good place to sleep and all a fellow has to do is to keep a little pep in himself so he can obey orders immediately and he gets along fine. I really like it. My papers have not returned, so I am not assigned to any certain company as yet, but I think I will be fitted out this week.
> Yesterday I went to a baseball game and saw an Indian team play. While standing there, someone called out, "Ted." I looked around and saw a friend, an Indian boy from Fort Berthold, by the name of Albert Little Owl. With him was Dan Chase, Frank Chase's brother.
> I am trying out for the remount service, as these boys are also. As soon as I get out of quarantine, I think we will probably be together. Anyway, no matter where they put me, I am going to make good. I have the highest education of any man in my Barracks, so I may get a non-commissioned officer's rating to start with.
> Well Chris, here's a good luck to you and the people of old Yates.
> So long,

Ted enjoyed his service time in France. He wrote, "I say here that it was the greatest opportunity that I have ever had." While still in France, he took the opportunity to study some books to improve his education. He added, I do my work and find time to study some, because I want to make the best of all the time I have over here." In a report he filled out after the war, he indicated he was Assiniboine Sioux. In the 1920 U.S. Census, Ted was working as a laborer in Sioux County. Shortly after this he moved to the Red Lake Reservation, where he married Mary Equayzaince Sitting (1903-1933). They had four children, Ted, Adelia, Clifford, and Marpesa. Their son, Clifford, served in the Air Force during the Korean Conflict. In the 1940 U.S. Census, Ted was a patient at the VA Hospital in St. Cloud, MN. He later moved to Minneapolis. He married his second wife, Genevieve (1915-2004). Ted worked as a painter. He passed away in the VA Hospital in Minneapolis on Nov. 19, 1963, and is buried in Fort Snelling National Cemetery (Section K, Site 2136). Genevieve is buried next to Ted at Fort Snelling.[1]

**Many Wounds, George.** Army number 502,368; registrant, Sioux County; born, Fort Yates, ND, Nov. 15, 1891, of American parents; occupation, barber; inducted at Fort Yates on March 6, 1918; sent to Fort Logan, CO; served in 19th Recruit Company, Fort Logan, CO, to April 5, 1918; 20th Company, Coast Artillery Company, Manila Bay, Philippine Islands, to discharge. Discharged at San Francisco, CA, on Oct. 13, 1919, as a Private.

In the Census Roll for Standing Rock taken in 1903, George is listed with Tiberius Many Wounds and Pretty Beaver (Capawastewin). In the Census Roll taken in 1909, George is listed with Clara

Tatooed, his first wife. Clara was the sister of James Tattooed, a fellow veteran. George and Clara had several daughters, including Josephine and Jennie, who died as an infant. George and Clara separated.

When George registered for the draft on June 5, 1917, he was living in Fort Yates. After George entered the service in the spring of 1918, he sent this letter, dated May 5, 1918, back to the *Sioux County Pioneer*.

> Dear Friend,
> After being 31 days on the Pacific Ocean we just landed at Manila, Philippine Islands. We went thru where Dewey raised cain with the Spainards. But I don't think they had those big guns now on the coast. I think I could raise hell with the Kaiser if he showed up here.
> I am proud to say that I am the first American Indian in this place and I think I can hold my own. They say that this is the strongest fort in the world, and there are thousands of men here. I send my regards to all my friends. Send me your paper.

After George arrived back in the U.S., he summarized his service: "On the 5th of May we landed at Manila, then posted at Corregidor Island, Fort Mills, Fort Drum, and El Fraile. Then sent to Tienkin, China to relief the 15th Infantry. On our way to the states we were quarantined at Nakasaki, Japan for 18 days the transport *Sherman*. Took 47 days to make Frisco, Calif, on account of typhoons." George arrived back in Fort Yates on Oct. 18, 1919, one of the last Sioux County veterans to return home. The local newspaper reported that George had also served in Siberia, performing guard duty at some warehouses owned by Standard Oil Co. In one encounter with the Russians, several men in his company were wounded. George said that the Russians liked the Americans more than the Japanese or British. At his discharge, George had received a rating of Gun Pointer for the 14-inch battery that he served on.

After returning to Fort Yates, George married Mary Halsey (1890-1949). She had previously been married to John Howard and had several children whom George and Mary raised. In April 1922, the *Sioux County Pioneer* reported that George planned to open a barbershop in one corner of the hotel lobby in Fort Yates. He had traveled to Selfridge to purchase a barber chair. George then worked as a barber in Fort Yates. In the 1940 U.S. Census, George was shown as a disabled veteran receiving a pension. George had been a charter member of the Albert Grass Legion Post at Fort Yates. George and Mary had four sons who were in the service. John and Perry served in the Navy, and Antoine and Joseph served in the Army during WWII. George passed away during WWII, while their sons were at war. George died in his home on Sept. 18, 1943. He had been in ill health and had been planning on entering the VA hospital in Fargo. His wife and children, including John, Antoine, Joseph, Marion, Phyllis, Leona, Perry, Peter, and Anita survived him. He is buried at St. Peter's Cemetery in Fort Yates.[2]

**Martell, Alfred J.** Army number 3,477,915; registrant Sioux County; born, Belcourt, ND, April 27, 1897, of (nationality of parents not given); occupation, (not given); inducted at Fort Yates on Oct. 24, 1918; sent to North Dakota Agricultural College; served in Student Army Training Corps, to discharge. Discharged on Dec. 9, 1918, as a Private.

The Census Roll for the Turtle Mountain Reservation taken in 1905 lists him with his parents, Joseph and Mary Jane Martell. His parents moved to McLean County, where his father ran a stage line north of Washburn until the railroad came. In the 1910 U.S. Census, the family was running a restaurant in Andrews Township, McLean County. Alfred attended school in Max and began working on the local newspaper. He worked for a number of different newspapers during his career. When he registered for the draft on June 7, 1918, he was working for the *Sioux County Pioneer*. After serving with the Student Army Training Corps (SATC) at Fargo, he married Elinor Henderson in McIntosh, SD, on Aug. 8, 1921. They had a son, Curtis. Alfred served as both commander and adjutant of the Legion Post at Fort Yates. He also was the manager of the Fort Yates baseball team. In the 1930 U.S. Census, Alfred was living in McLaughlin and working as a printer for the county paper. He also had worked for the *McIntosh News* and the *Selfridge Journal*. In the 1940 U.S. Census, he was living in Fort Yates. His last position was as editor and printer for the *Sioux County Pioneer-Arrow* at Fort Yates. He passed away at the Fort Yates hospital on May 12, 1950. His wife survived him. He is buried in the Soldiers Field section of the Catholic cemetery in Fort Yates. The Albert Grass American Legion Post took charge of the military rites at the cemetery.[3]

**Martin, John.**   Canadian army number 2,129,367; registrant, Dell Dell, Manitoba; born, Belcourt, ND, May 30, 1893, of Canadian parents; occupation, laborer; enlisted at Brandon, Manitoba, on March 4, 1918; served in 43rd Battalion, Canadian Expeditionary Force, to discharge; overseas from Feb. 20, 1918, to (date not given); wounded, (date not given). Discharged at Winnipeg, Manitoba, on April 7, 1919, as a Private.

John and his older brother, Joseph, were the sons of Theofile and Elisa Martin. His parents and Joseph were listed in the Census Roll for the Chippewa of the Devils Lake Agency taken in 1890. In the 1906 Canada Census, John was living with his parents near Dauphin, Manitoba. In the 1910 U.S. Census, the family lived in Rolla. His parents are listed as Chippewa. According to Canadian military records, John was living with his mother in Duck Mountain, Manitoba, when he underwent a medical examination on Nov. 27, 1917. He enlisted in Brandon on Jan. 9, 1918, and arrived in England on March 4, 1918 aboard the S.S. *Megantic.* He landed in France on June 22, 1918, and served two months with the 43rd Battalion (Cameron Highlanders of Canada). He was hit with a machine gun bullet in the right thigh on Aug. 16, 1918, while fighting near Amiens, along the Somme River. While John was waiting to be picked up, a shell exploded near him, rendering him unconscious. When he regained consciousness, he right ear was bleeding. He was evacuated to England on Aug. 19, 1918, where his leg wound was dressed. He was in the hospital in England for five months before being shipped back to Canada in December 1918. He stayed in Canadian hospitals until his discharge on April 7, 1919, in Winnipeg. Because of his loss of hearing, he was declared as medically unfit. He had recovered from his leg wound and had no trouble walking.

John likely returned to Duck Mountain to live, and later moved to Boggy Creek, Manitoba. John married Winnie Samuel and in 1958, moved to North Surrey, British Columbia. John was living in Winnipeg when his brother, Joseph, died in 1962. John passed away in the Cedarhurst Private Hospital in Surrey on Dec. 24, 1974. He is buried in Vancouver, B.C.[4]

**Martin, Joseph M.**   Army number 125,861; not a registrant, enlisted prior; born, Bottineau, D.T., Nov. 16, 1885, of Canadian parents; occupation, laborer; enlisted at Fargo on May 7, 1917; sent to Jefferson Barracks, MO; served in Battery C, 6th Field Artillery (1st Division), to discharge.
Battery C fired the first American shell in the war. Grades: Private 1st Class, Nov. 25, 1917; Saddler, April 13, 1918; Private, June 11, 1919; Private 1st Class, June 11, 1919: overseas from July 29, 1917, to Sept. 10, 1919. Engagements: Defensive: Montdidier-Noyon. Offensives: Aisne-Marne; St. Mihiel; Meuse-Argonne. Defensive Sectors: Sommerviller, Ansauville, Saizerais, (Lorraine); Cantigny (Picardy). Discharged at Camp Dodge, IA, on Sept. 16, 1919, as a Private 1st Class.

Joseph, also known as Mose, was the older brother of John Martin. Joseph appears with his parents on the Census Rolls for the Chippewa of the Devils Lake Agency taken in the late 1880s. Around 1900, the Martin family moved back to Canada. On April 4, 1917, Joseph returned to Rolla, ND. Shortly after this, he traveled with Moses Fiddler to Devils Lake to see about enlisting. He continued on to Fargo, where he enlisted in the U.S. Army on May 7, 1917. While undergoing training in Arizona, he sent a letter home:

> I am in Douglas, Ariz., right along the border. I like army life. They treat me pretty well. We get good board and good places to stay. But it's awful hot out here. I am beginning to get used to it, but it's hotter every day. Good thing the nights are cold. We go through hard drilling 10 hours a day. We handle three-inch guns, six men and six horses to each gun. Three men ride horses and three ride the guns. I drive a lead tem in front. No grass grows here. All sand and mountains. When the wind blows, it is like a blizzard in North Dakota. Douglas is a fair sized city. The people are mostly Spaniards and Mexicans. We are one mile from the city, but street cars run right thru the camp. There are about 6000 cavalry and artillery now in camp here. The infantry left for the front a few days ago. Give my regards to my friends. Hope to see them all after the war, and I will try to do my best on the front.

He served with the First Infantry Division, spending more than two years in France. He was able to speak and write French and German and served as an interpreter. He was discharged after exposure to gas had caused him to be disabled. The 6th FA unit history lists his home address as Duck Mt., Manitoba.

Joseph returned to Rolla, and on Aug. 23, 1921, he married Virginia Bercier (1898-1985). They lived in Rolla until 1925, when they moved to Devils Lake where Joseph worked as a carpenter. He was a member of the VFW and the American Legion. Joseph passed away at his home in Devils Lake on June 28, 1962. His wife and seven children, Joseph, Jr., Irene, Louis, Frances, Regina, Walter, and Duane, survived him. He is buried in Devils Lake Cemetery.[5]

**Mason, Joseph.** Army number, none; registrant, Rolette County; born, Belcourt, ND, Dec. 14, 1891, of American parents; occupation, farmer; enlisted in Company G, 2nd Infantry, North Dakota National Guard, at Rolla, on July 16, 1917; served in Company G, 2nd Infantry, North Dakota National Guard, to discharge. Discharged at Camp Greene, NC, on Oct. 9, 1917, as a Private, Surgeon's Certificate of Disability.

In the Census Roll of the Turtle Mountain Band of Chippewa taken in 1906, Joseph his listed as the adopted son of Day after Day (Nepetakezik), and his wife, Elise Lenoir. In the 1910 Census, Joseph was a student at the Fort Totten boarding school. In the Census Roll taken in 1914, he is listed with his wife, Rose Peltier. When Joseph registered for the draft on June 5, 1917, he was hauling poles with a team, and providing support for his family, including his mother. He has discharged a few days after his National Guard unit arrived in North Carolina. Joseph re-registered in 1918. At that time he was working for Olof Johnson of Overly, ND. In the 1930 U.S. Census, he was living on the Fort Berthold Reservation and working as a laborer. He later moved back to Fort Totten, where he died on Sept. 30, 1956. His is buried in St. Jerome's Catholic Cemetery in Benson County.[6]

**McCloud, Joseph.** Canadian army number 475,160; not a registrant, enlisted prior; born, Belcourt, ND, Aug. 26, 1895, of Canadian-American parents; occupation, electrician; enlisted in the Canadian Expeditionary Forces, at Winnipeg, Manitoba, on Aug. 2, 1915; assigned to 90th Canadian Rifles, to (date not given); 11th Reserve Battalion, Canadian Infantry, to (date not given); 8th Battalion, to (date not given); 18th Reserve Battalion, to (date not given); Mounted

Rifle Depot, to (date not given); Canadian Forestry Corps, to (date not given). Grades: Lance Corporal, Nov. 8, 1917; Corporal, April 17, 1918; Sergeant, April 4, 1919; overseas, (dates not given); wounded, June 16, 1916; wounded, seriously, July 26, 1916. Engagements: not given. Discharged in England, on July 15, 1919. Declared legally dead by the District Court of Burleigh County, on Sept. 21, 1931.

Joseph was the son of Legloire and Margaret McCloud. After enlisting in Winnipeg, Joseph arrived in France on May 4, 1916. On June 16, 1916, he was slightly wounded in his hand and returned to duty that same day. On July 25, 1916, he was assisting two men who were wounded in the fighting at Ypres. Private McCloud was hit with shrapnel in his right shoulder, left knee, and chin. The wounds in his chin and knee healed properly, but his shoulder wound became infected, and bothered him from time to time. It was determined that a piece of shrapnel was still under the skin, but the medical officers did not think it needed to be operated on, and discharged him as "fit for duty." He was serving with the 8th Battalion, which were known as the "Little Black Devils." While stationed at Seaford on the south coast of Sussex, Corporal McCloud was given permission to marry. Records indicate that his wife's name was Jessie. When Sgt. McCloud was discharged on July 15, 1919, he indicated that he would be living on York Street in Broadstairs, Kent. It is not known when he returned to the United States. Nor is it known when Joseph passed away. There is a gravestone marker for him in St. Ann's Cemetery in Belcourt.[7]

**McKay, Henry Stanilaus.** Army number 4,797,162; registrant, Benson County; born, Minnewaukan, ND, July 30, 1896, of American parents; occupation, laborer; inducted at Minnewaukan on Aug. 28, 1918; sent to Camp Lewis, WA; served in 166th Depot Brigade, to discharge. Discharged at Camp Lewis, WA, on Dec. 9, 1918, as a Private.

Henry was the son of Luke McKay (Hapanzi) and Mary Louise (Hdaiwankewin). In the 1910 U.S. Census, he was a student at the Fort Totten Boarding School. He also attended the boarding school at Carlisle, PA. When he registered for the draft before the war, he was working with his father. He was listed as of short stature and medium build. After the war, Henry married Laura Lohnes. In the 1930 U.S. Census, Henry was a farm laborer at the School of the Little Flower in St. Michael. In the Census Roll for the Devils Lake Sioux taken in 1937, Henry and Laura are listed with their daughters, Gertrude and Dorothy. They had several children who died as infants, including Delores and Henry, Jr. In the 1940 U.S. Census, Henry held the position of assistant dairyman. Henry passed away on April 2, 1945, when a tractor he was operating tipped over near Fort Totten. He is buried in St. Michael's Cemetery.[8]

**McLaughlin, James Sidney.** Sidney was born on March 18, 1894, in Fort Yates. He was the son of Harry and Annie McLaughlin. He was the grandson of James McLaughlin. In the Census Roll for Standing Rock Reservation taken in 1894, he is listed with his parents and an older sister. At Christmas of 1904, Frank Fiske took a photo of Sidney serving as an altar boy at the Catholic Church in Fort Yates. He married Zelda LeCompte. When Sidney registered for the draft on June 5, 1917, he was farming and providing support for his wife and first son, Melvin. On July 24, 1917, he traveled to Bismarck with his brother, Henry, and his cousin, Ray Lyon, to enlist in the ND National Guard regiment that Captain A.B. Welch was recruiting for. Henry failed the physical exam, while Sidney and Ray were accepted. Before the 2nd Infantry Regiment had left for initial training at Camp Greene, NC, Sidney had been promoted to Corporal. The 2nd Regiment was known as the "Smashed Second" because so many men were transferred to other units. By the end of the war, Sidney was promoted to Sergeant. He likely continued to serve in the 161st Ambulance Company with his cousin, Ray Lyon.

After the war, he returned to North Dakota on July 15, 1919. Sidney and Zelda had seven children: Melvin, Roletta, Geraldine, James, Willis, Harry Michael, and Maurine, as listed in the Census Roll for 1927. Their son, Michael, served in the Army during WWII. For awhile the family lived in Corson County, SD. Sidney and Zelda were later divorced. When Sidney registered for the Selective Service in 1942, he was living in Los Angeles. Sidney moved to Grants Pass, OR, in his later years, and passed away in a Roseburg, OR, hospital on Jan. 22, 1977. He is buried in Williamette National Cemetery (Section L, Site 2586) at Portland, OR.[9]

**Mead, Gabriel.** Army number 4,046,252; registrant, Benson County; born, Tokio, ND, Feb. 14, 1895, of (nationality of parents not given); occupation (not given); inducted at Minnewaukan on Aug. 18, 1918; sent to Camp Custer, MI; served in 160th Depot Brigade, to desertion. Deserted from Camp Custer, MI, on Nov. 15, 1918.

In the Census Roll for the Devils Lake Sioux taken in 1912, Gabriel was listed with his parents, Michael (Wasicuanamani) and Nancy (Winona) Mead. Gabriel married his wife, Mary, on Oct. 7, 1916. When he registered for the draft on June 5, 1917, he indicated that he was in "poor health." After he was inducted in the summer of 1918, he probably should have been given a medical discharge. After he left Camp Custer when the war was over, he attempted to get medical treatment, without success. In May 1919, he went to see a doctor in Devils Lake, but he did not receive treatment. He passed away suddenly on May 24, 1919, in a day coach at the Devils Lake railroad station while waiting for his train to depart. He is buried in St. Michael's Cemetery in Mission Township.[10]

**Means, Wesley William.** Navy number 1,422,329; not a registrant, under age; born, Pine Ridge, SD, Nov. 11, 1899, of American parents; occupation, student; enlisted in the Navy at Minneapolis, MN, on May 3, 1918; served at Naval Training Station, Great Lakes, IL, to June 12, 1918; Naval Air Station, Pauillac, France, to Nov. 11, 1918. Grades: Apprentice Seaman, 151 days; Seaman 2nd Class, 41 days. Discharged at Minneapolis, MN, on Aug. 18, 1919, as a Seaman.

Wesley was the son of Eugene and Nellie Means, who were enrolled members of the Oglala Sioux at Pine Ridge. His father worked as a financial clerk at the agency in Fort Yates.

After the Armistice was signed, Seaman Means was in the transport service with the U.S. Navy. He served as a member of an USN Nucleus Crew #2. Subsequently, he served on the USS *Imperator*, and the USS *Eten.* Both of these ships were former German passenger liners that were commissioned by the Navy for transporting servicemen back to the U.S.

In the 1920 U.S. Census (taken on Jan. 17, 1920), Wesley was working as a laborer in an auto factory in Detroit. In May 1920, he returned to Fort Yates after enrolling in the Sweeney Auto School in Kansas City, MO. Wesley played baseball for the Fort Yates team. Wesley was one of the charter members of the American Lgion Post in Fort Yates. On July 6, 1922, Wesley married Alma Short in Fort Yates. In the 1930 U.S. Census, Wesley and Alma lived near Fort Yates with their children, Lavinia, Wesley, Jr., and Mary. Wesley was working as a laborer doing cement work. In the mid-1930s, he married Louisa Agaard. In the 1940 U.S. Census, the family was living in Fort Yates and Wesley had a good paying job as a steam-fitting mechanic. Sometime after this, the family moved to California. There was a huge shipyard in Vallejo, so he likely went out there during WWII. In 1954, Wesley became a resident of the Veterans Home in nearby Yountville, CA. He passed away there on June 13, 1978. His daughter, Mrs. Richard Carter, survived him. He is buried in Monument Hill Park in Woodland, CA.[11]

**Menz, William.** Army number 2,143,791; registrant, Sioux County; born, Fort Yates, ND, April 23, 1891, of German-American parents; occupation, farmer; inducted at Thunderhawk, SD, on Sept. 18, 1917; sent to Camp Dodge, IA; served in Battery E, 338th Field Artillery, to April 1, 1918; Company I, 326th Infantry (82nd Division), to discharge; overseas from April 29, 1918, to May 29, 1919. Engagements: Offensives: St. Mihiel; Meuse-Argonne. Defensive Sectors: Lucey and Marbache (Lorraine). Discharged at Camp Dodge, IA, on June 8, 1919, as a Private; Surgeon's Certificate of Disability, 10%.

William was born at his father's ranch along the Cedar River, north of Morristown, ND. In the 1900 U.S. Census, he was a student at the boarding school in Fort Yates. He later attended the boarding school in Genoa, NE, where he learned the printer's trade. When he registered for the draft on June 5, 1917, he was working on his brother-in-law's farm near Thunderhawk.

William summarized his military service in a statement he sent to Joseph Dixon. "While in the world war, I have say that I have went through without a scratch, but although I suffered considerable I thought I was doing my duty. In the Argonne Forest, where we were under constant fire from Artillery, from the Germans, we nevertheless pushed our way forward, until the signing of the Armistice. I served one year overseas, and six months in U.S.A." Earlier he had written to Dixon that "through what I have went through during the war, and the experiences I had, has helped me a great deal, and would do it again if the country needs me again."

On Aug. 17, 1922, he married Christine Halsey, who worked as a nurse at the agency hospital. William and Christine had a daughter, Fay Marie. William passed away on Aug. 3, 1925, in the agency hospital in Fort Yates. His final illness was caused in part by his having been gassed during the war. He is buried in St Peter's Cemetery in Fort Yates. Christine had been expecting at the time of William's death. William, Jr., was born some months later. Christine then married Robert Zahn.[12]

**Merrick, Joseph Jr.** Army number 3,681,397; registrant, Benson County; born, Devils Lake, ND, March 12, 1895, of American parents; occupation farmer; inducted at Minnewaukan on June 27, 1918; sent to Camp Dodge, IA; served in Company F, 313th Ammunition Train (88th Division), to discharge; overseas from Aug. 17, 1918, to May 29, 1919. Engagement: Defensive Sector: Center (Alsace). Discharged at Camp Dodge, IA, on June 11, 1919, as a Private.

Joseph was the son of Joseph and Agnes (Wambdiahewin) Merrick. In the Census Rolls for the Devils Lake Sioux, their family name is also spelled Myrick. In the 1910 U.S. Census, Joseph was a student at the Fort Totten boarding school.

When he registered for the draft on June 5, 1917, he was farming with his father near Warwick. After the Armistice was signed, Private Merrick's commanding officer, 1st Lt. Donald Bleifress stated that Merrick was "regarded as unusually good man by whites." Merrick had served with Joseph Court in the 313th Ammo Train in France. After the war, Merrick's sister, Julia, married Court.

After the war, Joseph married Emma Longie (1905-1979) in St. Michael. They had three sons and a daughter, Mary Rose. Of their sons, Raymond and Frank served in the Army in WWII, while Clarence served during the Korean Conflict. In the 1940 U.S. Census, Emma was working as a housekeeper for Albert Hallsten in Twin Tree Township, Benson County. Joseph died in 1943.[13]

**Molash, David J.** Army number 2,787,125; registrant, Sioux County; born, Chamberlain, SD, Sept. 25, 1893, of American-Bohemian parents; occupation, farmer; inducted at Fort Yates on

May 25, 1918; sent to Camp Lewis, WA; served in Company D, 348th Machine Gun Battalion (91st Infantry Division), to discharge. Grade: Private 1st Class, March 3, 1919; overseas from July 6, 1918, to April 2, 1919. Engagements: Offensives: Meuse-Argonne; Ypres-Lys. Defensive Sector: Aubreville (Lorraine). Discharged at Camp Dodge, IA, on April 22, 1919, as a Private 1st Class.

David and his brother, George, were the sons of James and Johanna Molash. Their uncle was William Molash, known as Turkey Track Bill. The Molash family was part Chippewa, French and Spanish, according to Bill. They started to farm near Fort Yates in the early 1900s. When David registered for the draft on June 5, 1917, he was farming near Fort Yates and providing support for his parents and younger siblings. About a year later, he traveled to Camp Lewis with a contingent of men from Sioux County. He sent a letter back to his parents writing, "he is getting on fine, and reads the *Sioux County Pioneer* sent to Mike Halsey." David served in the 348th Machine Gun Battalion with Lawrence See the Elk and Asa Redstone, as well as several other men from the Rosebud Reservation. He sent a number of letters home, which were published by the *Sioux County Pioneer*. On July 27, 1918, he wrote, "I have seen all kinds of country good and poor. I did not get seasick coming over. I thought that I would get sick the first day but didn't. I am staying in a little village with the French people." David arrived back in the U.S. on April 2, 1919. The next day he wrote from Camp Upton, NY:

> I will now drop you a line and let you know that I have arrived in New York safe and sound. In good health, I left St. Nazaire, France, the 25th of March, and landed in New York the 2nd of April at 10 a.m. and am glad to be back in the good old U.S.A. I expect to be home soon. I don't know how long I will be at Camp Upton. I am checked for Camp Dodge for demobilization. Well, Chris, I have seen some big sights in France. Of course, I can't complain. I think I take the U.S.A. for my home. I can tell you more about it when I get home, and then I can tell you of all the places I've been while over there. The weather in France and Belgium is too damp, it rains mostly all the time. When I was up on the Argonne drive, we didn't have no blankets or overcoats, just raincoats, believe me I put in some time. The 91st Division was up there 9 days before being relieved, and it rained most of the time, but it isn't very cold. We didn't have no snow to speak of, we had just enough to cover the ground."

David returned to Fort Yates and married his first wife, Clara. In the 1930 U.S. Census, He and Clara lived in Fort Yates, where he worked as a baker in a bakeshop. In the 1940 U.S. Census, David was working as a farm manager in La Prairie Township near Janesville, WI. He married Florence Gillbank (1903-1976) on Feb. 22, 1952, in Beloit, WI. He had been a charter member of the American Legion in Fort Yates. He also had been past commander and district commander of the Veterans of World War I, VFW, and the Cooties. In the 1958 Beloit *City Directory*, he was working for the Department of Public Works. David passed away at the VA Hospital in Madison, WI, on Sept. 3, 1971. His wife and daughter, Mrs. Addison Long, as well as two sons, James and Leroy Gillbank, survived him. He is buried in Calvary Cemetery in Beloit, WI.[14]

**Molash, George.** Army number 4,039,946; registrant, Sioux County; born, Kennebec, SD, March 18, 1897, of American parents: occupation, farmer; inducted at Fort Yates on July 26, 1918; sent to Camp Custer, MI; served in Company C, 40th Infantry (14th Division), to discharge. Discharged at Camp Sherman, OH, on Jan. 19, 1919, as a Private.

When George registered for the draft on June 5, 1917, he was working on the family farm near Fort Yates. While George was at Camp Custer training with the 14th Division, he sent a letter back to his parents. He wrote, "So don't worry folks. I will try to see Dave when I get over there. Please send me the *Sioux County Pioneer*."

In March 1918, he became engaged to Annie Vermillion. He likely married her before he went in the service. They had several children, including George, Jr., and Marie. They were later divorced. On Sept. 13, 1937, he married Clara Wolfer (1906-1993). George lived in Walker, SD, and was a construction worker. He passed away from a short illness in the VA Hospital in Miles City, MT, on Aug 19, 1967. He is buried in McIntosh, SD. George had also been a charter member of the American Legion Post at Fort Yates.[15]

**Simon Monette, Pat Lizotte, 1917 (other unknown)**

Simeon Monette and Patrick Lizotte were inducted in Montana on Sept. 18, 1917. The unknown man may be from Montana. *State Historical Society of North Dakota*

**Monette, Simeon.** Army number 2,259,197. Simeon was born St. Joseph, Dakota Territory, on Aug. 8, 1885. He was the son of Tousainte and Caroline Monette. In the 1900 U.S. Census, he was listed as a Chippewa student at the Fort Totten boarding school. In the 1910 U.S. Census, he lived with his parents In Olga Township, Cavalier County. When he registered for the draft in July 1917, he was farming near Medicine Lake, MT. He was inducted at Plentywood, MT, on Sept. 18, 1917. He served initially with the Headquarters Company, 362nd Infantry Regiment at Camp Lewis, WA. On July 23, 1918, he transferred to the 5th Ordnance Guard Co. On Nov. 15, 1918, he was promoted to Private 1st Class, and was discharged on April 15, 1919. He did not go overseas. In the 1920 U.S. Census, he worked as a hired man near Medicine Lake. In the 1930 U.S. Census, he worked as a farm laborer for Wilfred Parent in Sheridan County. He never married. He passed away at the VA Hospital in Hot Springs, SD, on April 9, 1970. He is buried in the Black Hills National Cemetery (Section E, Site 1221).[16]

**Montreil, Martin.** Army number 54,254; not a registrant, under age; born, Belcourt, ND, Sept 14, 1897, of American parents; occupation farmer; enlisted in Company D, 2nd Infantry, North Dakota National Guard, at Devils Lake, on June 30, 1917; called into federal service, World War, on July 15, 1917; served in Company D, 2nd Infantry, North Dakota National Guard, to Oct. 13, 1917; Company L, 164th Infantry, to Jan. 12, 1918; Company H, 26th Infantry, to Aug. 28, 1918; Company L, 26th Infantry (1st Division), to discharge; overseas from Dec. 15, 1917, to Sept. 2, 1919. Engagements: Defensive: Montdidier-Noyon. Offensives: Aisne-Marne; St. Mihiel; Meuse-Argonne. Defensive Sectors: Ansauville and Saizerais (Lorraine); Cantigny (Picardy). Discharged at Camp Dodge, IA, on Sept 24, 1919, as a Private.

Martin was the son of Francis and Adele Montriel. His last name was later spelled as Montreal. His father worked for the Indian Police. In the 1910 U.S. Census, Martin was a student at the Fort Totten boarding school. In the 1920 U.S. Census, he lived with his parents. In 1921, he moved to South Dakota, and worked for the Fred La Plante Ranch in La Plant. In August 1932, he married Isabelle J. Traversie at St. Theresa Church in White Horse, SD. They lived at the Cheyenne Agency, where Martin started working for the BIA. He worked for 22 years until retiring in 1960, after moving to Eagle Butte. He later worked for Sioux SuperValu. He passed away in a Rapid City Hospital on Feb 18, 1974. His wife and two daughters, Joan and Rosalee, as well as his sons, Nino, Terry, and Gary, survived him. He is buried in the Black Hills National Cemetery (Section C, Site 1054).[17]

Barney Mulhern (left, seated), Ed Two Horses (right, seated) and
Milan White Eagle (standing). *Todd Hanson*

**Mulhern, Barney.** Army number 2,858,765; registrant, Sioux County; born, Cannon Ball, ND, May 30, 1896, of American parents; occupation, farmer; inducted at Fort Yates on April 30, 1918; sent to Camp Dodge, IA; served in Company F, 350th Infantry, to May 16, 1918; Company K, 358th Infantry (90th Division), to discharge; overseas from June 20, 1918, to Nov. 20, 1918; wounded, severely, Sept. 12, 1918. Engagements: Offensive: St. Mihiel. Defensive Sector:

Villers-en-Haye (Lorraine). Discharged at Fort Sheridan, IL, on Feb. 11, 1920, as a Private; Surgeon's Certificate of Disability, 15%.

Barney was the son of Bernard (J.B.) and Maggie Louise (Ohitawin) Mulhern. Bernard was born in Ireland and served briefly with the U.S. Navy in the Civil War. After the war, he enlisted in the 31st Infantry, and served as a baker at Fort Rice. In the 1910 U.S. Census, Barney was a student at the Bismarck Boarding School. His mother was listed as Yanktonai.

Barney served in Company K, 358th Infantry (3rd Battalion) with Ed Two Horses. Barney was wounded on the opening day of the St. Mihiel Offensive. Ten other men from his company were killed that day near Fey-en-Haye. According to their regimental history, "the 2nd and 3rd Battalions followed by the 1st Battalion went over the top, advancing across a country covered with old trenches and wire entanglements, and which afforded the enemy an excellent field of fire.... At the close of the days fighting approximately five percent of the fighting strength of the 2nd and 3rd Battalions lay dead on the battlefield, but the proportion of German dead was overwhelmingly in excess of our losses, not counting the huge toll in prisoners.... Everything possible had been prepared ahead of the battle so as to take care of the wounded.... These wounded men were a wonderful inspiration to all them by the brave and cheerful manner they exhibited, and seemingly their wounds caused only one regret and that was that they had to go back to the hospitals and leave their comrades to fight the enemy without them." Barney returned to the U.S. shortly after the Armistice, but was not discharged for over a year. He had been wounded in his legs, according to A. B. Welch.

Barney returned to Cannon Ball and married Melda Manz. They had a number of children, including two boys, Patrick and William, who died as infants. Barney never fully recovered his health from his war service. He passed away on May 15, 1931, while working in his garden. Nearly 400 people turned out for his funeral service. The funeral was conducted under the auspices of Blue Earth Post of the American Legion and the Indian War Mothers Association. Barney's wife and two young daughters survived him. He is buried in St. Elizabeth's Cemetery in Cannon Ball. His obituary stated "A happy and lovable character known to many has passed in the death of Barney Mulhern and a brave soldier has answered the last long roll to join the ever-growing ranks of patriots who have gone before." [18]

**Munnell, James Walter.** Army number 54,136; not a registrant, under age; born, Leech Lake, MN, Oct. 30, 1898, of American parents; occupation, student; enlisted in Company I, 1st Infantry, North Dakota National Guard, at Wahpeton, on April 9, 1917; called into federal service, World War, on July 15, 1917; served in Company I, 1st Infantry, North Dakota National Guard (Company I, 164th Infantry), to Jan. 13, 1918; Company H, 26th Infantry (1st Division), to discharge. Grades: Private 1st Class, Nov. 22, 1917; Corporal, Feb. 27, 1918; Sergeant, Sept. 21, 1918; overseas from Dec. 15, 1917, to Sept. 4, 1919; wounded, slightly, May 29, 1918. Engagements: Offensive: Meuse-Argonne. Defensive Sectors: Ansauville and Saizerais (Lorraine); Cantigny (Picardy). Discharged at Camp Grant, IL, on Sept. 25, 1919, as a Sergeant. Cited in General Orders No. 63, Headquarters, 1st Division, AFG, Neuweid, Germany, Aug. 7, 1919. The Division Commander cites the following officers and men for gallantry in action and devotion to duty... "Sergeant James W. Munnell," ... in the Meuse-Argonne Offensive, Oct. 4, 1918, for fearlessly advancing alone and locating enemy machine guns that were holding up the advance of our infantry. Entitled to wear a silver star.

James grew up on the Leech Lake Reservation with his family. In 1917, he was a student at the boarding school at Wahpeton, ND. He was one of a group of students who enlisted in the North Dakota National Guard a few days after President Wilson declared war on Germany. James had a younger brother, David, who also enlisted while he was attending school at Flandreau, SD. David died in the service on Sept. 17, 1919, and is buried at Onigum, MN. James served in the same company in France with Charles Ellis and Joseph Lockwood, who were fellow students from Wahpeton. James was wounded in May shortly after the First Division had driven the Germans from the town of Cantigny. The Germans made six counter-attacks against the Americans, but were unsuccessful. After the Armistice, Sgt. Munnell's commanding officer, 1st Lt. A. C. Rowe stated: "I have known this soldier for a year and find him efficient as a sergeant."

James Munnell. *Richland County Roster*

After the war, James returned to Minnesota. A photo of him in uniform was published in a roster of the veterans from Richland County, ND. In the 1920 U.S. Census, he was living in St. Paul. In the 1920s, he married Lois McEwen. In the 1930 U.S. Census, the family was living in Walker, MN. James' mother also lived with them. In the Census Roll for Leech Lake Consolidated Chippewa taken in 1937, James and his wife are listed with five children, Barbara, Dorothy, James Jr., Lucille and Stanley. Sometime after this, the family moved to Everett, WA, where James worked as a manufacturer's representative in retail merchandising. He passed away in the VA Hospital in Spokane, WA, on April 10, 1971, and is buried in Willamette National Cemetery (Section R, Site 517).[19]

**Murphy, James Charles.** Army number 2,559,195; registrant, Sioux County; born, Shields, ND, April 22, 1895, of American parents; occupation, farmer; inducted at Fort Yates on March 29, 1918; sent Camp Dodge, IA; served in Company A, 1st Training Battalion, 163rd Depot Brigade, to April 20, 1918; Company D, 139th Infantry (35th Division), to discharge. Grade: Private 1st Class, Aug. 1, 1918; overseas from May 3, 1918, to April 28, 1919; wounded, slightly, Sept. 30, 1918. Engagements: Offensive: Meuse-Argonne. Defensive Sectors: Gerardmer (Alsace); Grange-le Comte (Lorraine). Discharged at Camp Dodge, IA, on May 7, 1919, as a Private 1st Class.

Jim was the son of Joshua "Spud" Murphy and Frances Eagle Man. When Jim registered for the draft on June 5, 1917, he was farming near Shields. He was of medium height and stout build. When he arrived at Camp Dodge, he was one of five men from the Standing Rock Reservation who were selected as riding instructors. Three other men from Indian Country served with Private 1st Class Murphy in Company D, 139th Infantry. They were John Elk and Tom Graybull, and Fred Wheeler from Elbowoods. Murphy was wounded while the 139th Infantry was driving the Germans from the town of Exermont. He was struck in the left arm with a machine gun bullet. He had a number of other close calls, as their unit was hard hit in the Meuse-Argonne Offensive. In an evaluation by his commanding officer, Captain Gus Gehlbach, Private 1<sup>st</sup> Class Murphy was described as an "exceptionally good scout."

After Jim returned home, he ranched near Shields. He was one of the charter members of Shields American Legion Post #190. In the 1930 U.S. Census, he was living with his sister, Annie Skye. He never married. He passed away on Aug. 5, 1950, and is buried in St. James' Cemetery in Porcupine, ND. Military rites were conducted by the American Legion.[20]

**Nagel, John Jack.** Army number 4,041,749: registrant, Mercer County; born, Elbowoods, ND, Dec. 12, 1896, of American parents; occupation, farmer; inducted at Stanton on July 24, 1918; sent to Camp Custer, MI; served in 160th Depot Brigade, to Aug. 18, 1918; Headquarters Company, 41st Field Artillery, to Oct. 28, 1918; 42nd Field Artillery, to discharge. Discharged at Camp Dodge, IA, on Jan. 28, 1919, as a Private.

Dan Chase (seated), Albert Little Owl (standing, left) and Jack Nagel (standing, right) were inducted in Stanton on July 24, 1918 and traveled to Camp Custer, MI. *Four Bears Museum*

Jack was the son of John and Mattie (Ta-na-ca-hun) Nagel. His father was from Germany and had served in the Civil War. After John passed away in 1904, Mattie married Charles Grinnell. Mattie did not receive her Civil War widow's pension until 1971. She passed away on Jan. 6, 1975, at the age of 108. In the 1910 U.S. Census, Jack was a student at the boarding school in Bismarck. He also had attended school at Fort Stevenson, ND, and Santee, NE. After this he lived in Montana for a number of years, returning to ND in 1917, when he registered for the draft. He spent his military service at Camp Custer. He returned to Elbowoods after his discharge and married Sadie Smith. They ranched near Halliday in Dunn County. In the Census Roll for the Fort Berthold Reservation taken in 1939, they are listed with their children, Geraldine, John, Jr., Delbert, Thomas, Wilbur, and Vera. Thomas and Wilbur were twins. John, Jr., served in the U.S. Navy during WWII. Wilbur also served in the Navy, while Thomas served in the U.S. Army. Jack passed away at the Air Force Hospital in Minot on June 10, 1977. His sons, John and Wilbur, as well as his daughters, Geraldine and Vera, survived him. He is buried at Red Butte Community Cemetery, east of Twin Buttes. Military rites were conducted by Twin Buttes Community Post No. 303, American Legion.[1]

**Necklace, Mark.** Army number 4,705,175; registrant, McLean County; born, Fort Buford, ND, Dec. 25, 1891, of American parents; occupation, farmer; inducted at Washburn on Aug. 28, 1918; sent to Camp Lewis, WA; served in Company L, 44th Infantry, to discharge. Grade: Private 1st Class, Jan. 21, 1919. Discharged at Camp Lewis, WA, on March 25, 1919, as a Private 1st Class.

In the Census Roll for the Mandans taken in 1898, Mark is listed with his father, Coyote Necklace, and his mother, Comes Out Every Year, as well as two younger sisters. Before the war, he married Jessie Black Hawk. When he registered for the draft on June 5, 1917, he was farming and providing support for his father and Jessie. They lived at Van Hook. Mark served in the Army at Camp Lewis with Robert Dancing Bull. Charles Yellow Bird had traveled with them to Camp Lewis, so he likely was in their unit also. Sgt. Tom Rogers was a recruit instructor while Mark and Robert were at Camp Lewis. After the war, Mark returned to his farming operation.

After his wife, Jessie, died in 1936, he married Lottie Horn (1903-1967). They farmed in the rural Parshall area. In the Census Roll for the Fort Berthold Reservation taken in 1939, Mark and Lottie are listed with two daughters, Pauline and Frances. He was the treasurer of the Water Buster Clan. Mark passed away in the Stanley Hospital on Dec. 23, 1962. His wife and four daughters, Frances, Pauline, Margie, and Marigold survived him. He is buried in the Old Scouts Cemetery near White Shield.[2]

# O

**Old Mouse, Arthur.** Army number 3,775,409; registrant, Dunn County; born, Fort Berthold, D.T., July 1889, of American parents; occupation, farmer; inducted at Manning on Aug. 8, 1918; served in Company D, 10th Battalion, Infantry Replacement and Training Camp, Camp MacArthur, TX, to Sept. 2, 1918; Company 22, September Replacement Draft, to death; overseas from Sept. 23, 1918, to death. Died of pneumonia on Oct. 7, 1918; remains returned to U.S. on Oct. 12, 1920, and buried at Elbowoods.

In the Census Roll for the Mandans taken in 1903, Arthur is listed with his parents, Little Wolf and Buffalo Woman, as well as a sister and brother. Arthur played baseball for a team at Elbowoods. He married Ollie Horn. In the Census Roll for the Mandans taken in 1918, Arthur and Ollie are listed with three children, including Lee and Frieda. After Arthur died, his widow married Doug Standish, a fellow veteran. Arthur is now buried in Independence Congregational Cemetery near Mandaree.

**One Feather, Henry.** Henry was born on June 3, 1896, the son of Antoine (Wiyakawanjila) One Feather and Wiciqua. Antoine had served with the Indian Police, and received a pension. In the 1910 U.S. Census, Henry lived with his family in Corson County, SD. When Henry registered for the draft on June 20, 1917, he was living in Fort Yates and working for the government school. Henry entered the Army on July 22, 1918, and served with Headquarters Troop, 19th Division, at Camp Dodge, IA. On Aug. 6, 1918, Henry wrote a letter from Camp Dodge, IA, to the editor of *The Sioux County Pioneer*:

> Dear Chris,
> Will write you a few lines to let you know that I am getting along fine in army life so far, and hope that I will make good.
> Will you send my *Sioux County Pioneer* here to Camp Dodge. Will close here and send you my best regards. Give my best regards to my folks and friends at home.

Henry was discharged on Jan. 28, 1919. The 19th Division was demobilized at Camp Dodge, IA, in February 1919. In 1918, Henry had married Clara Lucy Swift Cloud in McIntosh, SD. In the 1930 U.S. Census, Henry and Lucy were living in Fort Yates, where Henry was working as the night watchman for the government school. He later ranched near Bullhead, SD. He married Ruby Gayton in Sioux Falls, SD, on July 29, 1935. In the Census Roll for Standing Rock taken in 1940, Henry and Ruby are listed with two daughters, Corrine and Beverly. Henry passed away in Bullhead on Feb. 7, 1956, and is buried in the Catholic Cemetery in Bullhead, SD.[1]

**P**

**Packineau, David.** Army number 2,139,963; registrant, McLean County; born, Elbowoods, ND, Nov. 27, 1892, of American parents; occupation, farmer; inducted at Washburn on April 2, 1918; sent to Camp Dodge, IA; served in 163rd Depot Brigade, to April 21, 1918; Company G, 139th Infantry (35th Division), to discharge; overseas from May 3, 1918, to April 24, 1919. Engagements: Offensive: Meuse-Argonne. Defensive Sectors: Grange-le-Comte (Lorraine); Gerardmer (Alsace). Discharged at Camp Dodge, IA, on May 2, 1919, as a Private.

In the Census Roll for the Gros Ventre (Hidatsa) taken in 1898, David was listed with his mother, Rattles Medicine, and his grandfather, Poor Wolf. In the Census Roll taken in 1906, he is listed with his mother and stepfather, White Duck. David attended day school in Elbowoods from 1902 to 1909. In September 1909, he was enrolled for five years at Carlisle boarding school with his brother, Charles, and sister, Ruth. He was taught the blacksmith trade. While a student, he was sent on "outings" to work for three different landowners. He received $10 per month. In the 1910 U.S. Census, he was working for Alva Osmun of Delaware, NJ. In the spring of 1912, he and his brother tried to run away from the school, but Charles was killed by a train in Altoona, PA. David brought Charles back to North Dakota for burial.

> Home's the place we head for in our sleep.
> Boxcars stumbling north in dreams
> don't wait for us. We catch them on the run. (Erdrich)

After completing his military training at Camp Dodge, David was transferred to Camp Mills, NY, until sailing to England from Hoboken, NJ. After arriving in France on May 11, 1918, the men were quartered near the town of Eu. While stationed there, the Americans received some training from English soldiers. However, they could not get used to British rations, especially when tea was served at breakfast. When the 35th Division was transferred to the Alsace-Lorraine region in eastern France, they took part in the fighting. Private Packineau spent about 40 days in the trenches. However, he came down with bronchitis and spent a month in Base Hospital #81. After the Armistice was signed, the 35th Division was stationed near Commercy, near the Meuse River. The men were as a rule in unheated billets, hay lofts, and the like, and there was the chronic shortage of clothing. Colds and pneumonia grew alarmingly. The men were very glad when the day came to board ship and sail back home.

After arriving back in North Dakota, David married Elizabeth Yellow Bird (1898-1977). She was a sister to Charles Yellow Bird, who also served in the war. David and Elizabeth had six children. Four of their sons served in the military. Calvin and Lambert served in the Army; David in the Navy; and Tracy served with the Marines during the Korean Conflict. David was well known in his community. He was a charter member of the Joseph Young Hawk American Legion Post No. 253, and served as Vice Commander. He passed away in his home on Jan. 28, 1939. His wife and six children, Camille, Calvin, David, Jr., Lambert, Clement, and Tracy, survived him. He is buried in the Old Scouts Cemetery near White Shield. Military rites were conducted by the Legion Post.[1]

**Parisien, Louis.** Army number 3,693,216; registrant, Rolette County; born, Samschal, ND, June 20, 1890, of American parents; occupation, farmer; inducted at Rolla on Aug. 30, 1918; sent to Camp Dodge, IA; served in 163rd Depot Brigade, to discharge. Discharged at Camp Dodge, IA, on Dec. 6, 1918, as a Private; Surgeon's Certificate of Disability, 80%.

In the Census Roll for the Turtle Mountain Reservation taken 1916, Louis is listed with his parents, Edward and Blondin Parisien, as well as a younger sister. When he registered for the draft on June 5, 1917, he was working as a laborer near Thorne. He was single. In the 1920 U.S. Census, Louis lived with his father. Louis died on Aug. 2, 1926, and is buried in Alcide, ND.[2]

Chaska Parkin. *State Historical Society of North Dakota, 1952-1922*

**Parkin, Charles Lewis.** Army number 2,236,921; not a registrant, enlisted prior; born, St. Paul, MN, Aug. 15, 1882, of American parents; occupation, civil engineer; enlisted at Fort Snelling, MN, Jan. 6, 1914; sent to Camp Travis, TX; served in Company G, 2nd Battalion, Engineers, to (date not given); Company C, 9th Engineers, to Sept 14, 1917; Company C, 315th Engineers, to March 1, 1918; Headquarters Company, 315th Engineers, to March 27, 1918; Headquarters Troop, 35th Division, to April 8, 1918; 110th Training Headquarters and Military Police, to July 3, 1918; Company A, 110th Military Police, to Aug. 5, 1918; Company H, 137th Infantry (35th Division), to Nov. 17, 1918; Headquarters Detachment, 5th Engineers, to discharge. Grades: Sergeant, June 8, 1917; 1st Sergeant, July 1, 1917; Regimental Sergeant Major, Sept. 17, 1917; Sergeant 1st Class, Dec. 13, 1917; Regimental Supply Sergeant, March 1, 1918; Private, March

26, 1918; Cook, June 17, 1918; Private, July 3, 1918; overseas from May 3, 1918, to Dec. 31, 1918; wounded, slightly, Sept. 29, 1918. Engagements: Offensives: Meuse-Argonne. Defensive Sectors: Gerardmer (Alsace); Grange-le-Comte (Lorraine). Discharged at Camp A.A. Humphreys, VA, on April 7, 1919, as a Private.

Charles was known as Chaska. He was the son of John Kennedy and Annie Galpin Kennedy. His father had come to Fort Yates as the chief clerk for Major McLaughlin, but died in 1883. Chaska's mother died soon after. His mother's sister, Alma Parkin, and her husband adopted the young child. Chaska attended the Fort Yates Boarding School, some Mandan schools, St. John's Academy in Collegeville, MN, and the De La Salle Institute in Chicago. As a boy he rode with the cowboys on the Parkin Ranch and clerked in the family store. After finishing his schooling, he worked as an engineer for the Northern Pacific Railroad in North Dakota and Montana.

As a soldier, Chaska served with the Engineers Corps under Pershing on the Mexican Border. Private Parkin was wounded and gassed in France while advancing with the 35th Division on its attack on the town of Exermont. He received a Purple Heart. Following the war, he served as a recruiting sergeant in the Southwest. He also served in Manila, Nicaragua, Canal Zone, and Panama. His career with the Army spanned more than 25 years. He passed away at the U.S. Soldier's Home in Washington, D.C., on Jan. 18, 1938. He was buried in St. Peter's Cemetery in Fort Yates. American Legion members from the Posts in Bullhead, SD, Fort Yates and Cannon Ball performed the military Rites. The Commander of the Cannon Ball Post at that time was Richard White Eagle.[3]

**Paul, Marcel.** Army number 4,037,055; registrant, Rolette County; born, St. John, ND, May 15, 1897, of American-Canadian parents; occupation, laborer; inducted at Rolla on July 22, 1918; sent to Camp Custer, MI; served in Company L, 77th Infantry, to discharge. Discharged on Jan. 28, 1919, as a Private.

In the Census Roll for the Turtle Mountain Reservation taken in 1907, Marcel's father, Antoine, is listed as a widower, with three other children besides Marcel. When Marcel registered for the draft on June 5, 1917, he was living in St. John and working as a laborer. He was of medium height with a slender build. Marcel was in Company L, 77th Infantry with Mike Bercier. In the Census Roll taken in 1933, he was listed as living in St. Paul, MN. The 1954 City Directory for St. Paul lists him as a laborer living on Rice Street. He continued to live in St. Paul until he was admitted to the VA Hospital in Hot Springs, SD, where he passed away on Nov. 24, 1971. He remained single. He is buried in the Black Hills National Cemetery (Section C, Site 1124).[4]

**Peltier, Robert Ben.** Army number 473,676; not a registrant, over age; born, Fort Capall, Saskatchewan, April 24, 1885; citizenship, alien; enlisted at Bottineau, on April 15, 1918; sent to Jefferson Barracks, MO; served in Battery B, 13th Battalion, Field Artillery Replacement Draft, to discharge. Discharged at Jefferson Barracks, MO, on Aug. 28, 1918, as a Private; Surgeon's Certificate of Disability, 10%.

Robert was the son of Paul and Louise Peltier. In the 1910 U.S. Census, Robert lived with his parents. After the war, He first married Mary Adele Swain. He later married Clemence Azure, and finally, Marceline Brien. He resided in Belcourt for most of his life. He passed away in the Belcourt Hospital on Nov. 16, 1959. His wife and two sons, Joseph and Peter survived him. He is buried in St. Ann's Cemetery in Belcourt.[5]

**Perkins, Henry.** Army number 3,083,301; not a registrant; born, Berthold, ND, Sept. 20, 1899, of American parents; occupation, farmer; enlisted at Jefferson Barracks, MO, on June 24, 1918;

served in Company F, 43rd Infantry, to discharge. Discharged at Camp Bowie, TX, on Jan. 18, 1919, as a Private.

Henry was the son of Yellow Bear and Big Chief Woman. In the Census Roll taken in 1906, he is shown with the name, Wahurunaka. In the Census Roll for the Arikara taken in 1917, Henry was listed with his wife, Elizabeth Price (1898-1978), and their daughter, Esther. Elizabeth was a sister to Stephen Price, who also served briefly during the war. Henry's unit, the 43rd Infantry Regiment, was part of the 15th Infantry Division undergoing training at Camp Logan, TX. On Dec. 4, 1918, a battalion was transferred to Camp Bowie, where Private Perkins was discharged. After the war, he returned to the Nishu area to ranch.

In the Census Roll for Fort Berthold taken in 1932, Henry and Elizabeth are listed with two sons, Sybert, and Gilbert, and seven daughters, Esther, Evangeline, Lorraine, Regina, Frieda, Melda, and Florentine. Both of their sons served in the U.S. Army during WWII. Henry passed away on May 3, 1946. He was hit by the box of a passing truck while standing on the river road between Elbowoods and Nishu. He had stopped to make an adjustment on his car, and had straightened up and stepped back as the truck passed him. He was buried at Nishu.

Henry's older brother, Clarence (1890-1975) was inducted in 1918. On June 24, 1918, he traveled from Washburn to Camp Dodge, IA, with a group of local men, including Harvey Hopkins and John Bears Tail. The *Washburn Leader* included him in a roster of servicemen from McLean County. It is not known when he was discharged.[6]

Henry Perkins (seated) and Philip Star were stationed with the
43rd Infantry at Camp Logan, TX. *Four Bears Museum*

**Plante, Daniel.** Army number 3,950,520; registrant, Rolette County; born, St. Joe, ND, Sept. 24, 1892, of American parents; occupation farmer; inducted at Rolla on Aug. 26, 1918; sent to Camp Lewis, WA; served in Company D, 76th Infantry, to discharge. Grade: Private 1st Class, Dec. 1, 1918. Discharged at Camp Lewis, WA, on Feb. 24, 1919, as a Private 1st Class.

In the Census Roll for the Turtle Mountain Chippewa taken in 1900, Daniel and his brother, Louis, are listed with their parents, John and Virginie Plante, as well as their other siblings. Daniel was a student at the boarding school in Carlisle, PA, for a number of years. He likely played in the band at Carlisle. During the war, Daniel's regiment was part of the 13th Infantry Division being trained at Camp Lewis. They completed their training just before the Armistice was signed, so they did not go to France.

In the 1920 U.S. Census, Daniel was living in Racine, WI, and working as a musician in a concert band. He was boarding with the parents of his wife, Harriet (Hattie) Cox. Shortly after this, Daniel and Hattie moved to Kalamazoo, MI, where Daniel worked for many years for Consumers Power Co. He retired in September 1957. Daniel passed away in Borgess Hospital in Kalamazoo on March 23, 1958. His wife (1897-1985) and two sons, Daniel, Jr., and Francis, (Brother M. Guerric O.C.S.O.), and his daughter, Mary, (Mother Mary St. John Vianney of Arc), survived him. Daniel is buried in Mt. Olivet Cemetery.[7]

**Plante, Louis J.** Army number 2,259,767; registrant, Sheridan County, MT; born, Volga, D.T., Feb. 4, 1888, of American parents; occupation, laborer; inducted at Plentywood, MT, on Oct. 2, 1917; sent to Camp Lewis, WA; served in 10th Battalion, 166th Depot Brigade, to Oct. 25, 1917; Company B, 362nd Infantry (91st Infantry Division), to discharge. Grade: Private 1st Class, Feb. 12, 1918; overseas from July 6, 1918, to April 15, 1919; wounded, slightly, Oct. 4, 1918. Engagements: Offensives: Meuse-Argonne; Ypres-Lys. Defensive Sector: Aubreville (Lorraine). Discharged at Fort D.A. Russell, WY, on May 2, 1919, as a Private 1st Class.

Louis was the older brother of Daniel. When he registered for the draft on June 5, 1917, he was farming near Dooley, MT. Private 1st Class Plante was wounded while the 91st Division was being relieved by the 32nd Division near Gesnes. On Oct. 4, 1918, German artillery fire caused 50 casualties among the 91st Division. Alongside these casualties was the loss of the many horses used by the artillery and supply units. Another North Dakota soldier who served in the 362nd Infantry remarked that he never forgot the sound of the wounded horses. After the Armistice was signed, the 91st Division was quartered near La Ferte Bernard, near Le Mans, France.

After the war, Louis was a member of 362nd Infantry Association. He was also active in the American Legion. Louis married Mary Ann Nicholas (1894-1974) on Nov. 23, 1920. Louis lived with his family in Devils Lake. Their children were Louis Jr., Eugene, Leo, Albert, Mary Edward and George. Eugene, Leo and Louis Jr. all served in the U.S. Army during WWII. Louis passed away suddenly on March 9, 1931, while attending a boxing program sponsored by the American Legion in Devils Lake. His wife and seven children survived him. Louis is buried in the Devils Lake Catholic Cemetery.[8]

**Poitra, Albert.** Army number 495,805; registrant, Lawrence County, KS; born, Thorne, ND, Feb. 5, 1896, of American-Canadian parents; occupation, student; enlisted at Kansas City, MO, on May 22, 1918; sent to Jefferson Barracks, MO; served in Company K, 3rd Infantry, to Jan. 18, 1919; Headquarters Company, 3rd Infantry, to discharge. Grade: Musician 3rd Class, Sept. 17, 1918. Discharged at Camp Eagle Pass, TX, on March 11, 1919, as a Musician 3rd Class.

In the Census Roll for the Turtle Mountain Reservation taken in 1896, 6 month old Albert is listed with his parents, Charles and Mary Poitra. In the 1910 U.S. Census, Albert was a student at the Fort Totten boarding school. He likely was a student at the Haskell boarding school in Kansas when he registered for the draft before the war. In the 1920 U.S. Census, he was still serving with the Army at Camp Eagle Pass, TX, which was on the Mexican border. He was with the 3rd Infantry, also known as The Old Guard. In the 1920s, Albert married Delia Desjardins (1895-1982). In the 1930 *City Directory*, Albert and Delia lived in Minneapolis. They changed the spelling of their name to Poitras. They had a son, Allen. Albert and Delia were later divorced, but Albert stayed in Minneapolis. He worked as a machinist. According to the 1956 Minneapolis *City Directory*, he was working as a maintenance man for the Bond Stores. Albert also served in WWII, as did his son, Allen. Albert passed away at the VA Hospital in St. Cloud, MN, on Aug. 8, 1974, and is buried in Fort Snelling National Cemetery (Section H, Site 1740).[9]

**Poitra, Charles F.** Army number, none; registrant, Rolette County; born, Belcourt, ND, April 15, 1896, of American parents; occupation, laborer; enlisted in Company G, North Dakota National Guard, at Rolla, on July 14, 1917; called into federal service, World War, on July 15, 1917; served in Company G, North Dakota National Guard, to discharge. Discharged at Camp Greene, NC, on Oct. 11, 1917, as a Private, by reason of physical disability.

In the Census Roll for the Turtle Mountain Reservation taken in 1906, Charles is listed with his parents, Joseph and Josephine Poitra, as well as three brothers and a sister. In the 1910 U.S. Census, he was a student at the Fort Totten boarding school. When he registered for the draft on June 5, 1917, he was working as a laborer for Norbert Poitra. Charles served with the National Guard, but was discharged shortly after his unit arrived in North Carolina. After the war, he married Beatrice Davis (1902-1939). In the 1930 U.S. Census, Beatrice's cousin, Frank Davis, lived with them. Frank was also a veteran. In October 1930, Charles was admitted to the veterans' hospital at Hot Springs, SD, for a checkup on symptoms of tuberculosis. He was discharged after about four months. In the Census Roll taken in 1937, Charles and Beatrice are listed with their children, John Pat, Melvin, Mary Stella, Sylvester, and Charles, Jr. Their son, Pat, served in the Army during WWII, while Sylvester served with the Army from 1950-53. Beatrice was a correspondent for the *Turtle Mountain Star*. After she died in 1939, Charles married Eveline. Charles died at his home on March 1, 1948. He is buried in St. Anthony Catholic Cemetery.[10]

Joe Pretends Eagle, photographed by Frank Fiske. *Dean Moos*

**Pretends Eagle, Joseph.** Army number 502,338; registrant, Sioux County; born, Fort Yates, ND, July 30, 1892, of American parents; occupation, farmer; inducted at Fort Yates on March 6, 1918; sent to Fort Logan, CO; served in Coast Artillery Corps, to discharge. Discharged at San Francisco, CA, on Aug. 5, 1918, as a Private; Surgeon's Certificate of Disability, 75%.

In the Census Roll for the Standing Rock Sioux Tribe taken in 1900, Joseph is listed with his father, Martin Pretends Eagle (Wanblikunza), and his mother, Earth (Tamaka), as well as a brother. Early in 1918, Joseph applied for voluntary induction. As a result, he was given a choice of training camps to be sent to. When Joseph was inducted, he traveled to Fort Logan with George Many Wounds. However, Joseph became sick and was admitted to a military hospital at Fort McDowell, Angel Island, California. He was given an early discharge for medical reasons.

In the early 1920s, Joe was known as an accomplished wrestler. He had defeated Johnie Lonien in a match at Wakpala around Christmas of 1919. In June 1921 he challenged a professional circus champion at McLaughlin, SD. He later wrestled against Sam Warford at Fort Rice. Joe married Benedicta Buffaloboy (1894-1981). In the Census Roll taken in 1933, Joseph and Benedicta are listed with their children, Alice, Joseph Jr., Josephine, Bernard, James, Leo, and Herbert. In the 1940 U.S. Census, he is shown as being disabled. His son, Herbert, served with the Army in Korea and Japan from 1950-53. Joseph passed away on Oct. 21, 1961, and is buried in St. Peter's Cemetery in Fort Yates.[11]

Joseph Pretends Eagle, 1917.
Ales Hrdlicka, photographer.
*National Anthropological Archives, INV 00595402.*

**Price, Stephen.** Stephen was born at Elbowoods on Aug. 14, 1894. In the Census Roll for the Arikara taken in 1909, he is listed with his parents, Hiram and Josephine Price, as well as his siblings. In the 1910 U.S. Census, Stephen was a student at the boarding school at Bismarck. When he registered for the draft in June 1917, he was farming for himself on the Fort Berthold Reservation. He was a tall man of medium build. The *Washburn Leader* reported that he was inducted on June 23, 1918, and was sent to Camp Dodge, IA, along with a number of other men from Elbowoods. The *Washburn Leader* continued to list him as serving in the military in their weekly roster that they published until the end of the war. It is not known when he was discharged. In the 1920 U.S. Census, Stephen lived with Morgan Jones on the Reservation. In the 1930s, he was married to Helen Gough (1904-1963). They were later divorced. Stephen died in Herrick Hospital, Berkeley, CA on July 25, 1976, and is buried in St. Paul's Cemetery near Garrison, ND.

## R

**Rabbit Head, John.** Army number 2,560,058; registrant, (place not given); born, Elbowoods, ND, March 1894, of (nationality of parents not given); occupation, (not given); inducted at Washburn on March 28, 1918; sent to Camp Dodge, IA; served in Company P, 163rd Depot Brigade, to death. Died of heart block on May 5, 1918.

In the Census Roll for the Gros Ventres (Hidatsa) taken in 1903, John was listed with his parents, Rabbit Head (Itakatush) and his mother, Not Touched (Irikitash), as well as his siblings. John is buried in Ft. Des Moines Post Cemetery (Section 4, Site 1).

John Elk (left) and John Red Bean
Camp Dodge, Iowa
*Todd Hanson*

**Redbean, John,** also known as **Redbear** (see photo previous page).  Army number 2,559,186; registrant, Sioux County; born, Fort Yates, ND, Sept. 20, 1890, of American parents; occupation, laborer; inducted at Fort Yates on March 29, 1918; sent to Camp Dodge, IA; served in 163rd Depot Brigade, to April 20, 1918; Company G, 329th Infantry (83rd Division), to discharge; overseas from May 3, 1918, to Jan. 31, 1919. Discharged at Camp Dodge, IA, on Feb. 12, 1919, as a Private; Surgeon's Certificate of Disability, 5%.

In the Census Roll for the Standing Rock Reservation taken in 1891, John is listed with his parents, Red Bean (Omnicaluta) and Clara. As a child, John was known as Brown Spider. A number of years later, Clara married Hugh Swiftbird. In the Census Roll taken in 1906, John Swiftbird is listed with his mother and stepfather. In the fall of 1916, John left Fort Yates for Canada where he enlisted in the Canadian Army on Oct. 25, 1916. He served for 11 months before returning to Fort Yates. He then worked as a laborer for the U.S. Indian Service before being inducted at Fort Yates. John traveled to Camp Dodge, IA, with 17 other men from the Fort Yates community. While at Camp Dodge, he had his photo taken with his friend, John Elk. A month after arriving at Camp Dodge, they were on their way to France. On April 28, 1918, the two Johns sent a letter back to the *Sioux County Pioneer* from Buffalo, NY. They had stopped in Niagara Falls, and had marched out to see the falls. They wrote that "We are doing fine. We hope to get the Kaiser Bill soon." They sailed to England on the *Carpathia*. John Redbean served with the 83rd Division, where he performed convoy and guard duty.  John Elk served with the 35th Division. While Private Redbean was in Europe, he wrote back to Fort Yates asking for a subscription to his hometown newspaper.

John returned to Fort Yates after the war. In April 1930, he went up to Portage La Prairie, Manitoba, to live with an uncle. The Census Roll taken in 1939 shows him living in Manitoba. In the 1940 U.S. Census, he was living with his brother, George, in Fort Yates. Sometime after this, he may have lived with Emma Kill Spotted (1895-1968). John passed away at the Fort Yates hospital on April 25, 1955, in the hospital at Fort Yates. About a year later, Emma requested a military headstone for John's grave in Big Lake Cemetery, south of Cannon Ball.[1] His relatives now use the name Red Bear.

**Red Fox, Ernest J.**  Army number 2,704,363; registrant, McLean County; born, Elbowoods, ND, Aug. 1, 1893, of American parents; occupation, farmer; inducted at Washburn on June 23, 1918; sent to Camp Dodge, IA; served in Company A, 352nd Infantry, to Aug. 7, 1918; 163rd Depot Brigade, to discharge. Grade: Bugler, Oct. 25, 1918. Discharged at Camp Dodge, IA, on March 8, 1919, as a Private.

Ernest was the son of Isaac and Julia Red Fox. In the Census Roll for the Arikara taken in 1909, he is listed with his stepfather, Mason Jones, and his mother and other brothers and sisters. One of his sisters was Nellie, who married Charles Yellow Bird, a fellow veteran. Ernest attended school at the Armstrong Day School and the boarding school at Wahpeton.

During the war, he went through training at Camp Dodge, IA, and later transferred to Camp Cody, NM. After the war, Ernest was a one-time heavyweight wrestler in the midwestern division of North Dakota. He first married Jessie Rogers, a sister to Tom Rogers, a fellow veteran. He married Veda Azure on Jan. 8, 1937. In the 1940 U.S. Census, he was working as a laborer with the CCC program. Ernest and Veda later moved to Minot. Ernest was a charter member of the Joseph Young Hawk American Legion Post, serving as Finance Officer. He died at the on the Minot Air Base hospital on Dec. 13, 1965. His wife and nine children survived him. The children were Beverly, Ernestine, Roxanne, Anatte, Kenneth, Kelsey, Dennis, Rocky, and Leland. Their son, Kenneth, served in the army in the Vietnam era. Ernest is buried in Memorial Cemetery south of Parshall. The Joseph Young Hawk American Legion Post conducted military rites.[2]

**Red Fox, George James.** Army number 503,331; registrant, Sioux County; born, Selfridge, ND, March 24, 1888, of American parents; occupation, rancher; inducted at Fort Yates on March 13, 1918; sent to Fort Logan, CO; served in 21st Company, Coast Artillery Corps, Fort Strong, MA, to May 12, 1918; Battery B, 71st Artillery, Coast Artillery Corps, to discharge; overseas from July 31, 1918, to Feb. 22, 1919. Discharged at Camp Dodge, IA, on March 7, 1919, as a Private.

In the Census Rolls for the Standing Rock Reservation taken in the early 1900s, George is listed with his father, Fred (Sungila luta), and his wife, Runs the Horses Off. In the 1910 U.S. Census, the family lived in Morton County. When George registered for the draft on June 5, 1917, he listed his address as Shields, ND.

George was inducted at Fort Yates on March 13, 1918, with George Santee. Together, they went to Fort Logan, and remained in the same unit for the duration of the war. While they were stationed in Fort Strong, MA, George Santee sent a letter back to the *Sioux County Pioneer* indicating that "we both are well, and getting along fine." The 71st Artillery sailed to England aboard the HMS *Margha* and the HMS *Anselm*. Upon arrival in France, they were billeted near Angers, and began training with 8-inch howitzers. However, the war ended before they had a chance to fire them at the enemy. The unit returned on the U.S. Transport *Manchuria*. "Following his return to the U.S., George remained in the service with Supply Company, 3rd Field Artillery, at Camp Grant, IL." George likely had reenlisted. The 3rd Field Artillery was one of the few U.S. Army units that actively recruited Native men. In the spring of 1920, recruiters traveled to Cannon Ball to sign up enlistees.

When the 1920 U.S. Census was taken in January, George was staying with his cousin, Joseph Murphy. By April of that year, George was ranching for himself. On Nov. 28, 1922, George married Alice Half in McIntosh, SD. In the Census Roll of the Standing Rock Reservation taken in 1927, George and Alice are listed with their daughters, Octavia and Mary Seraphine. In the 1930 U.S. Census, they were living in Corson County, SD. In the early 1930s, he married Mary Nationshield. In the Census Roll taken in 1937, George and Mary are listed with their children, Mary, Rosaline and George, Jr. George later moved into Bullhead, SD. He passed away in the hospital at Fort Yates on Oct. 14, 1964, and is buried in St. Aloysius Catholic Cemetery in Bullhead.[3]

**Redhorn, John George.** George was born on April 11, 1901, in Cannon Ball, ND. He spent his younger years in that community until his mother (Wastewin) remarried and moved to Kenel. George was too young to serve in the army during the war, but he did enlist in Cannon Ball in March 1920. Two Army recruiters came to town to recruit men for the 3rd Field Artillery at Camp Grant, IL. After George returned from service, he married Grace Bobtail Bear and lived in Kenel. In the Census Roll taken in 1933, George and Grace are listed with their two oldest children, Nelson and Dewey. George passed away from tuberculosis on Aug. 19, 1935. The *Sioux County Pioneer* wrote that he was easy going and friendly and that he did his best to serve everybody right. "His demise cast a shroud of sadness over our community that will not be lifted for many a day." He is buried in Kenel. His wife and three children survived him. In 1936, his widow married August Brought Plenty, a fellow veteran.[4] George's youngest son, William, was killed in action in Korea at the age of 17 and is buried in Arlington National Cemetery, VA.

**Redstone, Asa.** Army number 2,787,779; registrant, Sioux County; born, Cannon Ball, ND, Nov. 28, 1894, of American parents; occupation, farmer; inducted at Fort Yates on May 25 1918;

sent to Camp Lewis, WA; served in 166th Depot Brigade, to June 20, 1918; Company C, 348th Machine Gun Battalion (91st Division), to discharge; overseas from July 6, 1918, to April 2, 1919. Engagements: Offensives: Meuse-Argonne; Ypres-Lys. Defensive Sector: Aubreville (Lorraine). Discharged at Camp Dodge, IA, on April 22, 1919, as a Private.

In the 1900 U.S. Census, Asa (Hoksina Waste) lived with his mother (Good Woman). Asa attended school at Fort Yates. When Asa registered for the draft on June 5, 1917, he was living near Cannon Ball and farming for himself. Private Redstone's Battalion was part of the 91st Infantry Division, also known as the Wild West Division, as many of the men were from the western states. Asa was stationed in the same company as Lawrence See The Elk. Once they had completed their training at Camp Lewis, WA, it took them six days to travel by train to Camp Merritt, NY, where they were issued new uniforms which included steel helmets and hobnailed trench shoes. They sailed to England on ocean liners, which took another 12 days. The 91st Division played a very active part in the battle of Meuse-Argonne. However, Private Redstone's commanding officer, Captain Arthur Whitney, reported that Redstone was not part of the first assault because they were unable to find a gas mask to fit him. After the fighting was over, the 91st Division traveled to Belgium and Germany for occupation duty before returning to La Ferte Bernard, near Le Mans, France, where they were billeted for four months. They spent five hours daily performing drill exercises. Athletics and entertainment in the surrounding French villages occupied their afternoons and evenings. The men were very glad to return to their homes in the United States.

After the war, Asa married Susan One Horn. In the Census Roll taken in 1934, they are listed with their children, Seraphine, Virginia, Melvin, Cecelia, Courtney, Clara, and Isabelle. Courtney served with the U.S. Army in Korea. Asa passed away in the hospital in Fort Yates on Nov. 25, 1949.[5]

**Reed, Andrew.** Army number 3,084,402; not a registrant, under age; born, Nishu, ND, Feb. 22, 1899, of American parents; occupation, student; enlisted at Jefferson Barracks, MO, on July 1, 1918; served in Company K, 43rd Infantry, to discharge. Discharged at Camp Travis, TX, on April 2, 1919, as a Private.

Andrew was the son of Joseph Reed (Wi-ri-cis) and Lora Robinson (Sci-ta-pat). In the 1910 U.S. Census, Andrew was a student at the boarding school in Wahpeton. In the Census Roll for the Gros Ventres (Hidatsa) taken in 1913, Andrew is listed as the adopted son of Many Paints. In the Census Roll for the Arikara taken in 1918, Andrew is listed with his father and his father's wife, Red Eye, as well as his sister, Mamie. After he enlisted in the Army at Jefferson Barracks, MO, he was sent to Camp Logan, TX, where the 43rd Infantry Regiment was part of the 15th Infantry Division. Three other men from the Fort Berthold Reservation, Henry Perkins, Bill Deane and Philip Star, were also stationed with the 43rd Infantry at Camp Logan. However, they were in different companies. The Armistice was signed before they completed their training. Andrew had his hearing damaged during his training in Texas, but he did not receive a disability payment for it. Upon his return to North Dakota, he ranched and also had spent some winters working in lumber mills on the West Coast. He did not marry. Andrew eventually became deaf. Andrew died on June 11, 1958 when he was struck by a train in the Great Northern Railway yards near Minot. The train engineer indicated that he had blown the whistle when he saw Andrew near the tracks. Because of his loss of hearing, he could not hear the whistle of the locomotive. Andrew was carrying a piece of paper in his pocket, which said that he had lost his hearing following his military training. Andrew is buried in the Old Scout Cemetery near White Shield.[6]

**Reedy, Philip Graham.** Army number, none; not a registrant, enlisted prior; born, Fort Totten, D.T., Dec. 23, 1882, of American parents; occupation, physician and surgeon; appointed from civil life and commissioned 1st Lieutenant, in Officers Reserve Corps, April 14, 1917; called into active service as a 1st Lieutenant, Medical Corps, on June 13, 1917; sent to Fort Riley, KS; assigned to Medical Officers Training Camp, Fort Riley, KS, to Aug. 9, 1917; 16th Field Artillery, to April 1918; Medical Corps, Camp Greene, NC, to Oct. 31, 1918; 810th Pioneer Infantry, to Dec. 16, 1918; Medical Corps, unassigned, to discharge. Promoted: Captain, Nov. 25, 1917; Major, June 13, 1918. Principal Stations: Fort Riley, KS; Sparta, WI; Pittsburg, PA; Camp Greene, NC; Hoboken, NJ; Camp Dix, NJ; overseas from April 22, 1918, to Aug. 1, 1919. Discharged at Camp Dix, NJ, on Aug. 2, 1919, as a Major.

Philip was the son of Thomas and Agnes Reedy. Agnes was a niece of James McLaughlin. Philip was known as Hepan. Thomas was a blacksmith, manager of the gristmill and sawmill, as well as being in charge of the Indian Police at Fort Totten. In 1891, the Reedy family moved to Fort Yates. Philip's mother, a teacher, was Santee Sioux. In the Census Roll for the Standing Rock Reservation taken in 1899, Philip is listed with his mother and his older sister, Katie. Philip enrolled at St. John's in Collegeville, MN, at the age of 14. He also studied a commercial course in Chicago for two years. From 1904-1906, he ranched with his father. Then, Philip entered Northwestern Medical School in Evanston, IL. He graduated with a degree of Doctor of Medicine and Surgery in 1910. After graduating, he practiced medicine in South Dakota before moving to Regan, ND, arriving in March 1913. He married Rachel Nore O'Neill on Aug. 21, 1912. They had a daughter, Jane Patricia. In the 1915 North Dakota Census, Philip and Rachel were still living in Regan.

Philip Reedy. *State Historical Society of North Dakota, 1952-1931.*

Two years later, he enlisted in the Medical Corps. After his military training began, he wrote to his father at Fort Yates that he'd managed to lose weight. He said he entered training weighing 230 pounds, but managed to get his weight down to 185. Once he was promoted to Major, he served as surgeon on troop transports, making eight round trips to France. He also was stationed at Rotterdam, Holland as Post Surgeon, and later was sent to Antwerp, Belgium as Assistant Sanitary Inspector of Sector Nine, travelling through Belgium, Holland and Germany. An article in the *Casselton Reporter* mentions that he had received shrapnel wounds.

After the war, he and Rachel settled in Casselton, ND, to practice medicine. Rachel died on July 12, 1922, in a Seattle sanatorium. In 1928, he married Clara Gretter, a nurse. He and Clara had two sons. In the early 1920s, Philip's parents and his daughter, Jane, moved out to Seattle to live with his sister Katie's family. Philip served as health officer for the City of Casselton. He was active in the American Legion and served as Commander of the Rugg-Heille Post of Casselton, as well as the Florence Kimball Post in Lisbon. He also had been a member of the American Legion 40 and 8 Society in Fargo, the ND State Medical Society, American Medical Society, Association of Military Surgeons, and the Military Order of Foreign Wars. When he worked in South Dakota, he had been on the Corson County Medical Board. In 1935, Dr. Reedy moved to Lisbon to set up a medical practice. He died in his sleep on Dec. 18, 1936. At the time, his wife and sons were visiting Clara's family in Enderlin. Clara was expecting another child. Clara and two young sons, Thomas James and Robert Graham, survived him. A third son, James, was born the following June. James served as a Lieutenant with the U.S. Army in Vietnam. The two older sons of Philip and Clara also served in the U.S. Army. Robert served from 1951-52 and Thomas served from 1949-52. Philip is buried in Oakwood Cemetery in Lisbon. The Florence Kimball Legion Post and the ND National Guard 164th Service Company firing squad conducted military rites.[7]

**Rogers, Thomas Everett.** Army number 45,985; registrant, McLean County; born, Fort Berthold, ND, June 4, 1890, of American parents; occupation, farmer; enlisted in Company I, 2nd Infantry, North Dakota National Guard, at Bismarck, on Aug. 1, 1917; served in Company I, 2nd Infantry, North Dakota National Guard, to Oct. 5, 1917; 161st Ambulance Company, 116th Sanitary Train, to Nov. 14, 1917; Headquarters, 41st Division, to Jan. 9, 1918; Company A, 18th Infantry (1st Division), to Aug. 20, 1918; Headquarters Company, 44th Infantry, to discharge. Grades: Private 1st Class, March 11, 1918; Sergeant, July 2, 1918; overseas from Dec. 15, 1917, to Sept. 1, 1918. Engagements: Defensive: Montdidier-Noyon. Offensive: Aisne-Marne. Defensive Sectors: Ansauville and Saizerais (Lorraine); Cantigny (Picardy). Discharged at Fort D.A. Russell, WY, on, July 5, 1919, as a Sergeant. Cited in General Orders No. 15, Headquarters, 18th Infantry, France, Aug. 11, 1918, as follows: "Non-commissioned officer of great courage, initiative and intelligence. Always a volunteer for the most dangerous missions. Has, throughout his service with this regiment on the front, given proof of the highest qualities of the soldier, notably during the attack on Cantigny, May 28, 1918, and the battle south of Soissons, July 18th to July 22nd, on both of which occasions his service with the Intelligence Section of this regiment proved him to be a soldier of the highest type".

In the Census Roll for the Fort Berthold Reservation taken in 1900, Thomas (Ka-ta-nu-ta) is listed with his father, Thomas (Nu-ti-ha-ni), as well as his siblings. His mother was Yellow Calf Woman. In 1900, Thomas was attending school at the Browning Boarding School. He also attended the boarding school at Santee, NE. His sister, Jessie, married Ernest Red Fox, a fellow veteran, after the war. Jessie later married Stephen Price. Thomas was also known as Charges Alone (Skanatunawinag).

When Thomas arrived in France in January 1918, he was assigned to Company A, 18th Infantry along with Albert Grass, Richard Blue Earth, Joseph Young Hawk, and Joseph Jordan. Thomas served as a battalion runner. After the battle near Soissons, the 18th Infantry Regiment was relieved by the 15th Scottish Division, whom the Germans referred to as the "Ladies from Hell." They had problems dealing with fierce soldiers wearing kilts.

(Right)
-SKANATUNAWINAG-
(Charges Alone)

Born near old Fort Ber-
thold, about fifteen miles
west of old Fort Stevenson,
Fort Berthold Indian Reservation, North Dakota, June
4, 1891. Full blood Arikara
Indian, son of NUTIHANI,
(Young Snake) and SANINA-
KATA (Yellow Calf Woman)

Educated at Santee In-
dian School, Santee, Neb.
Name on rolls, is:
THOMAS E. ROGERS.

The necklace he is wear-
ing is made of beaver sk:
and grizzly bear claws,
and has been in the famil:
hundreds of years.

General Ferdinand Foch,
Marshal of France, at Bi:
marck, N. Dak., November
27, 1921, picked Tom out
of 27 Indians of the Fou:
tribes of the Upper Miss-
ouri, and remarked:"Tom
Rogers was the bravest
soldier in France".

General Foch, at that
time, was given the name
WAHKIA WATAKPE (Charging
Thunder)

Below:
Thomas E. Rogers and family

(Above)
SERGEANT THOMAS E. ROGERS,
enlisted Aug. 1, 1917, at
Bismarck, N. Dak.,in Co. I.,
2nd Reg. N. D. Inf., Capt.
A. B. Welch. Sailed for
Europe in Dec., 1917, landed
in England Dec. 24, 1917, ar
rived in France Jan. 1, 1918
with 164th Inf. transferred
to 18th U. S. Inf., Co. A.,
1st Div., in Jan. 1918, and
took part in all battles of
that Div., including the
battle of Soissons as Chief
of Indian Scouts. Two citations for bravery.

(Above)
THOMAS E. ROGERS, City
Letter Carrier at Mandan,
N. Dak., appointed, by Ex-
ecutive Order of President
Calvin Coolidge, Sept. 20,
1926, "In view of the val:
and very extraordinary mer
itorious service performed
by him".

Minnesota Historical
Society E99.1, p 11

106

Rogers served on scouting details that were conducted at night. One of the goals was to bring back a captured German. If the enemy soldier refused to surrender, Rogers usually killed the man and brought his uniform blouse back to the American lines. Rogers was known as "The Spectre" to his fellow soldiers. Sgt. Rogers was also credited with shooting 33 Germans in 30 days. Snipers were part of the Intelligence Section. Sgt. Rogers received the honor of being selected to return to the U.S. to help train selective service men. He was stationed with the 44th Infantry, which was part of the 13th Division undergoing training at Camp Lewis, WA. On his way out to Camp Lewis, he had a chance to spend a few days of furlough at Fort Berthold. Among the trainees in the 44th Infantry were Robert Dancing Bull and Mark Necklace. Both of them were promoted to Private 1st Class while Sgt. Rogers served as an instructor.

After the war, Thomas returned to Elbowoods. In the 1920 U.S. Census, he was boarding with Harry White Calf. He married Lucy J. Coffee at Washburn on Aug. 6, 1924. He received a presidential citation from President Calvin Coolidge that allowed him to enter the postal service without taking the civil service exams. He served as a mail carrier in Mandan from 1926 to 1932. Rogers' friend, A. B. Welch, was the postmaster in Mandan at that time. Thomas later worked as a government school bus driver and lived in Raub for a while. In the 1940 U.S. Census, he was driving the Elbowoods school bus. He was a member of the Little Shell American Legion Post No. 300. Thomas passed away in St. Joseph Hospital in Minot on April 17, 1965. His wife and sons, Bryan and Reginal, as well as four daughters, Darlene, Phyllis, Eleanor, and Celecaia survived him. He is buried in Memorial Congregational Cemetery south of Parshall. Graveside rites were conducted by the New Town Veterans of Foreign Wars Post and the Little Shell American Legion Post.[8]

**Rolette, Ernest Fred.** Army number 2,858,872; registrant, Williams County; born, Rolla, ND, March 5, 1893, of American parents; occupation, butcher; inducted at Williston on April 29, 1918; sent to Camp Dodge, IA; served in Company H, 358th Infantry (90th Division), to discharge; overseas from June 28, 1918, to April 2, 1919. Engagements: Offensives: St. Mihiel; Meuse-Argonne. Defensive Sectors: Villers-en-Haye and Puvenelle (Lorraine). Discharged at Camp Dodge, IA, on April 11, 1919, as a Private.

In the Census Roll for the Turtle Mountain Reservation taken in 1897, Ernest and his younger brother, Louis, are listed with their parents, Martin and Celina Rolette, as well as their other siblings. In the 1910 U.S. Census, the Rolette family was living in Williston, where Martin was working as a land locator.

Shortly after Ernest arrived at Camp Dodge, he was sent to Camp Travis, TX, for more intensive training. On June 9, 1918, the regiment started their train trip to New York City. On June 20, they sailed from Hoboken, NJ, for Liverpool, England, on the HMT *Euripedes*. On July 7, 1918, they arrived in LeHavre, France, and proceeded to their assigned billets for further training. On August 24, the 358th Regiment relieved the 18th Infantry near Fey-en-Haye. Early in the morning of September 12, the American and French artillery began a four-hour barrage of the Germans. Private Rolette was in the 2nd Battalion of the 358th Regiment, while Barney Mulhern and Ed Two Horses were in the 3rd Battalion. Together, the 2nd and 3rd Battalions went over the top and advanced across country covered with old trenches and wire entanglements. This was the day that Private Mulhern was severely wounded. Private Rolette was not wounded, but he definitely was exposed to gas during the remaining days of the war. After the hostilities ceased, the regiment took up a position near Stenay. From Stenay, the regiment marched about 100 miles to Daun, Germany, where they remained until the time came for them to sail home.

After the war, Ernest moved to Washington state. In the 1920 U.S. Census, Ernest and his father were living with the family of Ernest's sister in Chelan County, WA. Ernest was working as a laborer in a lumber mill. He married Caroline Abble (1896-1988) on March 3, 1924, in Clark County, near Vancouver, WA. In the Census Roll for the Turtle Mountain Reservation taken in 1932, Ernest was listed as living in Portland, OR. In the 1940 U.S. Census, Ernest was working as a meat cutter in a meat market in Portland. When he registered for the Selective Service during WWII, Ernest was living in Oakland, CA, and working for Todd Shipbuilding in Richmond. Ernest passed away on May 1, 1962, and is buried in Golden Gate National Cemetery (Section X, Site 1637).[9]

**Rolette, Louis Leo.** Army number 86,310; not a registrant, enlisted prior; born, Rolla, ND, Dec. 21, 1896, of American parents; occupation, pool hall clerk; enlisted in Company E, 1st Infantry, North Dakota National Guard, at Williston, on April 30, 1917; called into federal service, World War, on July 15, 1917; served in Company E, 1st Infantry, North Dakota National Guard (Company E, 164th Infantry), to discharge; overseas from Dec. 15, 1917, to Feb. 26, 1919. Discharged at Camp Dodge, IA, on March 11, 1919, as a Private.

Louis enlisted in the National Guard shortly after President Wilson declared war on Germany, and served with the 164th Infantry for the duration of the war. Many of the men who were not reassigned to combat units were used for guard duty in the port cities of France. After the war, Louis returned to Williston. In the 1920 U.S. Census, he was working as an assistant in a pool hall, while living in the Great Northern Hotel. In 1931, Louis entered the VA Hospital in Sawtelle, CA, near Los Angeles. In the Census Roll for the Turtle Mountain Reservation taken in 1934, Louis is shown as living in Tulsa, OK. In the 1940 U.S. Census, Louis lived in the Umatilla Hotel in Spokane and worked for himself as a novelties salesman. When Louis registered for the Selective Service during WWII, he was still working as a salesman in Spokane, WA. Louis passed away in Walla Walla, WA, after a long illness on Jan. 30, 1952, and is buried in Mountain View Cemetery in Walla Walla.[10]

**Santee, George W.** Army number 503,318; registrant, Sioux County; born, Standing Rock Reservation, March 14, 1896, of American parents; occupation, farmer; inducted at Fort Yates on March 13, 1918; sent to Fort Logan, CO; served in 21st Company, Coast Artillery Corps, Fort Strong, MA, to May 12, 1918; Battery B, 71st Artillery, Coast Artillery Corps, to discharge. Grade: Private 1st Class, Jan. 1, 1919; overseas from July 31, 1918, to Feb. 22, 1919. Discharged at Camp Dodge, IA, on March 7, 1919, as a Private 1st Class.

George was the son of Haskell Santee and Lucy White Weasel. In the Census Roll taken in 1904, George is listed with his parents, Haskell Santee (Isanyate) and Pretty Weasel (Hintunkasanwaste), as well as a brother and sister. George had been a student at the boarding school in Carlisle, PA. When he registered for the draft on June 5, 1917, he was farming and raising cattle near Cannon Ball. George entered the service with George Red Fox, both from the Porcupine district. They applied for immediate voluntary induction, so they were given a choice of where to do their training. They served together in the same unit. After initially reporting to Fort Logan, near Denver, they were transferred to Fort Strong, near Boston. On April 24, 1918, George Santee sent a letter back to the *Sioux County Pioneer* reporting that we "Like our army life fine. I am training for boxing now, so when I get to France I will be some boxer instead of a soldier." While in France, they were trained to fire the large 8-inch howitzers but did not get a chance to fire them in battle.

After the war, George returned to the Shields area and married Melda One Hawk (1900-1975) on June 9, 1919. He was a member of the American Legion Post at Shields. In the Indian Census Roll taken in 1939, they are listed with their daughter, Etta. They ranched in the Shields area. George passed away on July 17, 1962, while on his way to a Bismarck hospital. He is buried in St. James' Cemetery in Shields.[1]

**Sayers, Patrick Sebastian.** Army number 3,960,082; registrant, Rolette County; born, St. John, ND, Oct. 31, 1890, of Canadian parents; occupation farmer; inducted at Plentywood, MT, on July 24, 1918; sent to Camp Dodge, IA; served in Company No. 57, 15th Battalion, 163rd Depot Brigade, to Aug. 23, 1918; 36th Company, Labor Regiment, Camp Joseph E. Johnston, FL, to Sept. 21, 1918; Field Remount Squadron No. 340, Quartermaster Corps, to discharge. Grades: Corporal, Oct. 8, 1918; Private, Jan. 15, 1919; overseas from Oct. 27, 1918, to July 13, 1919. Discharged at Camp Dodge, IA, on July 21, 1919, as a Private.

Patrick was the son of Alexander and Adele Sayers. In the Census Roll for the Turtle Mountain Reservation taken in 1906, Patrick and his sister, Anna, are listed as orphans. Patrick married Mary St. Arnaud in Plentywood, MT, in 1914. They had two sons, Moses and Patrick Jr. When he registered for the draft on June 5, 1917, he was farming for Frank Bartley of Rolla. Patrick arrived in Europe with his unit toward the end of the war. His Remount Squadron was stationed at Merignac, France. After the war, Patrick's younger son passed away in Montana in 1925. As a result of Patrick's military service, he suffered from lung ailments. In the 1930 U.S. Census, Patrick was a patient at Battle Mountain Sanitarium near Hot Springs, SD. He stayed there for more than a year. After Patrick and Mary were divorced, he married Theresa Fayant in 1933 in Rolla. Patrick was a member of the Fred C. Wagner American Legion Post. He passed away from pneumonia in the Belcourt hospital on April 28, 1939. His wife and his children, Moses and Evelyn, survived him. A color guard and firing squad from the Fred C. Wagner American Legion Post provided military honors at the Rolla Cemetery.[2]

**See The Elk, Lawrence.** Army number 2,787,162; registrant, Sioux County; born, Fort Yates, D.T., Aug. 10, 1886, of American parents; occupation, farmer; inducted at Fort Yates on May 25, 1918; sent to Camp Lewis, WA; served in Company C, 348th Machine Gun Battalion (91st Division), to discharge; overseas from July 6, 1918, to April 2, 1919. Engagements: Offensives: Meuse-Argonne; Ypres-Lys. Defensive Sector: Aubreville (Lorraine). Discharged at Camp Dodge, IA, on April 22, 1919, as a Private.

In the Census Roll for the Standing Rock Reservation taken in 1905, Lawrence and his brother, Giles, were listed with their grandmother, Day (Anpetu). In the Indian Census Roll for 1909, Lawrence is listed with his wife, Rosa. When Lawrence registered for the draft on June 5, 1917, he was farming near Fort Yates.

On May 25, 1918, Lawrence was inducted with a group of Sioux County men who were sent to Camp Lewis, WA. The 91st Infantry Division was formed at Camp Lewis. Among the men who were sent there were George and Mike Halsey, who served together in the 361st Infantry Regiment, and Asa Redstone, who was assigned to Company C of the 348th Machine Gun Battalion with Lawrence. On June 9, 1918, the men from Sioux County sent a letter to Chris Christenson of the *Sioux County Pioneer*, along with a photo of Lawrence taken by an army photographer. They wrote, "We are anxious to get your paper and hear from you once in a while. All the Sioux County boys are well and happy." Lawrence and Asa served together in France. Though the 91st Division had a big part in the Meuse-Argonne offensive, Lawrence and Asa were not part of the initial assault. Their commanding officer, Captain Arthur St. J. Whitney reported that the supply people did not have gas masks large enough to fit Lawrence and Asa. In late October of 1918, the 91st Division took part in the fighting near Audenarde, Belgium. While the unit was in Belgium, they received orders that the official insignia for their division was a fir tree of green cloth, inscribed within a triangle. The Division remained in Belgium until December 1918, when they were assigned billets near Le Mans, France. When Lawrence returned home, he made a presentation in Lakota to the St. Joseph's Society, describing his experiences in Europe. He was honored with a generous silver offering by his appreciative audience.

Lawrence married Irene Loon. In the 1925 ND State Census, Lawrence and Irene had a son, John. Lawrence passed away at his home near Fort Yates on July 15, 1928. His wife and two children survived him. He is buried in the Catholic cemetery in Fort Yates. The American Legion Post conducted military honors.[3]

**Shambow, George R.** According to the 1900 U.S. Census, George was born on October 22,1899, the son of John and Lois Shambow. His place of birth is listed as Wolf Creek, WI, which is near the St. Croix River in Polk County. His family likely were part of the St. Croix Band of Ojibwe. The 1900 Census lists them as living in Sterling, which is adjacent to Wolf Creek in Polk County, WI. In the 1910 U.S. Census, George was living with his parents and siblings on the White Earth Reservation near Callaway, MN. Sometime after this, George became a student at the boarding school in Wahpeton. On April 9, 1917, he enlisted in Company I, 1st Infantry, North Dakota National Guard at Wahpeton, with a group of other students at the boarding school. George would have been 17 years old at that time. These men who enlisted were primarily from various bands of Ojibwe in Minnesota. George was transferred to Camp Greene, NC, in October 1917, with the rest of the ND National Guard soldiers. He was transferred to Camp Mills, NY, on Nov. 9, 1917, and to Camp Merritt, NJ, on Dec. 7, 1917, before sailing for England aboard the SS *Leviathan* on Dec. 14, 1917.

When these men from North Dakota arrived in France, many of them were reassigned to the 26th Infantry Regiment of the 1st Division. Most of the men who had enlisted together in Wahpeton served together in Company H of the 26ᵗʰ Infantry. George was promoted to Sergeant. After the Armistice, 1ˢᵗ Lieutenant Allen C. Rowe of Company H wrote, "I have known this soldier for a year and find him efficient as a Sergeant." A brief bio and a photo of George in his uniform were published in a roster of the soldiers from Richland County, ND.

George Shambow, *Richland County Roster.*

After the war, George returned to the White Earth Reservation in Minnesota. His mother had married Charles Wilkinson, who worked as a forester for the government. In the 1920 U.S. Census, George is listed as George Wilkinson and was living with his mother in Beaulieu Township, Mahnomen County. He was working as a laborer in a sawmill. George married Effie (Nah-zhuck) Bishop (1902-1935). They had several children, including Marvin, Lois and Cecelia. Effie suffered from tuberculosis and died at the Minnesota State Sanatorium. After Effie died, George moved to the West Coast, where two of his sisters lived. He lived in Chiloquin, OR, and worked as a logger. George passed away at the VA Hospital in Portland, OR, on Oct. 24, 1952. He is buried in Greenwood Hill Cemetery in Portland. Two sisters who also lived in Oregon and Washington survived him. His son, Marvin, survived him back in Minnesota. Marvin served with the U.S. Army in WWII and received the Purple Heart.[4]

**Sherman, Benedict.** Army number 572,813; registrant, Benson County; born, Fort Totten, ND, April 1890, of American parents; occupation laborer; inducted at Minnewaukan on March 20, 1918; sent to Camp Greene, NC; served in Company B, 58ᵗʰ Infantry, to April 5, 1918; Headquarters Casual Company, Camp No. 1, Camp Greene, NC, to May 4, 1918; Detention Camp, Camp Greene, NC, to June 1918; Company A, Casual Camp No. 1, to Aug. 20, 1919; 3ʳᵈ Company, Development Battalion No. 1, to Dec. 27, 1918; Provost Guard Company, Camp Greene, NC, to discharge. Grade: Private 1ˢᵗ Class, Feb. 1, 1919. Discharged at Camp Dodge, IA, on March 18, 1919, as a Private.

In the Census Roll for the Devils Lake Sioux taken in 1905, Benedict and Joseph are listed with their father, Joseph Sherman, and mother, Alice (Iawastewin). He attended the boarding school at Fort Totten. In the Indian Census Roll for 1912, Benedict is listed with his wife, Rose (Tahcaskawin). They had a daughter, Mary Jane, who died when she was 12 years old.

After his discharge, Benedict married Rosalie Bear (1895-1987) on Aug. 18, 1919. They farmed in the Fort Totten community. Benedict passed away in his home on Jan. 27, 1978. His wife and daughters, Rachel, Irene, and Cora, as well as his son, Vincent, survived him. Six children preceded him in death. Benedict is buried in St. Jerome's Cemetery, west of Fort Totten.[5]

**Sherman, Joseph.** Army number 572,702; registrant, Benson County; born, Fort Totten, ND, April 22, 1895, of American parents; occupation, laborer; inducted at Minnewaukan on March 12, 1918; sent to Camp Greene, NC; served in Company B, 58th Infantry (4th Division), to death; overseas from May 6, 1918, to death. Drowned on May 23, 1918, in the sinking of the *Moldavia*.

Joseph was Benedict's younger brother. When he registered for the draft in 1917, he indicated he was providing support for his father. Joseph and Benedict were inducted about a week apart and sent to Camp Greene, NC. Initially, they both were training with the 58th Infantry, but Benedict was reassigned. On April 21, 1918, the 4th Division began transferring by train to Camp Mills, NY. The 58th Infantry Regiment sailed aboard the RMS *Moldavia*, a refitted British liner. When the ship arrived during the night at a point midway between Land's End and the Isle of Wight, a German U-boat fired a torpedo that struck the *Moldavia*. "The explosion tore a gaping hole in the port side of the hull and shattered the compartment where the 'B' Company men were sleeping and the ladders leading to the deck above. Nearly all the men in the compartment were killed outright by the explosion." Fifty-six men died in that explosion. Several British destroyers rescued the remaining soldiers before the ship finally settled to the bottom in 150 feet of water. Joseph Sherman was the first man from North Dakota's Indian Country to die in the war. His name is included on a memorial to American MIAs at Suresnes American Cemetery and Memorial near Paris, France.

Joseph Sherman was asleep on the *Moldavia* when it was struck on the port side by a German torpedo on May 6, 1918. *Postcard, author's collection.*

**Short Baldhead, Benedict.** Benedict was born around 1888 in Fort Yates. In the Indian Census Roll taken in 1905, he is listed with his parents, Short Baldhead (Peslaptecela) and Short Woman (Winyanptecela). In the 1910 U.S. Census, he lived in Wakpala with his mother and worked as a laborer doing odd jobs. When he registered for the draft on June 5, 1917, he was a bronco buster at Fort Yates. He was inducted on July 26, 1918 and sent to Camp Custer, MI. Several weeks later the *Sioux County Pioneer* reported that he was given a medical discharge. Around this time he married Mary Brought. In the Census Roll taken in 1922, Ben and Mary are listed with their daughter, Bonnie. They lived in Bullhead. Ben passed away in his sleep on Aug. 16, 1924. He is buried in Black Horse Catholic Cemetery. Mary (1889-1967) later married Joseph Leaf.[7]

**Sleeps From Home, George.** Army number 3,954,592; registrant, Corson County, SD; born, Kenel, SD, Sept. 23, 1893, of American parents; occupation, rancher; inducted at McIntosh, SD, July 21, 1918; sent to Camp Dodge, IA; served in 41st Company, 163rd Depot Brigade, to Aug. 14, 1918; Company D, Development Battalion No. 1, to Sept. 13, 1918; Casual, in Hospital, to discharge. Discharged at Fort Des Moines, IA, on Dec. 23, 1918, as a Private, Surgeon's Certificate of Disability, 50%.

In the Census Roll for the Standing Rock Reservation taken in 1894, George is listed with his father, Oliver Sleeps From Home, and his mother, brother and grandmother. In the 1920 U.S. Census, George was living with his parents. He had developed some symptoms of tuberculosis, which is likely why he was given a 50% disability upon discharge from the Army. In January 1922, George entered Battle Mountain Sanitarium at Hot Springs, SD. He was discharged in May 1922. Around this time, he married Julia Yellow Fat (1902-1961). Julia had two brothers who served in WWI, including Martin, who died shortly after returning to South Dakota. The American Legion Post in Kenel was named in honor of Martin Yellow Fat. George was a member of that Post.

In 1921, George went to St. Paul, MN, for vocational training. George continued to ranch in Sioux County. In the Census Roll taken in 1940, George and Julia are listed with their children, Daniel, William, Mary, Margaret, Wallace, and Virginia. Their son, William, enlisted in the U.S. Army in 1942, and also served during the Korean Conflict. George died on Dec. 30, 1951, after being struck by a motor vehicle near Fort Yates. His wife and six children, including Daniel, William, Wallace, Loraine, Margaret, and Maxine, survived him. He is buried in St. Benedict's Cemetery in Kenel, SD.[8]

**Smith, John W.** Army number 55,278; not a registrant, under age; born, Fort Berthold, ND, Jan. 28, 1898, of American parents; occupation, farmer; enlisted in Company I, 2nd Infantry, North Dakota National Guard, at Bismarck, on Aug. 11, 1917; served in Company I, 2nd Infantry, North Dakota National Guard (161st Ambulance Company, 116th Sanitary Train), to Nov. 14, 1917; Company H, 164th Infantry, to Jan. 18, 1918; Company M, 26th Infantry (First Division), to discharge. Grades: Private 1st Class, July 1, 1918; Corporal, Sept. 6, 1918; Sergeant, Oct. 20, 1918; overseas from Dec. 15, 1917, to Sept. 2, 1919. Engagements: Defensive: Montdidier-Noyon. Offensives: Aisne-Marne; St. Mihiel; Meuse-Argonne. Defensive Sectors: Ansauville and Saizerais (Lorraine); Cantigny (Picardy). Discharged at Camp Dodge, IA, on Sept. 24, 1919, as a Sergeant. Cited in General Orders No. 1, Headquarters, 1st Division, Camp Zachary Taylor, KY, Jan. 1, 1920, for gallantry in action and especially meritorious services. Entitled to wear a silver star.

In the Census Roll for the Gros Ventres (Hidatsa) taken in 1899, John is listed with his father, Conrad Smith, and his mother, Mary Red Feather. In the 1911 Gros Ventres Census Roll, John is listed with his other brothers and his sister, Dora. After the war, Dora married Oscar Burr, a fellow veteran.

John was the first Hidatsa to enlist in the 2nd ND National Guard Regiment formed in Bismarck in the summer of 1917. Sgt. Smith served in Company M, 26th Infantry with Alphonse Bear Ghost and Louis Latraille. All three of these men from Indian Country were cited for gallantry and were eligible for the silver Citation Star. The Silver Star medal was not officially established until 1932. Sgt. Smith also received the French Fourragère, which is similar to a unit citation. After the fighting was ended, Sgt. Smith was rated by his commanding officer as a "very good scout and leader of men." After war, John filled out a report for Joseph Dixon, in which he wrote,

> I am proud that I was the first to enlist and spend more days in trenches than the rest of the boys from this Reservation. I've had some close calls too. While going over on the Soissons Drive July 18, 1918 a big Shell lit bout 2 ft to the right of me and exploded but didn't kill me. It killed two men on the right of me. I was just black with powder. That's all and if you don't call that luck. – Machine gun bullets tore my breeches all up the same day too.
> I think I'm the luckiest Grosventre.

John Smith. *Four Bears Museum*

In 1922, John married Nellie White Hawk (1904-1969), an enrolled member at Fort Peck. They farmed near Shell Creek until 1950, when the Garrison Dam was about completed. They went to live in Poplar, MT, for a number of years. When Nellie passed away in 1969, the family was still living in Poplar, MT. Sometime later, John moved back to North Dakota. John was the Sgt. at Arms for the Joseph Young Hawk Legion Post when it was chartered in 1934. His nickname was "Sarge." He also had been a member of the Beck-Sherven Legion Post at New Town, as well as the Valarian-Finley Post at Mandaree. He and Nellie had three daughters and five sons. Their son, Dell, served in the U.S. Army during the Korean Conflict. Their son, Theodore, also served in the Army. John passed away on April 19, 1977. His daughters, Lillie Mae, Joan, and Virginia, as well as his sons, Dell, Theodore, John, and Jess, survived him. He is buried in Shell Creek Cemetery.[9]

**Speaks Walking, Luke.** Army number 465,354; not a registrant, under age; born, Fort Yates, ND, March 20, 1900; occupation, student; enlisted at Flandreau, SD, April 13, 1918; sent to Jefferson Barracks, MO; served in 31st New York Coast Artillery Corps, Fort Wadsworth, NY, to June 17, 1918; Battery B, 74th Artillery, Coast Artillery Corps, to discharge. Grade: Private 1st Class, June 4, 1918; overseas from Sept. 23, 1918, to Dec. 22, 1918. Discharged at Camp Dodge, IA, on Jan. 9, 1919, as a Private 1st Class.

In the Census Roll for Standing Rock Reservation taken in 1902, Luke, also known as John, is listed with his father, Louis Speaks Walking (Iyamani), as well as his mother, Hairy Moccasin. Luke was a student at Flandreau when he enlisted in the Army. On April 6, 1918, he sent his parents a letter, which was published by the *Sioux County Pioneer.* This was shortly after his 18th birthday.

> Dearest Father and mother,
> I am going to ask or let my brothers and you both know that I plan to enlist in the army tonight. I am a man and want to show my love to our country and then to show my name to the country. We are going to leave here on Wednesday, April 10, for Sioux Falls to be examined. I have the name of my grandfather and which you gave me.
> You don't want to worry about me or cry for me. I am well off. We are going to join till the war is over, and if we should win the war we will (reach) the city of Berlin. If you are going to answer me, address it to Chas. Pierce, here and he will send them to us. I don't know if I will pass or not yet. There are lots of boys who enlisted already. I wish to enlist too. After we are examined I will let you know if I pass or not. We are going to come home after six months training to see you folks. Let some who can explain all this to you and read good to you so you will not be mistaken.
> I am getting along pretty good for this present writing and hope it will reach you as sure as it leaves me here.
> I wish you all and relations my best of wishes and regards and kiss every one of you, and close with love to you all, father, mother and brothers.

Luke sailed to Europe with the 74th Artillery aboard the transport USS *President Grant.* On the trip across the pond, 137 men on the ship died of the flu. Upon arrival in France, they were assigned to a camp at Mailly and Haussimont. They were a Railway Artillery unit that was to be trained in the firing of either the 400-mm or the 340-mm guns. Their training was not completed before the Armistice. They returned on the USS *Mongolia.*

After the war, Luke married Lucy Tiger. In the Indian Census Roll taken in 1924, Luke and Lucy are listed with their daughter, Julia. Lucy died of tuberculosis on May 20, 1926. On Jan. 18, 1927, Luke married Josephine De Rockbraine in McIntosh, SD. In the Indian Census Roll taken in 1928, Luke and Josephine are listed with their children, Charlotte and Oscar. Oscar died as a young child in 1932. At that time the family was living near Little Eagle, SD. In March 1928, Like was admitted to Battle Mountain Sanitarium near Hot Springs, SD, with some health problems, including partial deafness. The hospital at Hot Springs later became a VA facility. The deafness was probably due to having served in the artillery. His application to the hospital indicates he was receiving a pension, most likely for the deafness caused by being next to the big guns without adequate ear protection. He was discharged in April 1928. In the Indian Census Roll taken in 1936, Luke and Josephine are listed with Charlotte. Josephine passed away from tuberculosis on Aug. 24, 1945, in South Dakota. Luke had a heart attack and died at home on Nov. 23, 1962. He is buried in St. Mary's Cemetery in Bullhead.

**Spotted Bird, John.** John was born in Cannonball, ND on Sept. 7, 1894. His parents were Dan Spotted bird (Zitkanahdeska) and Hand (Nape). In the 1900 U.S. Census, John is also listed as Najiyapi. In the Census Roll for Standing Rock taken in 1903, John is listed as the stepson of Bears Heart. At Christmas in 1904, Frank Fiske took a photo of John serving as an altar boy at the Catholic Church in Fort Yates. In the Census Roll taken in 1915, John is listed with his wife, Mary White Twin.

John lived in Wakpala before the war. On June 24, 1918, he was inducted and sent to Camp Funston, which is located at Fort Riley, KS. Many of the men from Camp Funston were transferred to Camp Dodge, IA, in July 1918. John was assigned to Company B, 351st Infantry, which was part of the 88th Division. Straight Pine from Bullhead, SD, also served in Company B. By the end of July, men were painting "A.E.F." on their lockers, and the unit sailed to Europe in early August. After the war, Private 1st Class Spotted Bird noted, "I was at the front in the center sect of the Haute Alsace." The men from the 88th Division returned to the U.S. in June 1919.

In the Census Roll for Standing Rock taken in 1926, John is listed as divorced. In the 1920s, John moved to Fort Peck, MT, and married Virginia Powell (1907-1970), an enrolled member at Fort Peck. In the 1930 U.S. Census, John and Virginia are listed with their children, Josephine and Viola, as well as Virginia's mother, Helen Red Bird Sharp Eye. In the Census Roll for Fort Peck taken in 1936, there were two more children, Elaine and Gerald, added to their family. John worked as a farm laborer. The family lived near Brockton, MT. He passed away in the Poplar Community Hospital on July 24, 1966. He is buried in Fort Kipp Cemetery, near Brockton.[11]

**Standish, Douglas.** Army number 3,084,463; not a registrant; born, Independence, ND, Oct. 22, 1898, of American parents; occupation, farmer; enlisted at Bismarck on July 2, 1918; sent to Jefferson Barracks, MO; served in 7th Company, Coast Artillery Corps, to discharge. Discharged at Camp Dodge, IA, on Jan. 15, 1919, as a Private.

In the Census Roll taken at Fort Berthold in 1902, Douglas is listed with his parents, Peter (Aku-ru-ra-ha-ris) and Pollie (Ita-ki-wi-ash) Standish, as well as a sister, Ruth. During the war, Douglas likely was stationed along the East Coast. After the war, he married Ollie Horn (1895-1975). Ollie had been married to Arthur Old Mouse, who had died while serving with the Army in Europe. In the Census Roll taken in 1920, Douglas and Ollie are listed with their son, William, as well as Lee Old Mouse, the son of Arthur and Ollie. The family ranched near Mandaree. In the Fort Berthold Census Roll taken in 1939, Douglas and Ollie are listed with their children, Oliver, Polly and Leo. Douglas passed away on Dec. 15, 1965, at the hospital in Watford City. His wife and children, Polly, Oliver, Leo, and Lee survived him. He is buried in the Independence Congregational Cemetery.[12]

**Star, Philip Ward** (photo p. 96). Army number 3,084,365; registrant, Burleigh County; born, Ree, ND, Aug. 3, 1897, of American parents; occupation, farmer; inducted at Bismarck on July 1, 1918; sent to Jefferson Barracks, MO; served in Company H, 43rd Infantry, to discharge. Discharged at Camp Dodge, IA, on July 14, 1919, as a Private.

In the Census Roll for the Arikara taken in 1910, Philip is listed with his parents, Patrick and Dora Star, as well as his other siblings. In 1910, Philip was a student at the boarding school in Bismarck. He married Kate Hopkins (1902-1983) on June 18, 1917. Kate was the sister of Harvey and Dan Hopkins who both served in WWI. Philip enlisted in Bismarck on June 6, 1918, and was stationed with the 15th Infantry Division in Camp Logan, TX, and later at Camp Bowie, TX. After his discharge, he returned to farm near Elbowwoods. In the Census Roll for Fort Berthold taken in 1939, he and Kate are listed with their children, Ida, Margaret, McRoy, Evan, Glenn,

Woodrow, Theresa, Philip, Jr., and Alfonso. A number of their children served in the military. McRoy served in the U.S. Army from 1941-45, Margaret served from 1944-45, Philip, Jr. served in the USAF from 1951-55, and Alfonso also served in the U.S. Army. Philip died in the Elbowoods hospital after a short illness on April 17, 1950. He was buried in the Nishu Cemetery. The Young Hawk Post No. 253 of the American Legion of Elbowwoods officiated at military rites.[13]

**St. Arneaud, Alexander.** Army number 87,776; registrant, Rolette County; born, St. John, ND, Oct. 7, 1894, of Canadian-American parents; occupation, farmer; enlisted in Company D, 2nd Infantry, North Dakota National Guard, at Devils Lake, on June 30, 1917; called into federal service, World War, on July 15, 1917; served in Company D, 2nd Infantry, North Dakota National Guard, to Oct. 13, 1917; Company L, 164th Infantry, to discharge. Grades: Private 1st Class, Aug. 1, 1917; Corporal, Dec. 10, 1917; Sergeant, Oct. 19, 1918; overseas from Dec. 15, 1917, to Feb. 26, 1919. Discharged at Camp Dodge, IA, on March 13, 1919, as a Sergeant.

Alex was the son of John Baptiste and Julia St. Arnaud. His father had a trading post at St. John and freighted his own merchandise in Red River carts pulled by oxen. In the 1910 U.S. Census, Alex was a student at the boarding school at Fort Totten. According to the 1915 Iowa State Census, Alex was working in Huntington, IA. While serving in France with the 164th Infantry, Alex was a bayonet instructor and qualified as an expert rifleman.

After the war, Alex married Ernestine Wallett. They had a daughter, Leona. Ernestine died in 1921. Alex then married Louise (1897-1993). In the 1930 Census, Alex and Louise were living near Phoenix, where Alex worked as a truck driver. In the 1940 Census, they lived in Parker, AZ, with their daughter, Mary Margaret. Alex was working as a carpenter's helper on a dam construction project on the Colorado River. In 1945, they moved to Yuma and Alex worked for the Bureau of Reclamation as a machinist and blacksmith. He died in Parkview Baptist Hospital in Yuma on March 6, 1961. His wife and daughters, Leona and Mary Margaret, survived him. He is buried in Desert Lawn Memorial Park in Yuma, AZ.[14]

**Family of John B. and Julia St. Arnaud, 1918.**

Alex was photographed with his family before departing for overseas duty. *State Historical Society of North Dakota*

**St. Germain, Philip.** Army number 2,271,229; registrant, Sheridan County, MT; born, St. John, ND, April 1, 1892, of Canadian-American parents; occupation, laborer; inducted at Plentywood, MT, on Oct. 2, 1917; sent to Camp Lewis, WA; served in 136th Company, 34th Battalion, 166th Depot Brigade, to Oct. 25, 1917; Battery E, 348th Field Artillery (91st Infantry Division), to

117

discharge; overseas from July 14, 1918, to March 30, 1919. Discharged at Fort D.A. Russell, WY, on April 20, 1919, as a Private.

Philip was the son of Francis and Alphonnine St. Germain. He sometimes used the name, Joseph. His sister, Rosalie, married Patrick Desjarlais who also served in WWI. Philip went overseas with the 91st Division, also known as the Wild West Division. Their motto was "Let'er buck." They arrived in England on July 26, 1918. Upon arrival in France, the 348th Field Artillery Regiment was assigned to a training camp (155 mm guns) near Clermont-Ferrand. They trained separately from the infantry, and did not take part in the combat operations that the infantry conducted. After the Armistice, the artillery regiments were moved into Germany, where they occupied the village of Wittlich until February 1919.

Philip returned to North Dakota upon being discharged. He married Alice La France (1914-1973) in the 1930s. In the 1940 U.S. Census, Philip and Alice lived in Baxter Township of Rolette County with their children, John, Phyllis, and Delores. Philip worked as a laborer on a WPA project. The family later moved to Cle Elum, WA. Philip worked as a laborer in the lumbering business. Philip passed away in Modern Care Convalescent Center in Seattle on March 28, 1985. He is buried in Laural Hill Memorial Park in Cle Elum, WA.[15]

## T

**Tatankamani, George.** Army number 4,046,253; registrant, Benson County; born, Tokio, ND, Sept. 1, 1892, of American parents; occupation, laborer; inducted at Minnewaukon on Aug. 18, 1918; sent to Camp Custer, MI; served in 160th Depot Brigade, to discharge. Discharged at Camp Custer, MI, on Jan. 11, 1919, as a Private.

In the Census Rolls for the Devils Lake Sioux taken in the early 1900s list George with his father, Tatanbdi and his wife, Louisa. George was also known as Itewanbdi. In 1916, he married Lucy. In the 1920 U.S. Census, George is listed with his wife, Lucy, and his sister-in-law, Helen Goodhouse. He was later married to Mabel and had a daughter, Ruth. In the late 1920s, he moved to South Dakota. In the Census Rolls taken in the 1930s, he is listed as living at Sisseton, SD. In the 1940 U.S. Census, George was living in Benson County, ND, and working as a farm laborer. He later moved back to South Dakota. He was living near Browns Valley when he died on July 2, 1975. He is buried in St. Peter's Cemetery in Sisseton, SD.

**Tattoed, James.** Army number, none; registrant, Sioux County; born, Cannon Ball, ND, March 18, 1896, of American parents; inducted at Fort Yates on Sept. 18, 1917; sent to Camp Dodge, IA; served in Battery E, 338th Field Artillery, to discharge. Discharged at Camp Dodge, IA, on Oct. 10, 1917, as a Recruit, Surgeon's Certificate of Disability.

In the Census Roll for Standing Rock taken in 1902, James is listed with his parents, Tattoed and Couch (Oyake), as well as his brothers and sisters. His oldest sister, Clara, later married George Many Wounds, who also served in WWI. His father passed away shortly after that. James was also known as Blue Lips. In October 1910, his mother, Oyanke, gave her permission to have James enrolled for five years at the boarding school in Carlisle, PA. While living in Carlisle, he worked for a number of families in the surrounding area doing general farm work. He was paid $8 per month. He was not trained in a particular trade. He voluntarily left the school in May 1914 and returned to North Dakota. He had hurt his arm and had been in the hospital at Carlisle for a short time.

On July 4, 1917, James took part in the rodeo at Fort Yates. He was hurt while riding a bronco and entered the Fort Yates hospital. This was not long before he entered the military service. He received a medical discharge, which may have been related to earlier injuries. On May 5, 1919, he married Melda McLean at St. Peters Catholic Church in Fort Yates. The local paper reported that Mendelssohn's Wedding March was played, with the musicians including Joe Pretends Eagle and Frank Fiske. This was followed by a dance in the school hall. At that time, James was employed as the disciplinarian at the school. James was active in sports. He played outfield for the Fort Yates baseball team after the war. He also was active in wrestling, traveling to Aberdeen for some matches. In 1920, he retained the title of lightweight champion of North Dakota after defending himself against Loyd Solmon, who was 20 pounds heavier. In later years, his son, Morris, was an active boxer.

In the Census Roll at Standing Rock taken in 1930, James and Melda are listed with their children, William, Marie, Morris, and Margaret. Melda died of pneumonia at the Fort Yates Hospital on Jan. 1, 1933, leaving James with six children, including a three-month-old infant. James then married Cecelia Goodiron in the mid-1930s. In the 1940 U.S. Census, they were living in Fort Yates, where James worked as a construction laborer. In the 1940s, he moved out to Sacramento, CA. He passed away at a hospital in Mendocino, CA, on March 17, 1963. He is buried in Wakpala, SD.[1]

**Tetrault, Albert Manual.** Army number 4,037,098; registrant, Rolette County; born, St. Joseph, ND, Dec. 25, 1892, of (nationality of parents not given); occupation, student; inducted at Rolla on July 22, 1918; sent to Camp Custer, MI; served in Company B, 40th Machine Gun Battalion, to discharge. Discharged at Camp Dodge, IA, on Feb. 7, 1919, as a Private.

Albert was the son of Joseph and Matilda Tetrault. When he registered for the draft on May 30, 1917, he was a student at the Carlisle boarding school, Carlisle, PA. He served there as a Captain in the cadets. While he was stationed at Camp Custer, he was training with the 14th Infantry Division. The Armistice was signed before their training was completed. In the 1920s, he moved to Morgantown, WV, where he married Beulah Kryder. In the 1930 U.S. Census, Albert continued to live in Morgantown, where he worked as a carpenter in building construction while Beulah was a teacher. They had a daughter, Jane. Beulah died on Feb. 1, 1935. When Albert registered for the Selective Service during WWII, he was working for E.I. Du Pont Co. in Morgantown, WV. In his later years, Albert retired and moved to Lake Wales, FL. He passed away in Winter Haven Hospital, Winter Haven, FL, on March 2, 1994, at the age of 101. He is buried in Lakeview Crematory in Winter Haven.[2]

**Tetrault, Alfonce.** Army number 3,957,818; registrant, Towner County; born, Neche, ND, Jan. 9, 1894, of American parents; occupation, farmer; inducted at Cando on July 22, 1918; sent to Camp Dodge, IA; served in 37th Labor Regiment, Quartermaster Corps, to Sept. 29, 1918; Field Remount Squadron No. 341, to discharge; overseas from Oct. 27, 1918, to July 5, 1919. Discharged at Camp Dodge, IA, on July 14, 1919, as a Private.

Alphonse was the son of Patrick and Mary Tetrault. In the 1900 U.S. Census, he lived with his parents on the Turtle Mountain Reservation. When he registered for the draft on June 5, 1917, he was farming with his father east of Cando, ND. During the war, the Field Remount Squadron was part of the Veterinary Corps. Alphonse was trained at Camp Joseph E. Johnston, FL, before sailing from New York for France. After the war, Alphonse returned to North Dakota. In the 1920 U.S. Census, he lived with his sister near Cando. Nicholas Dauphinais, another returned veteran, lived with them as a hired man. Alphonse moved to Missouri with his parents. In the 1930 U.S. Census, they lived outside of St. Louis, in Lincoln County, MO. Alphonse was working as a laborer for a telephone company. He later married Bertha Johnson (1905-1991), and lived in St. Charles, MO. He worked as a machinist for Fulton Iron Works. He passed away at Rockwood Manor in St. Louis on Jan. 26, 1958. He is buried in St. Peter's Cemetery in St. Charles, MO.[3]

**Thomas, James.** Army number, none; registrant, (not given); born, Belcourt, ND, Jan. 15, 1896, of (nationality of parents not given); occupation, (not given); enlisted in Company G, 2nd Infantry, North Dakota National Guard, at Rolla, on July 16, 1917; served in Company G, 2nd Infantry, North Dakota National Guard, to discharge. Discharged on Aug. 6, 1917, as a Private.

James was the son of William and Clemence Thomas. In the Census Roll for the Turtle Mountain Reservation taken in 1897, James is listed with his parents. On April 21, 1914, James married Melanie Houle. When he registered for the draft on June 5, 1917, he was supporting his wife and two children, William and Rita Mary. In 1921, they had another daughter, Mary Louise. Melanie died on Nov. 5, 1922. He then married Mary Matilda Demontigny (1900-1960) in the early 1930s. Mary's first husband, Greg Bercier, had died in 1930. James and Mary lived in Rolla and had several children. James died suddenly on June 2, 1937, in Rolla and is buried in Belcourt.[4]

**Traversie, Alexander.** Army number 968,274; registrant, Burleigh County; born, Fort Yates, ND, Nov. 15, 1896, of American-Swedish parents; occupation, student; enlisted at Bismarck on Aug. 1, 1917; sent to Jefferson Barracks, MO; served in Medical Officers Training Camp, Fort Ogelthorpe, GA, to Aug. 13, 1917; Medical Department, Base Hospital No. 6, to July 15, 1918; Medical Detachment, 4th Infantry (3rd Infantry Division), to discharge; overseas from Oct. 3, 1917, to March 3, 1919; wounded, slightly, Oct. 14, 1918. Engagements: Defensive: Champagne-Marne. Offensives: Aisne-Marne; St. Mihiel; Meuse-Argonne. Discharged at Fort Snelling, MN, on June 6, 1919, as a Private; Surgeon's Certificate of Disability, 75%.

Alexander was the son of Gus and Augusta Traversie. Gus acted as an interpreter and a driver for the government paymaster on the Standing Rock Reservation. Gus died in 1901. Augusta was born in Sweden and had come to the U.S. as a young girl. At Christmas in 1904, Frank Fiske took a photo of Alex as an altar boy at the Catholic Church in Fort Yates. In the 1910 U.S. Census, Alexander was a student at the Bismarck boarding school. In December 1913, Augusta gave her permission to have Alexander enrolled at the boarding school in Carlisle, PA, for a three-year period. He had a hard time adjusting to school life in Pennsylvania, and troubles with some of the local people in town. At school, he got in trouble after losing his math book, *Milne's Progressive Arithmetic - First Book.* In the summer of 1916, his mother wrote to the school with her subscription for the school newspaper, *The Arrow.* She also asked if the school could teach her son how to drive a car. Later that year, Alexander was appointed manager of the boys' basketball team. He term at Carlisle ended with the school year in June 1917. After returning to Fort Yates, he enlisted in the Medical Department in Bismarck. His mother became a member of the War Mothers group in Fort Yates.

As a soldier of the 3rd Infantry Division, Alexander was involved in some of the heaviest combat, from Chateau Thierry to the Meuse-Argonne. When he returned to Fort Yates in June 1919, the local newspaper reported that "he and his comrades were without food for days at a time when the forward drives were on, the German return artillery fire being such as to prevent the bringing up of supplies. Their hunger was appeased at times, though, by the finding of food supplies in the captured German dugouts. He was at a hospital at Fort Snelling, MN, for four months, and is serving as district court bailiff."

Alexander's leg was amputated because of his wounds. In the 1920 U.S. Census, He was living in Minneapolis and working as a machine operator. Sometime after this he moved into the National

Home for Disabled Volunteer Soldiers, later a VA hospital, in Milwaukee, WI. Alexander continued to live in Milwaukee. He was still there when his mother died in hospital in Mandan in 1937. When Alexander registered for the Selective Service in 1942, he was living in Milwaukee.[5]

**Turner, Paul.** Army number 3,084,593; not a registrant; born, Elbowoods, ND, March 15, 1898, of American parents; occupation, farmer; enlisted at Bismarck on July 2, 1918; sent to Jefferson Barracks, MO; served in 18th Company, Coast Artillery Corps, Fort McKinley, ME, to Sept. 11, 1918; Fort McKinley September Automatic Replacement Draft, to Dec. 23, 1918; 15th Company, Coast Artillery Corps, Fort McKinley, ME, to discharge. Discharged at Fort McKinley, ME, on March 17, 1919, as a Private.

Paul (I-pa-da-kis) was the son of Crow Turns and Hunts Medicine. In many of the Indian Census Rolls he is listed as Allen Turner. In the Census Roll for Fort Berthold taken in 1901, he is listed with Crow Turns, Medicine Hunts and his brother, Samuel. In the 1906 Indian Census Roll, he is listed as the stepson of White Finger Nails. After his discharge from the Coast Artillery, he re-enlisted in the 14th Cavalry, stationed at Fort Sam Houston, TX. He was in Texas when the 1920 U.S. Census was taken. A contemporary booklet for returned vets reflected military humor:

> "The cavalry must be a lucky branch of the service to be in," observed the doughboy.
> "Why?" asked the pill roller.
> "Just think how many horseshoes they carry around with them."

Paul married Gladys Bassett (1905-1967) of Elbowoods at Manning on May 18, 1921. In the 1930 U.S. Census, Paul and Gladys were farming, and his stepfather was living with them. In the Indian Census Roll taken in 1939, Allen (Paul) and Gladys are listed with their children, Hazel, Nina, Primrose, Medora, and the twins, Allen Paul, Jr., and Frances Jane. Allen Paul served in the U.S. Army during the 1950s, and was stationed at Camp Chaffee, AR, when his father passed away on Aug. 31, 1955, at the VA Hospital in Fargo. Gladys and children, including Nina, Primrose, Medora, Allen Paul, Jr., Frances Jane, Tillie Mae, Rebecca, and Matthew survived him. Five children preceded their father in death. Paul is buried in Independence Congregational Cemetery near Mandaree.[6]

**Two Bears, Edward.** Edward was the son of Stephen and Henrietta Two Bears. Born on April 24, 1899, he was a brother to Joseph, who served with the 88th Division in France. Edward attended school in Bismarck. When he registered for the draft on Sept. 12, 1918, he was working as a section hand for the NP Railroad. He enlisted in the Army in March 1920, after several Army Recruiters attached to the 3rd Field Artillery Regiment at Camp Grant, IL, came to Cannon Ball. After his discharge he worked as a farm laborer and lived near Mandan. In 1938, he married Mable Blue Earth who was the sister of Richard Blue Earth. Mable passed away in 1952. Edward passed away in a Bismarck hospital on Sept. 5, 1959, and is buried at Cannon Ball.[7]

**Two Bears, George.** George was the son of Joseph and Mary Two Bears. He was born on June 16, 1899, in Breien, ND. He attended school in Fort Yates. When he registered for the draft on Sept. 12, 1918, he was working in Breien. He also enlisted with his cousin, Edward, in March 1920. They served together in the 3rd Field Artillery at Camp Grant, IL. After his discharge, he ranched near Breien. He married Esther Twiggs (1908-1966) in Breien on Nov. 28, 1927. George passed away in a Bismarck hospital on Feb. 11, 1970. His daughter, June, as well as his sons, William, Donald, and Vincent survived him. He is buried in St. Gabriel's Episcopal Cemetery in Cannon Ball.[8]

**Two Bears, Joseph.**  Army number 2,703,602; registrant, Sioux County; born, Cannon Ball, ND, April 18, 1894, of American parents; occupation, farmer; inducted at Fort Yates on June 23, 1918; sent to Camp Dodge, IA; served in Company M, 349th Infantry (88th Division), to discharge. Grade: Private 1st Class, Nov. 29, 1918; overseas from Aug. 9, 1918, to May 30, 1919. Engagement: Defensive Sector: Center (Alsace). Discharged at Camp Dodge, IA, on June 11, 1919, as a Private 1st Class.

In the Indian Census Rolls taken before 1900, Joseph is listed as Kutepi. In the Census Roll for 1894, Kutepi was listed with Stephen and Henrietta Two Bears, as well as Stephen's brother, Basil, who later became the stepfather of Albert Grass. In the 1900 U.S. Census, Joseph (Wahacankagi) is listed with his parents, Stephen (Matononpa) and Esther (Tarchaoyewastewin). Joseph attended school in Fort Yates.

When he registered for the draft on June 5, 1917, he was working at odd jobs in Cannon Ball. Joseph trained with the 88th Infantry Division at Camp Dodge, IA. He served in Company M, 349th Infantry Regiment along with Frank Young Bear. Upon arrival in France, the Division was assigned a training area near Semur. By the end of September 1918, the men were issued steel helmets and gas masks before being moved into the trenches at Centre Haute Alsace. Most of the division was not directly involved in the fighting in the final Meuse-Argonne Campaign. Private 1st Class Two Bears was described by his commanding officer as "a good all-around soldier." After the Armistice, the soldiers moved to a billet near Gondrecourt, where they were occupied with schools, sports activities, and cultural pursuits. The men were eager to return to the U.S. by then. When the soldiers from the Midwest finally arrived back at Camp Dodge, IA, each man was given a $60 bonus and a red chevron to put on their left sleeve to denote discharge. This permitted them to continue to wear their uniforms. The men had been issued new outfits complete, and were entitled to take home with them a gas mask, helmet, and other equipment and clothing. A photo of Pvt. 1st Cl. Two Bears was published in *Memoirs of France and the 88th Division*.

JOSEPH TWO BEAR
Pvt., 1st cl., Co. M., Cannon Ball, N. D.

*Minnesota Historical Society*

After returning home, Joseph married Dora Tail (1903-1997). Their oldest son, Gilbert, was born in 1922. The family continued to live in Cannon Ball. In the Census Roll for Standing Rock taken in 1937, Joseph and Dora are listed with their children, Gilbert, Patrick, Neal, Selma, and Marie. Joseph was a member of the American Legion. Gilbert, Patrick, and Neal all served in the military. Gilbert was in the U.S. Army in North Africa and Europe during WWII. Neal was with the U.S. Army from 1950-1953. Patrick served with the U.S. Navy during WWII, and also served in the U.S. Army in Korea. Joseph's youngest brother, Mandan, also served in the U.S. Army during WWII. In 1945, Joseph moved with his family to Mandan. In the 1951 *Mandan City Directory*, he was listed as a farmer. Joseph passed away at the VA Hospital in Sturgis, SD, on June 3, 1967. His wife and children, Gilbert, Patrick, and Neal, Mrs. One Horn, Mrs. Conica, and Mrs. Kottre survived him. A son and a daughter preceded him in death. He is buried in St. Elizabeth's Catholic Cemetery in Cannon Ball.[9]

**Two Crows, John.** Army number 2,560,095; registrant, McLean County; born, Elbowoods, ND, March 3, 1890, of American parents; inducted at Washburn on March 28, 1918; sent to Camp Dodge, IA; served in 153rd Depot Brigade, to April 20, 1918; Company I, 138th Infantry, to May 29, 1918; Company D, 129th Machine Gun Battalion (35th Division), to discharge; overseas from May 2, 1918, to Feb. 12, 1919. Engagement: Defensive Sector: Gerardmer (Alsace). Discharged at Camp Dodge, IA, on March 3, 1919, as a Private.

In the Census Roll for the Fort Berthold Reservation taken in 1900, John (Wa-its-kis-ki-tsi-ris) is listed with his mother, White Woman, and a brother and sister. John played baseball for a team at Elbowoods. When he registered for the draft before the war, he was farming. In the Census Roll taken in 1918, John is listed with his first wife, Ermel (1904-1975). After the war, John prepared a statement of his military service for Joseph Dixon.

> "I went to Washburn, North Dakota, then to Camp Dodge, Iowa where I was in training for 22 days. From here I was transferred to Camp Mills, Long Island, New York. Then I entered Co. I – 138th Infantry, and was transferred to Bordeaux, France. Immediately on my arrival here I was transferred to Company D – 129th Machine Gun Battalion. Without hesitation we were rushed to the 'French Front', where we were occupied with the 'guns' for a period of 29 days without intermission. After a few days fighting we succeeded in capturing 5 Germans. These I with one of my friends took back to a "Prisoner's Camp." Now I was sent back to a Camp Detachment – and I then served as a Military Police until the Armistice – a period of about 2 months. Received an honorable discharge at Camp Dodge, Iowa."

After the war, John returned to Elbowoods. In the Indian Census Roll taken in 1922, John and Ermel are listed with their two sons, Willis and Mason. John married Mary Fast Dog (1902-1965) on Nov. 21, 1929, at Van Hook. After becoming ill in June 1936, John had some friends in Elbowoods take him to the VA Hospital in Fargo. Unfortunately, he passed away at the hospital on June 10, 1936. His wife and children, Veronica, Byron, Willis, Mason, and Olivia survived him. His son, Mason, served with the U.S. Navy during WWII. Mason was married to Carolyn White Bear, who was the first woman from the reservation to enlist in the Navy's WAVES during WWII. John is buried in St. Anthony's Catholic Cemetery.[10]

**Two Horses, Edward.** Army number 2,858,764; registrant, Sioux County; born, Cannon Ball, ND, July 15, 1896, of American parents; occupation, rancher; inducted at Fort Yates on April 30, 1918; sent to Camp Dodge, IA; served in Company F, 350th Infantry, to May 16, 1918; Company K, 358th Infantry (90th Division), to discharge; overseas from June 20, 1918, to March 22, 1919; wounded, gassed, Sept. 29, 1918. Engagements: Offensive: St. Mihiel. Defensive Sectors:

Villers-en-Haye and Puvenelle (Lorraine). Discharged at Camp Dodge, IA, on April 15, 1919, as a Private.

Edward was often listed in the Census Rolls as Frank E. Two Horses. He was the son of Benedict and Scholastica Two Horses. When he registered for the draft on June 5, 1917, he was working at odd jobs. In April 1918, Edward made an application to the Fort Yates Selective Service Board for voluntary induction into the army. Not long after he arrived at Camp Dodge, IA, he and Barney Mulhern were transferred to Company K, 358th Infantry and sent to Camp Travis, TX. From there, they went to Camp Mills, NY. While at Camp Mills, Edward sent a letter to the Fort Yates paper stating, "Well, I have a spare moment, so will write a line or two. I am down here with a pleasant company, and feel all o.k., and hope you are the same. Simply wanted to ask you if you send the *Sioux County Pioneer* to my folks. So will say goodby to you." Two Horses and Mulhern sailed to Europe aboard the HMT *Walter Castle*.

Both he and Barney became casualties during the fighting in France. After the war, Edward prepared a statement that he sent to Joseph Dixon.

> I was with the AEF 90th Division. Landed in France July 7, 1918. We were in the front line trenches in August this line called Toul sector. Then we stayed there until the big drive begin on Sept. 12-18. We went over the top in early in morning before the sun rise up. I was a battalion runner. I went through the machine gun bullet whizzle & shell bursted and German airplane dropping bombs at us but I never get a scratch to get by with it. The next morning I was lost in the woods. I don't know where I was at. I thought myself I was in German ground or no mans land but after finally I know where I am. After week later I was gassed because my mask is torn by surprise big shell exploded.

Edward Two Horses.
*Todd Hanson*

After the war, Edward married Alice Bighead (1899-1957). In the Census Roll for Standing Rock taken in 1931, Frank (Edward) and Alice were listed with their children, Harding, Melda, Grady, and Ray. In the 1940 U.S. Census, Edward was living in Fort Yates. All three of their sons served in the military. Harding served in the U.S. Army during WWII, and was discharged as a Sergeant. Grady and Ray served with the Army during the Korean Conflict. In his later years, Edward moved to Minneapolis, where he passed away in Camellia Nursing Home on March 26, 1966. His wife and sons, Harding and Grady, preceded him in death. Edward is buried in Fort Snelling National Cemetery (Sect. J, Site 626).[11]

V

**Valley, John B.** Army number, none; registrant, Rolette County; born, Walhalla, D.T. Dec. 17,1886, of American parents; occupation, laborer; enlisted in Company G, 2nd Infantry, North Dakota National Guard, at Rolla, on July 14, 1917; called into federal service, World War, on July 15, 1917; served in Company G, 2nd Infantry, North Dakota National Guard, to discharge. Discharged at Camp Greene, NC, on Oct. 9, 1917, as a Private; Surgeon's Certificate of Disability.

John was the son of John and Julia Vallie. Shortly after his birth, the family moved to Belcourt. He married Mary Jane LaFountain (1896-1970) at Thorne on Jan. 14, 1915. Mary Jane's brother, Moses, enlisted in the North Dakota National Guard with John on July 14, 1917. John farmed in the Belcourt area after the war. In the Indian Census Roll taken in 1937, John and Mary are listed with their children, Emil, Eleanor, Joseph, Mary Jane, Daniel, Helen, and Cecelia. John died in the Rolette Hospital on Aug. 21, 1969. His wife and children, Eleanor, Mary Jane, Cecelia, Joseph, Emil, and Daniel survived him. He is buried in St. Anthony's Cemetery west of Belcourt.[1]

**Vallie, John.** Army number 82,143; registrant, Big Horn County, MT; born, Belcourt, D.T., Aug. 1, 1886, of (nationality of parents not given); occupation, (not given); inducted at Hardin, MT, on Oct. 3, 1917; served in Company D, 163rd Infantry, to March 26, 1918; Company I, 164th Infantry, to discharge. Grade: Private 1st Class, Oct. 12, 1918; overseas from Dec.15, 1917, to July 5, 1919. Discharged on July 17, 1919, as a Private 1st Class.

In the 1900 U.S. Census, John and his brother, Abraham, lived with their mother, Sophia, on the Turtle Mountain Reservation. When John registered for the draft on June 5, 1917, he was working near Lodge Grass, MT. In the 1920 U.S. Census, John was single and lived with his brother, Abraham, and Abraham's wife, Eliza, on the Crow Reservation. He was working as a farm laborer. He also lived for some time near Custer, SD. In 1930, he was admitted for several months to the veterans' hospital (Battle Mountain Sanitarium) near Hot Springs. He married Mabel Laverdure. In the Census Roll for the Turtle Mountain Reservation taken in 1934, John and Mabel are listed as living in Wyola, MT, with their sons, Aloysius and Joseph. Joseph died in 1935 after being kicked by a horse. John later moved to Billings. He became ill at his home and was taken to a Billings hospital, where he died on April 10, 1962. He is buried in Custer Battlefield National Monument (Section B, Site 1276).[2]

W

**Wallette, Gregory.** Army number 4,576,299; registrant, Rolette County; born, Belcourt, ND, Jan. 9, 1896, of (nationality of parents not given); occupation, laborer; enlisted in Company G, 2nd

125

Infantry, North Dakota National Guard, at Rolla, on July 13, 1917; called into federal service, World War, on July 15, 1917; served in Company G, 2nd Infantry, North Dakota National Guard, to discharge. Discharged on Oct. 9, 1917, as a Private, Surgeon's Certificate of Disability.

Gregory was the son of Mr. and Mrs. Moses Wallette. He was living in Belcourt when he registered for the draft in June 1917. Gregory was given a medical discharge four days after his unit arrived at Camp Greene near Charlotte, NC. After the war, he married Josephine Charette (1909-1999) on Sept. 9, 1926. They had a son, Henry. In the 1940 U.S. Census, Gregory was living in Belcourt and working on road construction. In 1942, the family moved from Belcourt to Nebraska. In 1946, they moved to Minot, where Gregory worked as a laundry man at Trinity Hospital. When he turned 65, he retired and moved back to the Turtle Mountain Reservation. Gregory passed away at his home on Dec. 5, 1975. His wife and son survived him. Gregory is buried in St. Ann's Cemetery.[1]

**Wallette, Norman Joseph.**   Army number 3,309,100; registrant, Dewey County, SD; born, Carman, Manitoba, Nov. 1, 1897; naturalized citizen; occupation, farmer; inducted at Timber Lake, SD, on June 23, 1918; sent to Camp Funston, KS; served in 164th Depot Brigade, to July 29, 1918; Company M, 69th Infantry, to discharge. Discharged at Camp Funston, KS, on Feb. 1, 1919, as a Private.

Norman was the son of Mr. and Mrs. Raphael Wallette. He moved to the U.S. at the age of 16. When Norman registered for the draft on June 5, 1917, he was living in Whitehorse, SD, on the Cheyenne River Reservation. He was working as a day laborer for Antoine Azure. During the war, his regiment was part of the 10th Infantry Division. After his discharge, he married Catherine Azure (1901-1978) at Belcourt in 1919. They continued to live in Belcourt. They had a son, David, who served in the U.S. Navy during WWII. Norman passed away in a Minot hospital on June 13, 1972. His wife and son survived him. He is interred in St. Ann's Cemetery.[2]

**Warren, Joseph John.**   Army number 5,124; not a registrant, under age; born, Belcourt, ND, May 13, 1897, of American parents; occupation, laborer; enlisted in Company G, 2nd Infantry, North Dakota National Guard, at Rolla, on July 18, 1917; served in Company G, 2nd Infantry, North Dakota National Guard, to Oct. 5, 1917; 164th Field Hospital Company, 116th Sanitary Train, to March 16, 1918; Company B, 302nd Battalion, Tank Corps, to Aug. 14, 1918; Company C, 303rd Battalion, Tank Corps, to discharge. Grades: Corporal, Aug. 15, 1917; Private, April 12, 1918; overseas from Dec. 11, 1917, to March 17, 1919. Discharged at Camp Dodge, IA, on April 7, 1919, as a Private.

Joseph was the son of William and Mary Rose Warren. In the Census Roll taken in 1899, he is listed with his parents, a brother, Alfred, and a sister, Mary. In the 1910 U.S. Census, Joseph was a student at the boarding school at Fort Totten. Joseph was one of a large group of men who enlisted in the ND National Guard at Rolla in July 1917. While their unit was still in North Dakota, both Joseph and his friend, Edward Brien, were promoted to Corporal. They continued to serve together in the 164th Field Hospital until March 16, 1918, when they both transferred to Company B, 302nd Battalion, Tank Corps. The 302nd Battalion trained in Langres near Bourg at the AEF Tank Center commanded by Captain George Patton.

In 1922, Joseph married Nora Jollie (1901-1989), who had three brothers who served in the military. They lived in Belcourt until 1925, when they moved to Wilton. In the 1930 U.S. Census, the Warren family was living near Wilton, ND, as Joseph was working as a coal miner in Ecklund Township, Burleigh County. They had three children: Ruth, Edward, and Joseph, Jr., at that time. In the 1930s, Joseph went to Arizona for a training program for the CCC. After this he became a foreman for a CCC crew. Later he went to work on the Alaskan Highway. In the Indian Census Roll taken in 1937, they had two more children, William and Nora. Nora worked as a cook for the employees at the Fort Totten School. In the 1940 U.S. Census, Joseph was working on road construction at Belcourt. In 1944, the family moved out to Vallejo, CA. Joseph and Nora started working at the Mare Island Shipyard, where many surface ships and submarines were constructed. Joseph's son, William, served in the U.S. Navy during the Korean Conflict. Their son, Edward, was a radio operator for the Air Force and died in a plane crash over Africa. Joseph passed away in Vallejo on Dec. 18, 1967. He and Nora are buried in All Souls Cemetery near Vallejo, CA.[3]

**Welch, Alfred Burton.** Army number, none, not a registrant, enlisted prior; born, Afton, IA, Sept. 26, 1876, of American parents; occupation, merchant; commissioned Captain and assigned to Company A, 1st Infantry, North Dakota National Guard, at Bismarck, on June 9, 1913; called into federal service on June 19, 1916, for Mexican border duty and served there until discharge; discharged from federal service at Fort Snelling, MN, on Feb. 14, 1917, and resumed National Guard status; called into federal service, World War, on March 26, 1917; placed on supernumary list, April 13, 1917; recalled into active duty, April 15, 1917, and assigned to Company I, 2nd Infantry, North Dakota National Guard (116th Ammunition Train), to Oct. 28, 1918; 3rd Ammunition Train, to discharge; overseas from Dec. 13, 1917, to Aug. 26, 1919. Engagements: Offensive: Meuse-Argonne. Discharged at Camp Dodge, IA, on Oct. 7, 1919, as a Captain. Previous military record: Spanish-American War, Company D, 1st Infantry, Washington National Guard, from May 6, 1898, to Nov. 1, 1899; Philippine Insurrection, from Feb. 4, 1899, to Oct. 9, 1899. Entitled to wear Spanish War Service Medal, by reason of his service with Company D, 1st Washington Volunteer Infantry.

Alfred was known as A. B. for much of his life. As a youth, he had lived with his family in the 1880s in South Dakota, near Fort Randall, where he had frequent contact with native people. In the late 1880s, the Welch family moved out to Washington State. In the 1892 Washington Territorial Census, Alfred was living with his parents, William and Mary Welch, near Tacoma, where his father was a Methodist minister. Alfred attended Puget Sound University and enlisted in the Washington National Guard. After the Spanish-American War, he moved to Bismarck, ND. He worked as a land agent for Hackney, Boynton Land Co. Around 1902, he married Adelaide Clark. In the 1910 U.S. Census, he was working in real estate, while Addie was working as a laundress at a local hotel.

A.B. had become a friend of Yanktonai Chief John Grass, also known as Charging Bear, and his son. After Chief Grass's son died, Grass decided to adopt Welch in a ceremony held at Fort Yates on June 5, 1913. Captain Welch was twice "taken prisoner" by ceremonial war parties, and then released when Charging Bear would say, "This man is my friend." The warriors voted on whether Welch was worthy of this honor. One negative vote would have stopped the adoption. Welch was accepted by the warriors and given his adoptive father's name, Mato Watapke, or Charging Bear. Over 500 people attended the ceremony, which included speeches, converging of elders, drumming, dancing, and singing. Chief Grass presented Welch with a specially-made pipe and Welch gave Grass a gold watch. One of the other elders who spoke for Welch was Red Tomahawk, who finished his talk by saying, "The sun is hot or I would say more. If at any time I need a friend, I will call on you." Welch gave the people a barbecue, furnishing two steers, 100 pounds of coffee, a wagonload of hardtack, and 100 pounds of tobacco.

As a Captain with the ND National Guard, Welch served with Company A, 1st Infantry Regiment along the Mexican border in 1916. After returning to North Dakota in February 1917, his company was assigned to guard the NP Railway bridge across the Missouri. By July 1917, he was assigned the duty of recruiting men for Company I, 2^nd Infantry Regiment. He made a concerted effort to enlist men from Indian Country around the state. Many men did travel to Bismarck from the Standing Rock Reservation and the Fort Berthold Reservation to enlist. He had first met with Chief John Grass to discuss how he felt about the young men from the Standing Rock Reservation serving in the U.S. Army. After receiving Chief Grass's approval, his grandson, Albert Grass, was the first man from Standing Rock to enlist in the new unit being formed. Once the recruiting was completed, Welch traveled with the other ND soldiers to Camp Greene, NC, where many of the ND soldiers were split up and reassigned to other units. Welch eventually ended up as a Major in a Field Artillery staff position. He did not see action in the front lines. He was discharged on Oct. 7, 1919. Shortly after he returned, he took part in a victory celebration held on Standing Rock.

Welch served as Commander of the American Legion Post in Mandan from 1921-1922. In 1923 he was appointed Mandan's Postmaster. One of the other postal employees under Welch was Tom Rogers, from Fort Berthold. Welch remained Postmaster until 1934, while his wife, Addie, ran a dry goods store in Mandan. She had a reputation as a kind and generous person. After she passed away on Dec. 11, 1932, a special ceremony was held in her honor at Cannon Ball. The *Sioux County Pioneer Consolidated* wrote,

> Mrs. Welch for many years took a great deal of interest in the Indians of Standing Rock Reservation. While in her mercantile business she enjoyed an excellent trade from the Indians. It is a matter of fact that she probably donated or gave the people more garments than she ever sold. The poverty stricken Indians referred to her often as the "white angel," and gave her every respect and honor.

> At the ceremony held on Jan. 2, 1933, the Tribal Council of the Sioux was in charge, members of the White Horse Riders and the Brave Hearts, both noted Indian organizations, the Sioux County War Mothers Chapter, of which Mrs. Welch was an honorary member, and the Legion Auxiliary had a part in the rites.

> The Services included special dances, laudation of the deceased in Indian song, the singing of the Indian death song, and other ceremonies traditional with the Sioux.

Addie was buried back in Ohio, where her family was from. Major Welch continued to live in Mandan. As an adopted son of the Lakota, he had many friends who shared information on customs and ceremonies of the people in North Dakota. He kept extensive notes in recording information he received over the years. Welch passed away on June 30, 1945, in a Bismarck hospital. He was active in the Masons, so the funeral was held in the Masonic Temple. Representatives from the American Legion, the VFW color guard, and an honor guard from the ND National Guard took part in the ceremony. He is buried in Union Cemetery in Mandan.[4]

**Wheeler, Fred.** Army number 2,139,962; registrant, McLean County; born, Elbowoods, ND, June 24, 1894, of American parents; occupation, farmer; inducted at Washburn on April 2, 1918; sent to Camp Dodge, IA; served in Company D, 139^th Infantry (35^th Division), to discharge. Grade: Private 1^st Class, Nov. 14, 1918; overseas from May 2, 1918, to April 28, 1919. Discharged at Camp Dodge, IA, on May 7, 1919, as a Private 1^st Class.

As a child, he was known as Levi Bull. In the Census Roll for Fort Berthold in 1895, he is listed with his father, Lean Bull (Wi-di-ha-la-hi), and his mother, Owns Long Corn Silk. In the Census Roll taken in 1911, Levi is listed with Bears Arm and Owns Long Corn Silk. On the Census Roll taken in 1918, he was listed as Fred Wheeler.

Fred served with the 35th Infantry Division, which played a big role in the initial attack in the Meuse-Argonne Offensive. In an evaluation of Private 1st Class Wheeler, his commanding officer, Captain Gus Gehlbach wrote, "Courageous and possesses a large amount of good humor." After the war, Fred prepared the following statement for Joseph Dixon. "In the Argonne forest assisted in the capture of nine German prisoners. Took part in Battle at St. Mihiel. At the Battle of Verdun, went over the top and assisted in the capture of two prisoners. Was transferred to different sectors on the western front, including Alsace Lorraine, Verdun, St. Mihiel and Argonne forest." Fred was not wounded, but he was exposed to gas numerous times. That affected his health, and in later years he had some respiratory problems. When he worked with rounding up cattle, he had to be cautious.

Fred married Olive Hoffman after the war. They were later divorced. He then married Mary Deane (1900-1967), a sister to fellow vet, Bill Deane. Fred and Mary had a daughter, Aleta. Fred was a charter member of the Joseph Young Hawk American Legion Post formed in 1934 at Elbowoods. Fred farmed on the reservation. He passed away at the VA Hospital in Minot on Feb. 10, 1954. His wife and daughter survived him. He is buried in Queen of Peace Catholic Cemetery at Raub.[5]

**White, Abel.** Abel was born on Feb. 18, 1897, in South Dakota. In the 1900 U.S. Census, his parents are listed as Benedict (Skala) and Rose (Wanbliipiwin) White. Abel may have lived in North Dakota for a short time, or possibly attended school at Fort Yates. The military service record of his brother, George, was published by the ND Adjutant General. In the Census Roll for Standing Rock taken in 1905, Abel and his younger brother, George, are listed with their mother, Mary White, who later married Pius Shoots First. Abel enlisted in Company D, 1st South Dakota NG Regiment, likely in late summer of 1917. He was sent to Camp Cody, NM. After he returned home, he became a member of the Martin Yellowfat American Legion Post at Kenel. Abel was a good athlete. After the war, he often competed in foot races as well as playing center field for the Kenel baseball team. At the Standing Rock Fair held in 1921, Abel took 1st Place in the half mile race. He also took 2nd Place in the 220-yard dash. In the 1930 U.S. Census, Abel was living with his mother and stepfather. On Dec. 2, 1930, he married Elizabeth Red Bear in Kenel. Abel passed away in the McLaughlin Hospital on March 13, 1968. His wife survived him. He is buried in St. Thomas Cemetery in Kenel.[6]

**White, George.** Army number 465,344; not a registrant, under age; born, Standing Rock, ND, Jan. 1900, of (nationality of parents not given); occupation, (not given); enlisted at Jefferson Barracks, MO, on April 13, 1918; served in Infantry, Unassigned, Attached to 23rd Recruit Company, General Infantry, to discharge. Discharged on June 16, 1918, as a Private; Surgeon's Certificate of Disability, 100 %.

In the 1900 U.S. Census, George (Matoakicita) is listed with his parents, Benedict (Skala) and Rose. In the Census Roll taken in 1918, George and his brother, Abel, were listed with their mother, who was now married to Pius Shoots First.

When George was discharged at Jefferson Barracks, the Army felt he was too ill to travel by himself. Pvt. L. P. Boyd of the Medical Department was detailed to accompany George back to Fort Yates. George had first came down with pneumonia, which developed into tuberculosis. Unfortunately, George did not recover. He passed away on April 9, 1919, and is buried in St. Benedict's Cemetery in Kenel.[7]

**White Bull, Jacob.** Jacob was born in South Dakota on Oct. 25, 1895. In the Census Roll for Standing Rock taken in 1897, Jacob was listed with his parents, Jake (Cetanpahaakayanka) and Genevieve, as well as a sister and his grandmother. In the 1900 U.S. Census, the family is listed as living on the Standing Rock Reservation in North Dakota. Jacob attended the boarding school at Haskell for several years. He enlisted on June 24, 1918, and was sent to Camp Funston, KS. After completing some training there he was transferred to Camp Dodge, IA, where he was assigned to Company A, 351st Infantry Regiment. As part of the 88th Division, he went to France, though the division only reached the front lines just before the Armistice. Private 1st Class Whitebull's commanding officer wrote that Whitebull "had a splendid physique, character excellent. Shown special excellence in the Browning Automatic."

After his discharge on June 7, 1919, he returned to Kenel, SD. He married Julia Red Fish (1905-1973) in Selby on July 11, 1925. Jacob served as post historian for his Legion Post. In the Standing Rock Census Roll taken in 1937, Jacob and Julia are listed with their children, Cecil, Melvin, Cynthia, Frank, Patricia, Wilbert and Albert. Sometime after 1950, Jacob lived in Fort Yates for awhile. He later moved to Kenel, SD. He passed away on July 13, 1973, at the hospital in Fort Yates and is buried in Assumption Catholic Cemetery in Kenel.[8]

**White Eagle, Milan.** Milan was born at Cannon Ball on May 6, 1899. In the Census Roll for 1906, he is listed with his parents, Jerome (Situpi) and Genevieve White Eagle. When Milan registered for the draft on Sept. 12, 1918, he was farming. Milan was too young to be drafted. He enlisted on June 21, 1919. In the 1920 U.S. Census, Private White Eagle was stationed at Fort Sheridan, IL. On the day the census was taken, Milan was a patient in the hospital at Fort Sheridan. Upon his discharge, he returned to Cannon Ball, where he became a member of the Richard Blue Earth American Legion Post.

In the mid-1920s, he married Annie Grey Bull (1901-1933). In the 1930 U.S. Census, Milan and Annie are listed with their children, Melvin and Wesley, as well as Milan's father, Jerome. He and Annie had two more children, Earl and Victoria. Annie passed away from tuberculosis in 1933. In the Census Roll for 1937, Milan was listed with Josephine White Lightning. Milan's sons, Melvin and Earl, served in the U.S. Army in the post-WWII era. Wesley served with the Air Force during WWII. Milan passed away following a car accident south of Cannon Ball on June 16, 1956. He is buried at Cannon Ball.[9]

**White Eagle, Richard.** Army number, none; registrant, Sioux County; born, Cannon Ball, ND, Jan. 19, 1891, of American parents; occupation, farmer; enlisted in Company I, 2nd Infantry, North Dakota National Guard, at Bismarck, on July 23, 1917, 1917; served in Company I, 2nd Infantry, North Dakota National Guard, to discharge. Discharged on Aug. 10, 1817, as a Private, Surgeon's Certificate of Disability.

In the 1900 U.S. Census, Richard is listed as a student at the Standing Rock Industrial School. In the Census Roll taken in 1903, he is listed with his mother, Warta. On October 11, 1909, he married Margaret Jordan (1892-1963). In the 1910 U.S. Census, they are listed with their daughter, Melda. After the U.S. entered the war against Germany, Richard was one of the first people to travel to Bismarck to enlist. Albert Grass and Joseph Jordan had enlisted the previous day. However, Richard received a medical discharge. Back in Cannon Ball, Richard worked as a carpenter and operated a small farm to support his family. He and his wife had 23 children. Their son, Joseph, served as a Sergeant with the Army during WWII. Margaret had a reputation as a good cook and housekeeper. At one time, she had been employed in some of the finer Bismarck restaurants. In October 1959, Richard and Margaret celebrated their 50th wedding anniversary. Around 300 family members and friends helped them celebrate. Margaret passed away on July

19, 1963. Richard died about three months later on Oct. 22, 1963. They are buried in St. Elizabeth's Cemetery in Cannon Ball.[10]

**White Feather, Alex Joseph.** Army number 85,237; not a registrant, enlisted prior; born, Springbrook, WI, May 7, 1892, of American parents; occupation, stenographer; enlisted in Company A, 1st Infantry, North Dakota National Guard, at Bismarck, on June 29, 1916; called into federal service on June 29, 1916, for Mexican border duty and served there until discharge; discharged from federal service at Fort Snelling, MN, on Feb. 14, 1917, and resumed National Guard status; called into federal service, World War, on April 16, 1917; served in Company A, 1st Infantry, North Dakota National Guard (Company A, 164th Infantry), to Oct. 8, 1918; Company B, 116th Military Police, to Nov. 1, 1918; 1st Provisional Military Police Company, Depot Division, to Nov. 5, 1918; 217th Company Police Corps (267th Company, Military Police Corps), to June 7, 1919; Casual, to July 3, 1919; Demobilization Group, Camp Grant, IL, to discharge. Grades: Sergeant, Aug. 13, 1917; Mess Sergeant, March 8, 1918; Sergeant, June 19, 1918; Private, June 13, 1918; Private 1st Class, Nov. 2, 1918; overseas from Dec. 15, 1917, to June 29, 1919. Discharged at Camp Grant, IL, on July 15, 1919, as a Private 1st Class.

In the 1900 U.S. Census, Alex was a student at the Tomah Indian Industrial School, in Tomah, WI. In the 1905 Wisconsin State Census, he was living near Hayward with his parents, Antoine and Annie Slater. In early 1916, Alex received an appointment as assistant clerk at the Bismarck Boarding School. The following summer, he enlisted in the ND National Guard. After the war he returned to the Lac Courte Oreilles Reservation near Hayward, WI. The Census Roll taken in 1920 lists him as being single. In the 1920 U.S. Census, he was working as a laborer in a lumber camp near Solon Springs, WI. In the Lac Courte Oreilles Census Roll taken in 1937, Alex is listed as living on the Lac du Flambeau Reservation. In the late 1950s, he moved to Minneapolis. In 1958 he was living on Washington Ave. S. He later moved to the Kenesaw Hotel. He passed away at the VA Hospital in Minneapolis on Nov. 16, 1966. He is buried at New Post Cemetery on the Lac Courte Oreilles Reservation.[11]

**White Lightning, Paul.** Army number 4,040,237; registrant, Sioux County; born, Cannon Ball, ND, Aug. 19, 1890, of American parents; occupation, farmer; inducted at Fort Yates on July 26, 1918; sent to Camp Custer, MI; served in 160th Depot Brigade, to Aug. 29, 1918; Company I, 78th Infantry, to discharge. Discharged at Camp Dodge, IA, on Feb. 7, 1919, as a Private.

In the Census Roll taken in 1903, Paul is listed with his parents, White Lightning and White Deer, as well as his sister and two brothers. When Paul registered for the draft on June 5, 1917, he was farming near Cannon Ball. Paul trained at Camp Custer as part of the 14th Division, but the war ended before their training was completed. After the war, he married Margaret Red Ears. In the Census Roll taken in 1934, they are listed with their children, John, Luke, Edward, and Clara. In the 1940 U.S. Census, Paul was working with the CCC program near Fort Yates. His son, John, served in the U.S. Army during WWII. Luke served in the U.S. Navy. Paul was a member of the American Legion Post at Cannon Ball. He passed away at the Hettinger Community Nursing Home on April 1, 1973. His sons, John and Luke, as well as his stepson, Clyde Standing Bear, survived him. He is buried in St. Elizabeth's Cemetery in Cannon Ball.[12]

**Whiteman, Oscar.** Army number 2,787,561; registrant, Dunn County; born, Elbowoods, ND, June 1894, of (nationality of parents not given); occupation, stock raiser; inducted at Manning on May 25, 1918; served in Air Service, Signal Corps, to June 18, 1918; 90th Spruce Squadron, to discharge. Discharged on Jan. 3, 1919, as a Private.

Oscar was the son of Old Whiteman (Wa-shi-hi-esh) and Eagle Woman. In the Fort Berthold Census Roll taken in 1903, Oscar is listed with his parents and his other siblings. When he registered for the draft on June 5, 1917, he lived at Elbowoods and raised livestock. In a report prepared for Joseph Dixon, he indicated that he had enlisted at Dunn Center on May 25, 1918, and spent his army life at Vancouver Barracks, WA. In 1917, Oscar married Cora Hunts Along (1898-1943). They farmed in Dunn County. In the Census Roll taken in 1939, Oscar and Cora are listed with their children, John, Donald, Floria, Quentin, Oscar Jr., Emily, Wallace, Loretta and Willis. Quentin served in the U.S. Navy. Oscar passed away at St. Joseph's Hospital in Dickinson on July 31, 1954, and is buried in St. Joseph's Catholic Cemetery in Twin Buttes.[13]

**White Tail, David.** David was born at Elbowoods on Aug. 15, 1893. In the 1910 U.S. Census, Davis was a student at the Bismarck boarding school. In the Census Roll taken of the Arikara in 1912, David's parents are listed as White Tail and Eagle Woman. On July 26, 1918, the *Washburn Leader* published an article stating that David White Tail had been inducted in Washburn on July 22, 1918, and had traveled by train to Camp Custer, MI. David's name was listed in the weekly update of the roster of men serving from McLean County. It is not known when David was discharged. After the war, he married Mamie Reed. They farmed near Emmet, ND. They had six sons and three daughters. David and Mamie later were divorced. David passed away at the Garrison Hospital on May 15, 1955. His six sons, Ronald, Sanford, David Jr. Byron, Fay Arnold, and Sylvester, as well as a daughter, Mary Rose, survived him. Fay Arnold was stationed with the U.S. Army at Fort Ord, CA, at the time of his father's death. David is buried in Sacred Heart Cemetery in Emmet.[14]

**Wilkie, Cyprian Raphael.** Army number 3,950,504; registrant, Rolette County; born, Belcourt, ND, Jan. 20, 1890, of American parents; occupation, student; inducted at Rolla on Aug. 26, 1918; sent to Camp Lewis, WA; served in 38th Company, 10th Battalion 166th Depot Brigade, to Sept. 10, 1918; Battery A, 39th Field Artillery, to Oct. 4, 1918; Headquarters Company, 39th Field Artillery, to discharge. Discharged at Camp Lewis, WA, on Jan. 30, 1919, as a Musician, 2nd Class.

Cyprian and his brother, Peter, were the sons of Gabriel (Kabi-ush) and Mary Wilkie. When Cyprian registered for the draft on June 4, 1917, he was attending the boarding school at Carlisle, PA. He also indicated that he had attended the boarding school at Chilocco, OK, for four years. He likely had played in the school band at Carlisle. Cyprian remained single. He was self-employed as an upholsterer. In both the 1930 and 1940 Censuses, Cyprian worked as an upholsterer in St. Cloud, MN. His brother was also living in St. Cloud. Around 1942 Cyprian moved to Riverside, CA. He passed away on Jan. 24, 1974, in the VA Hospital in Long Beach, CA. He is buried in Los Angeles National Cemetery, Section 109, Row X, Site 5.[15]

Cyprian Wilkie, 1918

**Wilkie, Louis.** Army number, none; not a registrant, under age; born, Belcourt, ND, Aug. 10, 1898, of American parents; occupation, laborer; enlisted in Company G, 2nd Infantry, North Dakota National Guard, at Rolla, on July 13, 1917; called in federal service, World War, July 15, 1917; served in Company G, 2nd Infantry, North Dakota National Guard, to discharge. Discharged at Camp Greene, NC, on Oct. 11, 1917, as a Private; Surgeon's Certificate of Disability.

In the Census Roll for the Turtle Mountain Chippewa taken in 1906, Louis is listed with his parents, Albert and Josephine Wilkie, as well as two sisters and a brother. After Louis enlisted in the National Guard, he traveled to Camp Greene, NC, where he underwent a more intensive medical checkup. He was given a medical discharge due to trachoma. After returning to Belcourt, he married St. Ann Dauphinais. They had a son, Clifford, who served with the U.S. Army in Europe during WWII. Louis worked as a farm laborer. He passed away in his home on May 27, 1945. He is buried in Belcourt. His widow later married Louis D. Houle.[16]

**Wilkie, Peter Alfred.** Army number 2,163,706; registrant, Benson County; born, Belcourt, ND, July 19, 1893, of American parents; occupation, farmer; inducted at St. Paul, MN, on Feb. 15, 1918; sent to Camp Dodge, IA; served in Headquarters Company, 352nd Infantry, to Sept. 21, 1918; Company K, 352nd Infantry (88th Division), to discharge. Grades, Private 1st Class, May 1, 1918; Mechanic, Aug. 1, 1918; Private, Sept. 20, 1918; overseas from Aug. 16, 1918, to June 1, 1919. Engagement: Defensive Sector: Center (Alsace). Discharged at Camp Dodge, IA, June 16, 1919, as a Private.

Peter was a younger brother to Cyprian. In the 1910 U.S. Census, he was a student at the Fort Totten boarding school. When Peter registered for the draft on June 5, 1917, he was living near Leeds, ND, and working as a laborer for Charles Anderson. On the draft registration form, there was a question about prior military service. Peter wrote that he had been at the Carlisle Boarding School. Peter served overseas in the 352nd Infantry Regiment. Louis Bercier also served with him in Company K, 352nd Regiment. After the Armistice, the regiment was garrisoned near Gondrecourt, France. In May 1919, each soldier in the 88th Division received a bronze Cloverleaf Medal. The soldiers returned to the United States in June 1919. Sometime after his discharge, Peter moved to Minneapolis, MN. In the 1930 U.S. Census, he was living there with his wife, Eunice, and working as a plater for metal works manufacturer. In the early 1930s, he moved to St. Cloud, MN. He passed away at the VA Hospital in St. Cloud on Aug. 23, 1959. He is buried in Ft. Snelling National Cemetery Section H, Site 4857).[17]

**Winans, Robert.** Army number 2,858,911; registrant, McLean County; born, Elbowoods, ND, 1894, of American parents; occupation, farmer; inducted at Washburn on April 28,1918; sent to Camp Dodge, IA; served in Headquarters Company, 350th Infantry, to June 22, 1918; 163rd Depot Brigade, to discharge. Discharged at Camp Sherman, OH, on Jan. 8, 1919

In the Census Roll taken of the Arikaras at Fort Berthold in 1908, Robert is listed with his parents, Strikes Two and Plum Woman, as well as a brother and sister. In the 1910 U.S. Census, he was a student at the Bismarck Boarding School. In the summer of 1917, Robert first enlisted in Company I, 2nd Regiment, ND National Guard at Bismarck. On Oct. 1, 1917, a Bismarck paper published a roster of Company I, with Robert's name included. He likely received a medical discharge. Robert re-enlisted in Washburn the following spring. After first being sent to Camp Dodge, IA, he was transferred to several other camps in the U.S. They included Fort Crook, NE, Camp Funston, KS, and finally, Camp Sherman, OH. He did not go overseas. After his discharge, he returned to North Dakota. Around 1930, he lived in Canton, SD, for awhile. In the late 1930s, he was living at Nishu with the family of his cousin, Mrs. Hattie Waters. Robert passed away at the Waters home on March 23, 1939. He had not married. The local paper noted, "He was a very honest and faithful man in the service of his country." The American Legion Post at Elbowoods held a military burial for him. He is buried in the Old Scouts Cemetery near White Shield.[18]

# Y

**Yellow Bird, Charles.** Charles was born on the Fort Berthold Reservation on June 1, 1897. In the Census Roll for the Arikara taken in 1906, Charles is listed with his parents, Yellow Bird (Nikustakata) and Looking to be Chief (Steshanahwe), as well as his brothers and sisters. Two of his sisters later married men who served in the war. Leona married Bill Deane, and Elizabeth married David Packineau. In the 1915 North Dakota State Census, Charles was a student at the Wahpeton boarding school. Charles married Nellie Red Fox (1899-1988). Nellie had a brother, Ernest, who served in the war. When Charles registered for the draft on June 5, 1918, he was married and living near Elbowoods. On Aug. 30, 1918, the *Washburn Leader* reported that Charles had been inducted and went to Camp Lewis, WA, with a group of men from McLean County. Mark Necklace and Robert Dancing Bull were also in that group. Charles likely was assigned to the 44th Infantry with those others. Until the war ended, Charles was listed in the roster published weekly by the *Washburn Leader*. It is not known when Charles was discharged. For some reason, his service record was not published by the ND National Guard. Charles was one of the charter members of the Joseph Young Hawk American Legion Post formed at Elbowoods. In the 1920 U.S. Census, Yellow Bird and three of his children lived with Charles and Nellie. In the Fort Berthold Reservation Census Roll taken in 1926, Charles and Nellie are listed with two of their children, Dolly and Willard.

In the 1930s, the Civilian Conservation Corps (CCC) program was established on the Fort Berthold Reservation but did not have a permanent location. Families moved from project to project around the reservation. Charles Yellow Bird became the CCC foreman. In August 1939, the camp was located upriver from Elbowoods when Charles tried to help find the bodies of two young boys who had drowned in the Missouri. Charles had recently been discharged from the reservation hospital. He became exhausted and drowned on Aug. 31, 1939. His wife and children, Darlene, Willard, Harold Leroy, and Joyce survived him. The Joseph Young Hawk Legion Post conducted military rites at Nishu. "Two car loads of Legionnaires from Garrison attended and took part in the very impressive ceremonies, which were attended by the largest crowd ever gathered on the Reservation."[1]

**Young Bear, Frank.** Army number 2,703,601; registrant, Sioux County; born, Cannon Ball, ND, Dec. 14, 1892, of American parents; occupation, farmer; inducted at Fort Yates on June 23, 1918; sent to Camp Dodge, IA; served in Company M, 349th Infantry (88th Division), to discharge. Grade: Corporal, Dec. 5, 1918; overseas from Aug. 9, 1918, to May 30, 1919. Engagement: Defensive Sector: Center (Alsace). Discharged at Camp Dodge, IA, on June 11, 1919, as a Corporal.

In the 1900 U.S. Census, Frank is also listed as Iyawankantuya. In the Census Roll for Standing Rock taken in 1903, Frank is listed with his parents, Moses (Matocinca) and Pretty Rope (Tasinnawastewin), as well as two sisters. He attended school in Cannon Ball. When he registered for the draft on June 5, 1917, he was raising livestock near Cannon Ball. He was a tall man of slender build. As part of the 88th Division serving in France, Frank and Joseph Two Bears were together in Company M, 349th Infantry Regiment. Corporal Young Bear's commanding officer stated that he "demonstrated fitness for scouting, observing and reporting. Good humor at all times." After the Armistice, the 88th Division spent about six months stationed near Gondrecourt, France, before returning the United States.

After his discharge, Frank married Margaret Rattling Cloud (1901-1959). In the 1930 U.S. Census, they were listed with their children, Franklin, Kingman, Calvin, and Estelle. The family enjoyed doing traditional dancing. In the 1940 U.S. Census, Frank was working as a laborer with the CCC program. Frank was a member of the American Legion and the Veterans of Foreign Wars. Two of their sons served in WWII. Franklin was in the Army, and Kingman was in the Navy. Frank passed away in Cannon Ball on Nov. 30, 1966. His children, Franklin, Kingman, Calvin, Willis, Colleen, Marlene, Camella, Jacqueline, and Josephine survived him. He is buried in St. James Episcopal Cemetery in Cannon Ball.[2]

**Young Bear, Walter.** Army number 2,787,573; registrant, Dunn County; born, Elbowoods, ND, May 15, 1894, of American parents; occupation, rancher; inducted at Manning on May 25, 1918; sent to Camp Lewis, WA; served in Company D, 158th Infantry, to Sept. 20, 1918; Company C, 306th Infantry (77th Division), to discharge. Grade: Private 1st Class, Nov. 1, 1918; overseas from Aug. 12, 1918, to May 30, 1919. Engagements: Offensive: Meuse-Argonne. Defensive Sector: Foret-Argonne (Lorraine). Discharged at Camp Dodge, IA, on June 12, 1919, as a Private 1st Class.

In the Census Roll for Fort Berthold taken in 1901, Walter is listed with his parents, Young Bear (Nahpitsiraka) and Iron Woman (Uwatsawia), as well as his other siblings. When he registered for the draft on June 4, 1917, he was farming. After being drafted in May 1918, he was sent to Camp Lewis, WA. He was later transferred to Camp Kearney, CA, and finally to Camp Mills, NY, before going overseas. On Sept. 20, 1918, he was one of a group of about 700 men who were reassigned to the 306th Infantry as replacements at Le Claon, France. The 306th went over the top on Sept. 26, 1918, and remained in the front until the Armistice was signed. Once the fighting was over, the Private 1st Class Young Bear's unit was billeted in the vicinity of Luzy. Captain Ralph J. Sprague of Company C wrote that Young Bear "has very keen eyesight, sense of direction. Has done extraordinary individual work. As night worker, runner and verbal reporter is remarkable." The 306th Infantry returned to New York aboard the *Mt. Vernon* at the end of May 1919.

After returning to North Dakota, Walter married Pearl Burr (1903-1984). In the 1930 U.S. Census, Walter and Pearl were listed with six children, Thelma, Alonzo, Ivan, Jasper, Alisa and Clair. The family was farming in Dunn County. Their son, Alonzo, served in the Army during WWII. Walter passed away in St. Joseph's Hospital in Dickinson on Oct. 26, 1949. He is buried at St. Anthony's Catholic Cemetery near Mandaree.[3]

**Young Hawk, Joe.** Army number 46,008; registrant, McLean County; born, Fort Berthold, ND, Dec. 15, 1893, of American parents; occupation, farmer; enlisted in Company I, 2nd Infantry, North Dakota National Guard, at Bismarck, on Aug. 1, 1917; served in Company I, 2nd Infantry, North Dakota National Guard, to Oct. 5, 1917; 161st Ambulance Company, Camp Mills, NY, to Nov. 14, 1917; Company A, 164th Infantry, to Jan. 9, 1918; Company A, 18th Infantry (First Division), to discharge; overseas from Nov. 14, 1917, to Sept. 29, 1918; wounded, severely, May 6, 1918. Engagements: Defensive Sectors: Ansauville (Lorraine); Cantigny (Picardy). Discharged at Fort Snelling, MN, on May 26, 1919, as a Private; Surgeon's Certificate of Disability, 75%

In the Census Roll for the Arikaras taken in 1907, Joe is listed as "Richard Young Hawk" (Nutnarohanu). His parents were Young Hawk and Chief Lying Against. Young Hawk had served as a scout with Custer. After 1915, Richard was known as Joseph. He was one of the first men from Elbowoods to enlist for service in WWI. In January 1918, he was among the soldiers transferred from the 164th Infantry to the 18th Infantry. Sgt. Herman Brocopp, also with the 164th, described how "these men were loaded in open cattle cars in the depth of winter, the country covered in snow, in bitter weather." Joe was stationed with the 18th Infantry Regiment in the front lines in the spring of 1918. The men made frequent raids on the German trenches at night. On one of these raids, Private Young Hawk was wounded and gassed slightly and captured. There are several versions to the story of what happened to Young Hawk, as he himself talked about it very little. He turned on his captors and quickly killed three of them and brought two captives back to the American lines. As a result of being wounded in the leg, he spent seven months in French hospitals. His leg was later amputated. Supposedly after the surgery, he remarked that he would not be riding in any more rodeos.

In the 1920 U.S. Census, he was living at Elbowoods with his mother and his brother, Alfred. On Dec. 28, 1922, he married Grace Wilde Gillette. While recuperating from his wounds, he came down with tuberculosis and passed away in a Bismarck hospital on June 18, 1923. He was buried at Elbowoods. His grave has been moved to the Old Scout Cemetery near White Shield.[4]

Joseph Young Hawk (seated) with an unknown fellow soldier, probably a Sioux. Note the wound chevron on the right sleeve of the man behind Young Hawk. *Four Bears Museum*

**Young Wolf, Leo.** Leo was born on March 2, 1889 at Fort Buford. His father, Young Wolf, later settled in the Shell Village community on the Fort Berthold Reservation. In 1910, he married Fannie Davis (1890-1954). According to the *Washburn Leader*, Leo was inducted at Washburn on April 28, 1918, and traveled to Camp Dodge, IA. Two other local men who traveled with him were Frank Birds Bill and Robert Winans. Leo was listed on the roster of men serving that the *Washburn Leader* published until the end of the war. It is not known when Leo was discharged. Leo was a well-known rancher and farmer on the reservation. He had a son, Frank, who served in the Army. Leo passed away in St. Joseph's Hospital in Minot on Aug. 25, 1960. His daughter, Mrs. Minot Grady and son, Frank, survived him. He is buried in the Raub Catholic Cemetery.[5]

# Z

**Zahn, Francis Benjamin.** Army number 2,558,367; registrant, Sioux County; born, Cannon Ball, ND, May 4, 1891, of American parents; occupation, bookkeeper; inducted at Fort Yates on March 4, 1918; sent to Camp Dodge, IA; served in 351st Infantry, to discharge. Grades: Private 1st Class, April 10, 1918; Corporal, April 15, 1918. Discharged at Whipple Barracks, AZ, on May 24, 1919, as a Corporal; Surgeon's Certificate of Disability, 33 1/3 %.

Frank was the son of William Zahn and Kezewin Flying Cloud. His father, of German descent, had served in the U.S. Cavalry. Frank attended school at Fort Yates; Carlisle, PA; and the Riggs Institute in South Dakota. When he registered for the draft before the war, he was working as a clerk for the Indian Service at Fort Yates. After his discharge, he attended Aaker's Business College in Fargo. In the 1920 U.S. Census, he boarded with George Halsey in Fort Yates. Frank was a master of Teton and Yanktonaii dialects, as well as German and English. In 1911 he began working as an interpreter. He did interpretive work for several U.S. presidents, as well as military officers and Senators. In the 1940 U.S. Census, his occupation was listed as interpreter.

He married Gladys Fisher in Sioux Falls, SD, on May 5, 1947. He maintained a museum in his home at Fort Yates. He served on the Standing Rock Tribal Council and was a senior judge for Standing Rock Jurisdiction. He also was an accomplished violinist and artist. He had been active with the State Historical Society and was a former commander of several American Legion Posts. In the 1940s, he played in three movies in Hollywood, including "They Died With Their Boots On." Frank passed away in a Bismarck hospital on July 3, 1966. His wife and two sons, Frank and Louis, as well as his daughters, Winona and Maria, survived him. He is buried in St. Peter's Catholic Cemetery at Fort Yates. Military rites were conducted by the American Legion.[1]

Cpl. F. B. Zahn,
*Todd Hanson*

Ft. Yates, ND, Welcoming a returned Soldier, photo by F.B. Fiske.
*State Historical Society of ND*

# CHAPTER 3

## Honoring the Warriors

After the war, Major A. B. Welch described the honor accorded to the families of veterans on Standing Rock Reservation:

> The tents of the parents of soldier boys were decorated with pieces of red or black cloth, for among the Sioux, black is the color of war and red is the color which relates to bravery or wounds. The relatives of the soldiers were treated everywhere with the greatest respect and consideration, and even today at practically every gathering, it is a common sight to see some women come over to the grant [sic] of a tent of a mother of an ex-serviceman and sing a song in honor of the soldier and his relatives. When she is finished she will always utter a high tremolo, twice, and this will be answered from many quarters by other women who shout the name of the soldier and give this tremulous song of encouragement and victory.

### Victory Dance

When Major A. B. Welch returned to North Dakota in the fall of 1919, he received a visit from a committee from Standing Rock who were planning a great victory dance to which all the Indian soldiers would be invited. Here is his description of the event:

> There was erected a high pole upon which hung the skin of a wolf, representing the enemy, and the dancing took place around this. The returned soldiers had been invested with feather head dresses and the permission to wear paint had been conferred upon them and the right to take a warrior's place in the dance. I also was given the right to display three white feathers and two red ones. The white feathers represent wars engaged in and the red represent wounds received. I had taken with me some enemy helmets, swords, medals, etc., which I had obtained in the Argonne. After I had made a speech, and displayed these trophies, there was a rush to lay hands upon them and they were soon whisked out of my sight, to appear again in the next dance, which, to say the least, was a wild affair.

> After the dance the parties who had, or carried these war relics, gave money or horses or beef steers to the Red Cross Society for the honor of having carried them. I remember that the Indian who wore a silver helmet gave $50.00 and the one who dances with an enemy sword gave $25.00. An old Indian woman by the name of Mrs. Crow Ghost, who wore paint for me, made a liberal present for that debatable honor. Every soldier was sung for and flags were carried for those who had paid the supreme sacrifice, and as these were carried around, the people would advance and take hold of the flag, for an instant, and then run to the enemy and strike the post upon which the wolf skin hung. Trophies, including scalps, from battlefields were always brought home to the women in the olden times, and remembering this, I had several hundred buttons from the uniforms of the enemy, and these I presented to the women. These buttons and belt buckles were much sought after and are still highly prized by the women who received them.

In writing about the music of the Mandan and Hidatsa people, Frances Densmore stated, "It is the custom of many Indian tribes to honor their successful warriors by inserting their names in 'praise songs.' Some tribes insert the name of a new hero in an old song, the former name being withdrawn. The Mandan appear to have used the same song for several warriors, the different names being used in consecutive renditions." She added that Crow's Heart recorded a war song in which the honoree's name was followed by the words (in Mandan) *a' wado' du wade' duk washo' kiduts* ("Any land where I go, in front of me"), meaning that wherever they went to seek the enemy they were successful.[1] The Arikara Flag Song is still sung to honor all Indian veterans.

> Our friends, our Flag is now waving
> Over there, waving over enemy land.

Mato Watakpe (A. B. Welch) in center with Kangi Wanagi (Crow Ghost) and wife, Zuyala, winter of 1919-1920. Frithjof Holmboe, photographer. *State Historical Society of North Dakota, B0173*

## Deceased Veterans

Five men from North Dakota died overseas. The first casualty from North Dakota's Indian Country was Joseph Sherman, who died when the ship he was on was struck by a torpedo off the coast of Ireland. Harry Lean Elk and Arthur Old Mouse died of pneumonia. Their bodies were returned home in late 1920. Albert Grass and Richard Blue Earth both served in Company A, 18th Infantry Regiment and were killed in action. Their bodies were returned home for reburial in 1921.

Shortly after the end of the war, returned veterans began organizing local American Legion Posts. A number of Posts were organized in communities on the Standing Rock Reservation. Two of the earliest Posts were named in honor of men who had died in France. The Post at Fort Yates was organized in early 1920 by George Halsey, Joseph Jordan, and J.R. Harmon, and was named in honor of Albert Grass. There were 17 charter members. The first Commander of the Albert Grass American Legion Post was J.R. Harmon.[2] Harmon also helped organize a Post at Shields. Around that same time, a Post was organized in Cannon Ball and named in honor of Richard Blue Earth. The Richard Blue Earth American Legion Post was later moved to Solen.

A number of the North Dakota veterans lived in Kenel, SD, after the war. These men helped organize a Legion Post in Kenel, which they named in honor of Martin Yellow Fat. Martin had enlisted early in the war while he was a student at a government school in Rapid City. He fought with the Rainbow or 42nd Infantry Division. He took part in 19 engagements and was wounded. While returning back home, he died in a hospital in Aberdeen, SD.[3] One of the men who helped organize Post No. 232 was George Sleeps From Home, who was married to Martin's sister.

Shortly after the war, the agency superintendent at Fort Yates sent a report to the Commissioner of Indian Affairs stating that, according to his records, 129 men from Standing Rock had been in the service. Three men were killed in action. In addition to Albert Grass and Richard Blue Earth, Joseph Takes The Shield, Jr., died in combat. Joseph was from Wakpala, SD, and died on Nov. 1, 1918 while serving with Company B, 314th Battalion, Military Police. He had been drafted in 1917, and sent to Camp Funston, KS, for training. In January 1921, Joseph's father wrote to the Commissioner in Washington, D.C. requesting that his son be buried in a military cemetery. As a result of his request, Joseph Takes The Shield Jr. was finally buried on Aug. 15, 1921, at Arlington Cemetery (Section EUR. Site 2789). In a special ceremony on Memorial Day in 1924, President Calvin Coolidge placed flowers on his grave in the presence of his parents. After they returned to Wakpala, they arranged for a feast in honor of their son.[4]

An American Legion Post was organized in Elbowoods in 1934 and named in honor of Joseph Young Hawk, who died in Bismarck a few years after returning from France. Joseph Young Hawk, Albert Grass, and Richard Blue Earth had served with Company A, 18th Infantry Regiment, after having enlisted in the North Dakota National Guard in Bismarck in 1917.

## Marshall Ferdinand Foch

Marshall Ferdinand Foch, Commander-in-chief of the Allied Forces, visited Bismarck and Mandan in November 1921. As a guest of the North Dakota American Legion, Foch traveled to North Dakota in the private coach of W.W. Atterbury, vice-president of the Pennsylvania Rail Road. The French marshall had expressed a desire to meet some of the Native veterans who had performed outstanding service in France. Legion members from Elbowoods, Fort Yates, and Cannon Ball were invited. In a special naming ceremony, Foch received the name Charging Thunder. Red Tomahawk acted as the spokesman, and after the pipe ceremony, presented Foch with several gifts.[5] Around 2000 people attended the ceremony in the Bismarck City Auditorium. E. C. Means, the father of Wesley Means, acted as interpreter.

# Citations for Bravery

Larson listed the four cardinal virtues of a Lakota warrior as bravery, fortitude, generosity and wisdom.[6] Warrior traditions were strong among the people of the Northern Plains. Over 200 men from Indian Country served during the World War I era. According to military service records, twelve men were cited for bravery and gallantry. Records are incomplete for some veterans, so there likely were more men who deserved the recognition. This represents more than 5% of the number of men who served and is a higher proportion than among the overall population of North Dakotans who served. The **Table of Citations** lists the men who were recognized. Most of the soldiers cited by the U.S. military had enlisted in the North Dakota National Guard. Upon arriving in France, they were transferred to the First Division. Their service records indicate they were eligible to wear a small, silver star known as a Citation Star on their campaign ribbon. The Silver Star medal, created in 1932, later replaced these Citation Stars. Most of the soldiers cited by the French became eligible to wear the Fourragère, which is a braided cord worn over the left shoulder. It is similar to a unit citation award. Several men also received the Croix de Guerre.

## *Table of Citations*

| Soldier | Cited by U.S. | Cited by French |
|---|---|---|
| Alphonse Bear Ghost | x | x |
| Richard Blue Earth | x | x |
| August Brought Plenty | | x |
| John Brought Plenty | | x |
| Albert Grass | x | |
| James Jollie | x | x |
| Joseph Jordan | x | x |
| Louis Latrail | x | |
| Raphael Lyon | | x |
| James Munnell | x | |
| Thomas Rogers | | x |
| John Smith | x | x |

# Sources and Acknowledgments

All service records are written as printed in the *Official Roster of the North Dakota Soldiers, Sailors and Marines*, which was published under the direction of Brigadier General G. Angus Fraser in 1931 in Bismarck, ND. Additional information on the military units was obtained from *WWI Campaign and Service Credits*, published in 1996 by Planchet Press of Arlington, VA. The information on the civilian life for each veteran was obtained primarily from the U.S. Indian Census Rolls (1885-1940), the U.S. Census records, and draft registration files available at www.ancestry.com. Some local newspapers were used also, especially the *Sioux County Pioneer*, which was the only newspaper published on a reservation during the World War I era. Most of the other local newspapers did not have good coverage of events on the reservation. The back issues of the local papers are available at the State Archives of the State Historical Society of North Dakota in Bismarck, ND. The staff at the library was always helpful. Another source of information was death certificates from North Dakota and surrounding states. Death certificates were obtained from the District of Columbia for two men who are buried in Arlington Cemetery. The Montana Historical Society provided information on many of the men from that state.

Once the fighting was over, the U.S. military officials and some private organizations were interested in finding out how the Native servicemen had performed. Officers and NCOs were asked to evaluate the men who had served under them. Joseph K. Dixon, who had traveled around Indian Country as a photographer before the war, was also interested in recording how the war had affected the veterans. Working with Rodman Wanamaker, Dixon developed his own questionnaire that he sent to men on the reservations to complete. Dixon exchanged several letters with Joseph Gray Day. Dixon had plans for publishing a book on the war experiences of the men from Indian Country, but never was able to finish it. Those unpublished records are now part of the Wanamaker Documentation, William Mathers Museum, Indiana University, Bloomington, IN. Ellen Sieber helped us find the records and photos which pertained to North Dakota soldiers. Other unpublished material was obtained from the National Archives and Records Administration in Washington, D.C., and Kansas City, MO, (NARA). Records for some of the men who attended the boarding school at Carlisle, PA, were obtained from the NARA staff in Washington, D.C. Barbara Larsen, Archives Technician in Kansas City, very ably provided much information relating to the WWI veterans from the Plains Region (Record Group 75, Records of the Bureau of Indian Affairs, File code 610). Robert Barr, Mandan, ND, provided unpublished notes written by Alfred B. Welch. The staff at the Rolette County Museum in St. John, ND, kindly lent us their copy of *Memoirs of France and the Eighty-eighth Division*, by Edgar J. D. Larson. We want to thank Marilyn Hudson and Susan Dingle for reviewing our rough draft.

Many people have been very helpful in providing photos which help commemorate those who are gone. The initial receipt of a set of photos from Robert Barr and Todd Hanson was the start of this project back in 2010. Not long after that, we were able to copy the photos from the Four Bears Museum, thanks to Marilyn Hudson. Other photos have been obtained from the State Historical Society of North Dakota, Minnesota Historical Society, Chick LaRocque, Richard Birklid, Michael Rempfer, Dean Moos, the Smithsonian Institution, the William Mathers Museum, and the Cumberland County [PA] Historical Society.

## CHAPTER 1
### Ready for Action

1. Thomas A. Britten, *American Indians in World War I*, (Albuquerque, 1997), 37.
2. Wanamaker Documentation
3. "Indian School Notes," *The Wahpeton Times*, 19 April 1917, 1.
4. *Sioux County Pioneer*, 24 May 1917, 1.
5. *Sioux County Pioneer*, 24 May 1917, 1.
6. *Sioux County Pioneer*, 7 June 1917, 1.
7. Jerry Cooper with Glenn Smith, *Citizens as Soldiers: a History of the North Dakota National Guard*, (Fargo, 1986), 196.
8. *Turtle Mountain Star*, 26 April 1917, 8.
9. *Turtle Mountain Star*, 12 July 1917, 8.
10. *Devils Lake Daily Journal*, 30 June 1917, 1.
11. "Indians Dismissed From Service Account Trachoma Infection," *Devils Lake Journal*, 27 July 1917, 3.
12. *Turtle Mountain Star*, 26 July 1917, 1.
13. Cooper, 198.
14. Elizabeth Creevey Hamm, *In White Armor: The life of Captain Arthur Ellis Hamm, United States Army*, (New York, 1919), 76.
15. Alfred B. Welch, unpublished notes, no dates given.
16. "Ban Indian Company For 2nd North Dakota," *Sioux County Pioneer*, 19 July 1917, 1.
17. "North Dakota's Second Regiment Badly Broken Up," *The Palladium*, 11 Oct. 1917, 5.
18. *Sioux County Pioneer*, 9 Aug. 1917, 1.

## CHAPTER 2
### Roster of Veterans

### A

1. Montana Death Certificate; *The Billings Gazette*, 5 July 1974, H5; *The Ninth Infantry in the World War*, (Neuwied, Germany, nd), 35.
2. North Dakota Death Certificate; "Indians Recover After Drinking Debauch Friday," *Devils Lake World*, 12 Mar. 1930, 1.
3. Standing Rock Decimal Correspondence File Code 610, NARA, Kansas City; Susan A. Krouse, *North American Indians in the Great War*, (Lincoln, NE, 2007), 197-198; *Sioux County Pioneer*, 30 Jan. 1919, 1; South Dakota Death Certificate; *Sioux County Pioneer*, 6 Aug. 1954, 1.
4. Folder 1081, Box 25, MS71, Beecher Family Papers, Yale University Library; District of Columbia Death Certificate; "Illustrious Indian Dies at Capital," *Sioux County Pioneer*, 14 Mar. 1930, 1.
5. "World War I Veteran Dies; Services Held," *Turtle Mountain Star*, 29 Mar. 1956, 5.

### B

1. North Dakota Death Certificate; "World War I Veteran Dies," *Turtle Mountain Star*, 2 Jan. 1964, 6. The photo of Patrick and Louise Baker was first published in *St. Ann's Centennial, 1985*, p. 262, copied by the State Historical Society of North Dakota.
2. *Sioux County Pioneer*, 2 May 1918, 4; Wanamaker Documentation; Charles B. Fullerton, *The Twenty-sixth Infantry in France*, (Montabaur-Frankfurt, Germany, 1919), 68; *Sioux County*

*Pioneer*, 1 May 1919, 1; "Alphonse Bear Ghost services in Cannon Ball," *Morning Pioneer*, 6 July 1972, 10.

3. "Bearshield Cook and Baker," *Sioux County Pioneer*, 16 June 1927, 1; South Dakota Death Certificate.

4. Wanamaker Documentation; North Dakota Death Certificate.

5. North Dakota Death Certificate; "Services Held For Lifelong Resident," *Turtle Mountain Star*, 4 Nov. 1965, 6.

6. North Dakota Death Certificate; "Hold Funeral Services For Belcourt Man," *Turtle Mountain Star*, 6 March 1958, 1.

7. Edgar J. D. Larson, *Memoirs of France and the Eighty-Eighth Division*, (Minneapolis, 1920), 63; North Dakota Death Certificate; "Hold Services For Louis Bercier, 64," *Turtle Mountain Star*, 11 Aug. 1960, 12.

8. North Dakota Death Certificate; *Minot Daily News*, 22 Sept. 1962, 6.

9. Tom Benjey, *Doctors, Lawyers, Indian Chiefs*, (Carlisle, PA, 2008), 272-273; Montana Death Certificate; "Poplar Rites For Football Star, J. Bergie," *Poplar Standard*, 13 March 1970, 1; "Last Rites Held for Poplar Gridiron Star; His Game Too Much For 'Ike'," *Poplar Standard*, 20 March 1970, 2.

10. Montana Death Certificate; "Martin Bergie Passes," *Havre Daily News*, 5 Nov. 1976.

11. Wanamaker Documentation; Procter M. Fiske, *History of the Three Hundred Fiftieth Regiment of the U. S. Infantry*, (Cedar Rapids, 1919), 126; North Dakota Death Certificate; "Louis Big Horn Elk, Fort Yates man dies," *Morning Pioneer*, 29 Feb. 1972, 12.

12. Wanamaker Documentation; Jerome Forbes, (editor), *Our Book of Memories 338 FA*, n.d., 85; "Funeral Pending For Frank Birds Bill," *New Town News*, 4 Jan. 1968, 1.

13. North Dakota Death Certificate; *Devils Lake Morning Journal*, 31 Oct. 1968, 8.

14. "Special Indian Recruiting Party Visits Ft. Yates," *Sioux County Pioneer*, 1 April 1920, 1; North Dakota Death Certificate.

15. Wanamaker Documentation; North Dakota Death Certificate.

16. Ben Chastaine, *History of the 18th U.S. Infantry, First Division, 1812-1919*, New York (n.d.), 96; Wanamaker Documentation; "Returned Soldier-Hero Buried at Cannon Ball," *Sioux County Pioneer*, 22 Sept. 1921, 1.

17. North Dakota Death Certificate.

18. North Dakota Death Certificate; "World War Veteran Dies at Belcourt On Tuesday," *Turtle Mountain Star*, 15 Feb. 1940, 1. Photo of Brien copied from *St. Ann's Centennial, 1985*, 205.

19. Wanamaker Documentation; North Dakota Death Certificate; *Minot Daily News*, 10 Dec. 1956, 6.

20. Wanamaker Documentation; NARA, Kansas City; *Sioux County Pioneer*, 12 Sept. 1918, 1; North Dakota Death Certificate.

21. Social Security Administration, Application for account number.

22. "Robt. Bruce No. 2 In France," *Sioux County Pioneer*, 28 Feb. 1918, 1; "Million Dollar Band Coming to Lakota, Monday, Apr. 7th," *The Lakota American*, 27 March 1919, 1; South Dakota Death Certificate; *Rapid City Journal*, 25 Nov. 1968.

23. North Dakota Death Certificate; "Pat Brunelle Passes Away Friday, July 23," *Turtle Mountain Star*, 29 July 1937, 1.

24. *Oregonian*, 5 March 1966, 28

25. "James F. Buckley Dies At Camp Dodge, Iowa," *Sioux County Pioneer*, 25 April 1918, 1.

26. North Dakota Death Certificate.

27. North Dakota Death Certificate; "Services Monday for Oscar Burr, 75," *The McKenzie County Farmer*, 26 Feb. 1970, 5.

## C

1. Certificate of Marriage, Spokane, WA; Washington State Death Certificate.
2. *Sioux County Pioneer*, 19 June 1919, 1; "Guy Chapman, Fort Yates," *Bismarck Tribune*, 22 June 1972, 13.
3. *Sioux County Pioneer*, 30 Jan. 1919, 8; Wanamaker Documentation; "Fort Yates Soldiers Royally Entertained," *Sioux County Pioneer*, 8 May 1919, 1; North Dakota Death Certificate.
4. 1947 Grays Harbor City Directory, 48; Elerding Mortuary, Inc.; "Elmer Charlebois Dies Unexpectedly," *Daily World* (Aberdeen, WA), 7 Dec. 1948, 1.
5. Wanamaker Documentation; "Indian Boy, Victim Of Spanish Flu," *McLean County Independent*, 24 Oct. 1918, 1.
6. NARA, Record Group 75, File 1327, Folder 5532; Cooper, 188; Wanamaker Documentation; Britten, 107; *Dayton Daily News*, 27 March 1959, 34.
7. North Dakota Death Certificate.
8. *Camp Dodger*, 3 Feb. 1919 and 10 Feb. 1919, 4; Wanamaker Documentation; South Dakota Death Certificate.
9. NARA, Kansas City, MO; Edgar J. D. Larson, *Memoirs of France and the Eighty-Eighth Division*, (Minneapolis, 1920), 128; North Dakota Death Certificate.

## D

1. Eva Case and Harold Case, *100 Years at Fort Berthold*, (Bismarck, 1977), 277, 281; North Dakota Death Certificate; "Funeral Was Monday For Robert Cherries," *New Town News*, 22 Nov. 1973, 5.
2. *The History of Company M, 352nd Infantry, 88th Div., AEF*, (n.d.); North Dakota Death Certificate; "Nicholas Dauphanais Rites Here Saturday," *Fargo Forum*, 20 Jan. 1956, 6.
3. Wanamaker Documentation; North Dakota Death Certificate.
4. Wanamaker Documentation; *McLean County Independent*, 27 Jan. 1982, 3.
5. North Dakota Death Certificate; "Lifelong Resident of Belcourt Dies," *Turtle Mountain Star*, 13 May 1965, 5.
6. NARA, Kansas City; North Dakota Death Certificate.
7. North Dakota Death Certificate; "Pat Desjarlais Rites Are Held At Belcourt," *Turtle Mountain Star*, 5 Dec. 1946, 1.
8. Wanamaker Documentation; North Dakota Death Certificate; "Dunseith Man Loses Life In Harvest Field When Rack Overturns," *Turtle Mountain Star*, 17 Sept. 1953, 1.
9. Wanamaker Documentation; North Dakota Death Certificate.
10. "Special Indian Recruiting Party Visits Ft. Yates," *Sioux County Pioneer*, 1 April 1920, 1; North Dakota Death Certificate; "500 At Funeral," *Sioux County Pioneer*, 27 Oct. 1927, 1.
11. *Washburn Leader*, 17 May 1918, 3; North Dakota Death Certificate; *Minot Daily News*, 6 Aug. 1968, 6.

## E

1. "Special Indian Recruiting Party Visits Ft. Yates," *Sioux County Pioneer*, 1 April 1920, 1; "A. Eagle Boy, Fort Yates," *Mandan Roughrider News*, 4 April 1976, 7.
2. Wanamaker Documentation; Britten, 111; Claire Kenamore, *Story of the 139th Infantry*, (St. Louis, 1920), 38; North Dakota Death Certificate.
3. *In The World War: 1917-1918-1919*, Wahpeton, 1920), 87; Minnesota Death Certificate; "Charles Ellis Passed Away July 17, 1973," *Cass Lake Times*, 26 July 1973, 1.

# F

1. NARA, Record Group 75, File 1327, Folder 4725; North Dakota Death Certificate.
2. North Dakota Death Certificate; "Moses Fiddler Dies At Belcourt Friday," *Turtle Mountain Star*, 27 Oct. 1932, 1.
3. "Fiske-Cournoyer Wedding," *Sioux County Pioneer*, 26 June 1919, 1; *Selfridge Journal*, 24 July 1952, 1.
4. Wanamaker Documentation; *New Town News*, 10 April 1980, 2.
5. North Dakota Death Certificate; "Funeral Is Held For Belcourt Man," *Turtle Mountain Star*, 17 Dec. 1964, 2.

# G

1. "Man of Indian Blood Commissioned Captain U.S.A.," *Devils Lake Journal,* 18 Aug. 1917, 3; Benjey, 123-132.
2. North Dakota Death Certificate; "Indian Veteran Dies In Fargo Hospital," *Fargo Forum*, 21 Sept. 1925, 5.
3. Montana Death Certificate; *Miles City Star*, 11 Sept. 1978, 2.
4. South Dakota Death Certificate; *Sioux County Pioneer*, 14 July 1927, 8.
5. Wanamaker Documentation; "Funeral Today For Charles Grady Sr.," *New Town News*, 26 April 1973, 1.
6. Ben Chastaine, 48; "Funeral Rites for Albert Grass," *Sioux County Pioneer*, 26 May 1921, 1.
7. *Sioux County Pioneer*, 10 Oct. 1918, 1; "Joe Day, Shields Dies At Age 71," *Selfridge Journal*, 9 Oct. 1969, 1.
8. Wanamaker Documentation; Montana Death Certificate; *Wotanin Wowapi*, 23 Dec. 1982, 7.
9. Montana Death Certificate; "Death Claims B. Grey Hawk, Rites In Poplar," *Poplar Standard*, 28 Feb. 1964, 3.

# H

1. Wanamaker Documentation; *Story of the 91st Division*, (San Francisco, 1919), 90; "Heart Trouble Incurred Five Years Ago in Action Direct Cause of Geo. Halsey's Death," *Sioux County Pioneer*, 6 Dec. 1923, 1.
2. Harold Burton, *600 Days Service: A History of the 361st Infantry*, (Cleveland, 1919), 185; "Michael Halsey and Miss Tallbear Married," *Sioux County Pioneer*, 12 Jan. 1922, 1; South Dakota Death Index; *Rapid City Journal*, 17 Dec. 1970, 19.
3. *Oregonian*, 22 Dec. 1964, 37.
4. "Is Most Popular Man In Camp," *Washburn Leader*, 24 May 1918, 4; Wanamaker Documentation.
5. Welch, unpublished notes; District of Columbia Death Certificate.
6. North Dakota Death Certificate.
7. Wanamaker Documentation; Douglas R. Parks, *Myths and Traditions of the Arikara Indians*, (Lincoln, NE, 1996), 43; *Havre Daily News*, 29 Nov. 1982.
8. Wanamaker Documentation; Edgar J.D. Larson, 125; North Dakota Death Certificate; "Harvey Hopkins, Sr., 56 Dies Wed. in Rugby Hospital," *McLean County Independent*, 28 Feb. 1952, 1.
9. Montana Death Certificate; *Billings Gazette*, 1 May 1985, 8A.

## I

1. North Dakota Death Certificate.
2. "Special Indian Recruiting Party Visits Ft. Yates," *Sioux County Pioneer*, 1 April 1920, 1; North Dakota Death Certificate; "Coroner's Jury Finds Cannon Ball Man Dies of Diabetes," *Sioux County Pioneer-Arrow*, 7 May 1954, 1.

## J

1. George Wythe, *A History of the 90th Division*, (1920), 100; *Hiawatha Daily World*, 29 Aug. 1977.
2. North Dakota Death Certificate; *Turtle Mountain Star*, 24 May 1993, 15.
3. Minnesota Death Certificate; "Belcourt War Veteran Dies At Fort Snelling," *Turtle Mountain Star*, 7 March 1929, 6.
4. North Dakota Death Certificate.
5. Minnesota Death Certificate; *Mahnomen Pioneer*, 11 May 1934, 1.
6. *Devils Lake Journal*, 4 June 1979, 14.
7. Wanamaker Documentation; North Dakota Death Certificate; *Turtle Mountain Star*, 5 Jan. 1978, 8. The photo of Jollie copied from *St. Ann's Centennial,1985*, page 205.
8. Montana Death Certificate; "WW I Veteran Dies: Rites Held," *Turtle Mountain Star*, 18 Dec. 1958, 1.
9. California Death Certificate.
10. North Dakota Death Certificate; "Morgan Jones, Nishu, Dies Last Thursday," *McLean County Independent*, 23 April 1931, 1.
11. "Home From the War," *Sioux County Pioneer*, 19 June 1919, 1; South Dakota Death Certificate.
12. "Young Bride of Joseph Jordan Ends Own Life," *Sioux County Pioneer*, 4 Oct. 1917, 1; Ben Chastaine, 91; Wanamaker Documentation; Welch unpublished Notes; "Cannon Ball Man Dies," *Sioux County Pioneer-Arrow*, 30 Sept. 1949, 1.

## K

1. *Sioux County Pioneer*, 2 May 1918, 5; North Dakota Death Certificate.

## L

1. California Death Certificate. Photo copied from *St. Ann's Centennial, 1985*, p 205
2. North Dakota Death Certificate; *Minot Daily News*, 5 May 1964, 2.
3. Calvary Cemetery records, Evanston, IL. Photo from *St. Ann's Centennial, 1985*, 416.
4. North Dakota Death Certificate; "John Landry Dies: Funeral Set Friday," *Turtle Mountain Star*, 11 Feb. 1965, 1.
5. Washington Death Certificate; *Turtle Mountain Star*, 14 Dec. 1972, 6.
6. "Frank Longie Services Held," *Turtle Mountain Star*, 9 April 1970, 6A.
7. Wanamaker Documentation; Fullerton, 39; 1953 Green Bay *City Directory*, 418; *Green Bay Press-Gazette*, 7 April 1986, B9.
8. Wanamaker Documentation; 1964 Portland (ME) *City Directory*, 346; *Portland Press Herald*, 30 March 1964, 2.
9. Washington Death Certificate; *Oregonian*, 3 Aug. 1972.

10. *In the World War: 1917-1918-1919,* (Wahpeton, 1920), 91; Washington State Death Certificate; *Tacoma News Tribune,* 24 June 1986, B2.
11. Wanamaker Documentation; North Dakota Death Certificate; "Funeral Held for Martin Levings," *New Town News,* 7 Nov. 1974, 3.
12. North Dakota Death Certificate; *Turtle Mountain Star,* 27 July 1978, 8.
13. Wanamaker Documentation.
14. Susan Krouse, 29, 124; 1948-49 Bismarck *City Directory,* 175; North Dakota Death Certificate; "Little Chief Rites Set on Wednesday," *Bismarck Tribune,* 19 March 1956, 2.
15. Wanamaker Documentation; North Dakota Death Certificate; "Services Held For Albert Little Owl," *Killdeer Herald,* 5 March 1975, 4.
16. Service Records from Montana Historical Society. Photo of Lizotte copied from *St. Ann's Centennial, 1985,* 205.
17. "Albert Grass Lost in Action, Joseph Lockwood Missing," *Sioux County Pioneer,* 19, Sept. 1918, 1; *In The World War: 1917-1918-1919,* (Wahpeton, 1920), 91; N.A.R.A., Civilian Personnel Records, St. Louis, MO, 27 April 2011: numerous copies of correspondence relating to Joseph Lockwood as a civilian employee; *Greenbrier Independent,* 25 Aug. 1966.
18. Washington State Death Certificate; *Spokesman Review,* 17 Feb. 1968, 14.

## M

1. *Sioux County Pioneer,* 22, Aug. 1918, p. 4; Wanamaker Documentation; 1948 Minneapolis *City Directory,* 814; 1956 *City Directory,* 871; Minnesota Death Certificate.
2. "George M. Wounds Back From Siberia," *Sioux County Pioneer,* 23 Oct. 1919, p. 1; Wanamaker Documentation; North Dakota Death Certificate; *Sioux County Pioneer-Arrow,* 24 Sept. 1943, p. 1.
3. "Military Funeral For Fort Yates Editor," *Sioux County Pioneer-Arrow,* 19 May 1950, p. 1.
4. Canadian military records, Library and Archives Canada; British Columbia Death Certificate.
5. "Letter from Joseph M. Martin," *Turtle Mountain Star,* 5 July 1917, p. 8; North Dakota Death Certificate; "Joseph Mose Martin," *Devils Lake Daily Journal,* 29 June 1962, p. 6; *A History of the Sixth Regiment Field Artillery First Division,* Ransbach, Germany, June 1919.
6. North Dakota Death Certificate.
7. Canadian military records, Library and Archives Canada.
8. North Dakota Death Certificate; "Henry McKay Killed When Tractor Tips," *Benson County Farmers Press,* 6 April 1945, 1.
9. *Sioux County Pioneer,* 25 Oct. 1917, 1; *News Review,* 26 Jan. 1977, p. 14.
10. North Dakota Death Certificate; "Young Indian Late Soldier, Died Suddenly Aboard Train," *Devils Lake Journal,* 24 May 1919, p. 3.
11. Wanamaker Documentation; "Westley Means and Alma Short Married Thursday," *Sioux County Pioneer,* 13 July 1922, p. 1; *Napa Register,* 15 June 1978.
12. Wanamaker Documentation; "Menz-Halsey," *Sioux County Pioneer,* 24 Aug. 1922, p.1; North Dakota Death Certificate; "Death Summons William Menz," *Sioux County Pioneer,* 6 Aug. 1925, p. 1.
13. Wanamaker Documentation; The obituary for Joseph's widow states that he died in 1943. *Devils Lake World,* 28 March 1979, p. 10.
14. *Sioux County Pioneer,* 19 April 1919, 1; *Beloit Daily News,* 4 Sept. 1971, p. 2.
15. *Sioux County Pioneer,* 22 Aug. 1918, p. 4; Montana Death Certificate.
16. Service record, Montana Historical Society; South Dakota Death Certificate; Photo of Monette copied from *St. Ann's Centennial, 1985,* p. 205.
17. *Eagle Butte News,* 28 Feb. 1974, p.1.

18. W. L. McSpedden, *History and Statistics of the 358th Infantry*, (Gerolstein, Germany, 1919), 12; "Barney Mulhern, Indian World War Veteran of Cannon Ball, is Dead," *Siuox County Pioneer-Arrow*, 22 May 1931, 1.

19. *In The World War: 1917-1918-1919,* 93; Wanamaker Documentation; Washington State Death Certificate.

20. Wanamaker Documentation; "Murphy Moved Faster Than Bullets, Appears," *Sioux County Pioneer*, 15 May 1919, 1; North Dakota Death Certificate; "Funeral Services Held at Shields Last Week For Indian Rancher," *Sioux County Pioneer-Arrow,* 18 Aug. 1950, 1.

## N

1. Wanamaker Documentation; Eva and Harold Case, 431; "Funeral held for Jack Nagel, 81," *The Hazen Star*, 16 June 1977, 5.

2. North Dakota Death Certificate; "Mark Necklace Laid To Rest At Old Scout Cemetery Dec. 28," *New Town News,* 3 Jan. 1963, 1.

## O

1. NARA, Standing Rock Decimal Correspondence, File Code 610; South Dakota Death Certificate.

## P

1. NARA, Record Group 75, Records of the Bureau of Indian Affairs, File 1327, Folder 3712; Louise Erdrich, *Indian Boarding School: the Runaways*, in *Native American Literature:an anthology*, (Chicago, 1999), 625; Wanamaker Documentation; North Dakota Death Certificate; "Ft. Berthold Residents Are Called," *McLean County Independent,* 2 Feb. 1939, 1.

2. North Dakota Death Certificate.

3. District of Columbia Death Certificate; "Impressive Funeral Held in Honor of Chaske Parkin," *Sioux County Pioneer-Arrow,* 28 Jan. 1938, 1.

4. 1954 *St. Paul City Directory*, 588; South Dakota Death Certificate.

5. North Dakota Death Certificate; "Hold Funeral Services For War Veteran," *Turtle Mountain Star*, 26 Nov. 1959, 4.

6. North Dakota Death Certificate; "Henry Perkins Funeral Services Held Wednesday," *McLean County Independent*, 9 May 1946, 1.

7. *Kalamazoo Gazette*, 24 March 1958.

8. North Dakota Death Certificate; "Louis Plante Dies Suddenly," *Devils Lake Daily Journal*, 10 March 1931, 1.

9. 1956 Minneapolis *City Directory*, 1139; Minnesota Death Certificate.

10. North Dakota Death Certificate.

11. *Sioux County Pioneer*, 4 April 1918,1; 30 June 1921; 20 Oct. 1921.

12. *Washburn Leader*, 21 June 1918, 7; "Helen Gough, Arikara Leader and One of the State's Wealthiest Women, Dies," *McLean County Independent*, 21 Feb 1963.

## R

1. "Deserter Arrested Here," *Sioux County Pioneer*, 4 Oct. 1917, 1; *Sioux County Pioneer*, 9 May 1918; North Dakota Death Certificate; "Inquest Held on Cannon Ball Veteran Who Died at Agency Hospital," *Sioux County Pioneer-Arrow*, 6 May 1955, 1, Krouse, p. 102.

2. Wanamaker Documentation; North Dakota Death Certificate; *Minot Daily News*, 14 Dec. 1965, 6.

3. Krouse, 159; North Dakota Death Certificate.

4. "Special Indian Recruiting Party Visits Ft. Yates," *Sioux County Pioneer*, 1 April 1920, 1; South Dakota Death Certificate; "Taps Sound at Kenel for World War Veteran," *Sioux County Pioneer*, 23 April 1935, 1.

5. Wanamaker Documentation; North Dakota Death Certificate.

6. North Dakota Death Certificate; "Failed to Hear Train Coming, New Town Deaf Man Killed," *Minot Daily News*, 12 June 1958, 1.

7. *Sioux County Pioneer*, 12 July 1917, 1; "Rites for Reedy Held Sunday, 20th," *Ransom County Gazette*, 24 Dec. 1936, 1.

8. Krouse, 78; Minnesota Historical Society, E99.1. p 11 (photo file of Thomas Rogers); North Dakota Death Certificate; *Minot Daily News*, 19 April 1965, 6.

9. McSpedden, 12.

10. "Spokane Resident Taken by Death," *Union Bulletin* (Walla Walla, WA), 30 Jan. 1952, (published on www.findagrave.com)

## S

1. *Sioux County Pioneer*, 2 May 1918; *Sioux County Pioneer*, 12 June 1919, 1; North Dakota Death Certificate; "George Santee Retired Shields Rancher Dies," *Sioux County Pioneer-Arrow*, 19 July 1962, 1.

2. North Dakota Death Certificate; "Disabled War Veteran Dies Friday, April 28," *Turtle Mountain Star*, 4 May 1939, 1.

3. *Sioux County Pioneer*, 20 June 1918, 1; Wanamaker Documentation; "A Soldier Passes On," *Sioux County Pioneer*, 19 July 1928, 1.

4. Wanamaker Documentation; *In The World War: 1917-1918-1919*, 97; Oregon Death Certificate; *Oregonian*, 26 Oct. 1952, 11.

5. *Benson County Farmers Press*, 2 Feb. 1978, 14.

6. "Ship Carrying Soldiers Sunk," *The McLean County Independent*, 30 May 1918, 7; Christian A. Bach and Henry Noble Hall, *The Fourth Division: Its Services and Achievements in the World War Gathered from the Records of the Division*, (Garden City, NY, 1920), 43.

7. *Sioux County Pioneer*, 15 Aug. 1918, 8; South Dakota Death Certificate.

8. North Dakota Death Certificate; "Death Saturday of Ft. Yates Rancher May Prove First 1951 Highway Fatality for Sioux County," *Sioux County Pioneer-Arrow*, 4 Jan. 1952, 1.

9. Wanamaker Documentation; "Last Rights Held for John W. Smith Sr.," *New Town News*, 28 April 1977, 1.

10. *Sioux County Pioneer*, 2 May 1918.

11. NARA, Kansas City, File Code 610; Cecil Frank Brantner, *351st Infantry*, (St. Paul, 1919), 102; Krouse, 37; Montana Death Certificate.

12. North Dakota Death Certificate; "Douglas Standish At Mandaree For Services Dec. 18," *McKenzie County Farmer*, 23 Dec. 1965, 16.

13. Wanamaker Documentation; "Philip Star, 52, Elbowoods, Dies," *McLean County Independent*, 20 April 1950, 7.

14. NARA, Kansas City, File Code 610, Box 154; "Belcourt Pioneer Resident, 92, Dies," *Turtle Mountain Star*, 7 Nov. 1957, 1.

15. Washington State Death Certificate.

# T

1. NARA, Record Group 75, File 1327, Folder 1989; "McLean-Bluelips," *Sioux County Pioneer*, 8 May 1919, 1; *Sioux County Pioneer-Arrow*, 6 Jan. 1933, 1; California Death Certificate.
2. Florida Death Certificate.
3. Missouri Death Certificate.
4. North Dakota Death Certificate.
5. NARA, RG 75, File 1327, Folder 4797; "Sioux County Soldiers Returning to Homes," *Sioux County Pioneer*, 12 June 1919, 1; "Mrs. Traversie Played Leading Role in Taming of North," *Mandan Daily Pioneer*, 31 July 1937, 5.
6. Wanamaker Documentation; Dick Kennedy, *Soldier's Jokes and Stories*, nd; "Paul Turner Dies in Vets Hospital," *New Town and Sanish Sentinel*, 1 Sept. 1955, 1.
7. "Cannon Ball Rites Thursday for Edward Two Bears," *Mandan Daily Pioneer*, 8 Sept. 1959, 2.
8. "Rites Saturday," *Morning Pioneer*, 13 Feb. 1970, 5.
9. *Memoirs of France and the Eighty-Eighth Division*, 100; "Joseph Two Bear Dies; Rites at Cannon Ball," *Mandan Pioneer*, 6 June 1967, 3.
10. Wanamaker Documentation; North Dakota Death Certificate; "Fort Berthold Indian Brought to Fargo, Dies," *Fargo Forum*, 10 June 1936, 8.
11. Wanamaker Documentation; Minnesota Death Certificate.

# V

1. Montana Death Certificate; "John Vallie, 70, Dies in Hospital," *Billings Gazette*, 11 April 1962, 7.
2. North Dakota Death Certificate; "Longtime Belcourt Resident Succumbs," *Turtle Mountain Star*, 28 Aug. 1969, 2.

# W

1. *Turtle Mountain Star*, Dec. 1975.
2. *Minot Daily News*, 15 June 1972, 6.
3. *Vallejo Times-Herald*, 4 Oct. 1979.
4. Unpublished notes of A. B. Welch, from Robert Barr; "Body of Mrs. Welch Taken to Ohio Home," *Mandan Daily Pioneer*, 12 Dec. 1932, 1; "Special Rites of Rare Variety Held for Mrs. Welsh at Cannon Ball," *Sioux County Pioneer-Arrow*, 6 Jan. 1933, 1; "Colonel Welch Passed Away Saturday," *Mandan Daily Pioneer*, 30 June 1945, 1.
5. Wanamaker Documentation; North Dakota Death Certificate; *Minot Daily News*, 11 Feb. 1964, 6.
6. NARA, Kansas City, RG 75, Records of the Bureau of Indian Affairs, File Code 610; South Dakota Death Certificate.
7. "George White Discharged," *Sioux County Pioneer*, 4 July 1918, 1.
8. NARA, Kansas City, RG 75, File Code 610; Wanamaker Documentation.
9. North Dakota Death Certificate; "Killed Saturday in Car Accident Near North Fort Yates," *Sioux County Pioneer-Arrow*, 22 June 1956, 1.
10. *Sioux County Pioneer-Arrow*, 22 Oct. 1959, 1; North Dakota Death Certificate.
11. 1962 Minneapolis *City Directory*, 1480; Minnesota Death Certificate.
12. "Services Held for Paul White Lightning," *Selfridge Journal*, 5 April 1973, 1.
13. Wanamaker Documentation; North Dakota Death Certificate.

14. *Washburn Leader*, 12 July 1918, 1; North Dakota Death Certificate; "Rites Held for David White Tail," *McLean County Independent*, 19 May 1955, 4.
15. California Death Certificate.
16. North Dakota Death Certificate; "Louis G. Wilkie Dies," *Turtle Mountain Star*, 31 May 1945, 4.
17. *88th Division in the World War of 1914-1918*, (New York, 1919), 97; Minnesota Death Certificate; "Peter Alfred Wilkie Dies in Minneapolis (sic)," *Turtle Mountain Star*, 10 Sept. 1959, 1.
18. Wanamaker Documentation; North Dakota Death Certificate; "Shell Shocked War Veteran Takes Own Life at Nishu Home," *McLean County Independent*, 30 March 1939, 1.

### Y

1. "Thirty Boys Left for Camp Lewis," *Washburn Leader*, 30 Aug. 1918, 1; "Missouri River Brings Death to Yellow Bird, 41," *McLean County Independent*, 7 Sept. 1939, 1.
2. Wanamaker Documentation; North Dakota Death Certificate; "Services Saturday for Life-long Cannon Ball Man, " *Mandan Pioneer*, 2 Dec. 1966, 2.
3. Wanamaker Documentation; Julius O. Adler, *History of the 306th Infantry*, (New York, 1935), 60, 174; North Dakota Death Certificate.
4. Wanamaker Documentation; Cooper, 207; Krouse, 78; "Legion Honors Its Dead Hero," *McLean County Independent*, 21 June 1923, 1.
5. "More Boys Off For Service in the U.S. Army," *Washburn Leader*, 3 May 1918, 1; North Dakota Death Certificate; " Young Wolf's Funeral Set Near Raub," *Minot Daily News*, 27 Aug. 1960, 6.

### Z

1. "Frank B. Zahn, Historian, Judge, Dies Here Sunday," *Bismarck Tribune*, 5 July 1966, 10.

**Chapter 3**
**Honoring the warriors**

1. Frances Densmore, *Mandan and Hidatsa Music*, (Washington, D.C., 1923), 156-57.
2. "Albert Grass Post Elects its First Officers," *Sioux County Pioneer*, 25 March 1920, 1.
3. "Indian Soldier Died On His Way Home," *Sioux County Pioneer*, 18 Dec. 1919, 1.
4. NARA, FG 75, File Code 610, Correspondence relating to Joseph Takes The Shield.
5. "Indians Add Interest to Foch Reception," *Sioux County Pioneer*, 1 Dec. 1921, 1.
6. Robert W. Larson, *Gall*, (Norman, OK, 2007), 28.

# Bibliography

## Manuscripts

Alfred Burton Welch unpublished papers, copies received from Robert Barr, Mandan, ND.

Beecher Family Papers, MS71, Box 25, Folder 1081, Yale University Library.

Records of the Bureau of Indian Affairs, Record Group 75, National Archives.
    Carlisle Indian School Names, File 1327, Washington, D.C.
    Records Relating to Indians in WWI, File 610, Kansas City

Wanamaker Documentation, William Hammond Mathers Museum, Indiana University, Bloomington, IN.

## References

Adler, Julius Ochs. *History of the 306ᵗʰ Infantry.* New York City: privately printed, 1935.

Bach, Christian A., and Henry Noble Hall. *The Fourth Division: Its Services and Achievements in the World War Gathered from the Records of the Division.* Garden City, N.Y.: Christian A. Bach 1920.

Benjey, Tom. *Doctors, Lawyers, Indian Chiefs.* Carlisle, PA: Tuxedo Press, 2008.

Brantner, Cecil Frank. *351ˢᵗ Infantry.* St. Paul, MN: Randall Company, 1919.

Britten, Thomas A. *American Indians in World War I: At Home and at War.* Albuquerque: University of New Mexico Press, 1997.

Burton, Harold H. *600 Days' Service: A History of the 361ˢᵗ Infantry Regiment of the United States Army.* Cleveland: privately printed, 1919

Case, Eva and Harold Case. *100 Years at Fort Berthold: The History of Fort Berthold Indian Mission: 1876-1976.* 1977

Chastaine, Ben H. *History of the 18ᵗʰ U.S. Infantry.* New York: Hymans Publishing Company, 1919.

Child, Brenda J. *Holding Our World Together: Ojibwe Women and the Survival of Community.* New York: Viking Penguin, 2012.

Cooper, Jerry and Glenn Smith. *Citizens as Soldiers: A History of the North Dakota National Guard.* Fargo: North Dakota Institute of Regional Studies, 1986

Cyr, A. Brian. *Métis Veterans of Manitoba: From Buffalo to Battlefields.* Winnipeg: Manitoba Metis Federation, 2010.

Densmore, Frances. *Mandan and Hidatsa Music.* Washington: Government Printing Office, 1923.

Dorsey, George A. *Traditions of the Arikara.* Washington: Carnegie Institution, 1904.

Dunlay, Thomas W. *Wolves for the Blue Soldiers: Indian Scouts and Auxiliaries with the United States Army, 1860-1890.* Lincoln: University of Nebraska Press, 1982.

Durrett, Deanne. *Unsung Heroes of World War II: The Story of the Navajo Code Talkers.* Lincoln: University of Nebraska Press, 1998.

*88th Division in the World War of 1914-1918.* New York: Wynkoop Hallenbeck Crawford Company, 1919.

Erdrich, Louise. *Indian Boarding School: The Runaways,* in *Native American Literature.* Chicago: NTC/Contemporary Publishing Group, Inc., 1999.

Fiske, Proctor M. *History of the Three hundred Fiftieth Regiment of U. S. Infantry.* Cedar Rapids, IA: Laurance Press Company, 1920.

Flaherty, Thomas H. (edit). *The Way of the Warrior.* Alexandria, VA: Time-Life Books, 1993.

Fullerton, Charles B. *The Twenty-Sixth Infantry in France.* Montabaur-Frankfurt, Germany: Martin Flock, 1919.

Hamm, Elizabeth Creevey. *In White Armor: The Life of Captain Arthur Ellis Hamm, 326th Infantry, United States Army (1919).* New York: Knickerbocker Press. Reprint, Kessinger Publishing, 2010.

Holm, Tom. *Strong Hearts, Wounded Souls: Native American Veterans of the Vietnam War.* Austin: University of Texas Press, 1996.

Hoxie, Frederick E. and Jay T. Nelson (Edit). *Lewis and Clark and the Indian Country: The Native American Perspective.* Urbana: University of Illinois Press, 2007.

*In the World War: 1917-1918-1919, Richland County, ND.* Wahpeton, ND: Globe-Gazette Printing Co., 1920.

Kavanagh, Thomas W. *North American Indian Portraits: Photographs from the Wanamaker Expeditions.* Old Saybrook, CT: Konecky and Konecky, 1996.

Kenmore, Clair. *Story of the 139th Infantry,* St.Louis: Guard Publishing Co., 1920.

Kennedy, Dick. *Soldier's Jokes and Stories.* (No publisher or date).

Krouse, Susan Applegate. *North American Indians in the Great War.* Lincoln: University of Nebraska Press, 2007.

Larson, Edgar J. D. *Memoirs of France and the Eighty-Eighth Division.* Minneapolis: privately printed, 1920.

Lengel, Edward G. *To Conquer Hell: The Meuse-Argonne, 1918,* New York: Henry Holt and Company, 2008.

McNickle, D'Arcy. *Indian Man: A Life of Oliver LaFarge*, Bloomington: Indiana University Press, 1971.

McSpedden, W. L. *History and Statistics of the 358ᵗʰ Infantry, Ninetieth Division*, Gerolstein, Germany, 1919

Meldrum, T. Ben. *A History of the 362ⁿᵈ Infantry*, Ogden, UT: privately printed, 1920.

Owings, Alison. *Indian Voices*, New Brunswick: Rutgers University Press, 2011.

Parker, Dorothy R. *Singing an Indian Song: A Biography of D'Arcy McNickle*, Lincoln: University of Nebraska Press, 1992.

Parks, Douglas R. *Myths and Traditions of the Arikara Indians*, Lincoln: University of Nebraska Press, 1996.

Rosier, Paul C. *Serving Their Country: American Indian Politics and Patriotism in the Twentieth Century*, Cambridge: Harvard University Press, 2009.

Rubin, Richard. *The Last of the Doughboys*, Boston & NY, Houghton Mifflin Harcourt, 2013

Sprague, Donovin Arleigh. *Standing Rock Sioux*, Chcago, IL: Arcadia Publishing, 2004.
Strandberg, John E., and Roger J. Bender. *The Call of Duty: Military Awards and Decorations of the United States of America*, San Jose: R. James Bender Publishing, 1994.

Viola, Herman J. *Warriors in Uniform*, Washington, D.C.: National Geographic, 2007.

White, Bruce. *We Are At Home: Pictures of the Ojibwe People*, St. Paul: Minnesota Historical Society Press, 2007.

Wythe, George. *A History of the 90ᵗʰ Division*, privately printed, 1920.

# Index

## About the Authors

Mike Knudson has been interested in history and genealogy since high school. He served in the Peace Corps in Morocco, went back to school for his master's degree, then went to work as a forester with the Soil Conservation Service (now the Natural Resources Conservation Service) in North Dakota. He retired in 2011, and now has more time for research on family and military history, especially the World War I era.

Ann served 28 years in the North Dakota National Guard, and retired in 2012.

Mike is from Wisconsin, and Ann is from upstate New York. They met in college in Syracuse, NY. They have lived in North Dakota since 1977, in Wahpeton, Lisbon and Bismarck, and raised two children there.

The Knudsons published one previous book, *"Ransom County's Loyal Defenders,"* copyright 2010, ISBN 978-0-9821700-1. It is about World War I veterans with ties to Ransom County, ND, where the authors lived for seven years. Copies are available from the authors.

They are currently researching their next book, which will be about Native American service members from South Dakota who served in WWI.

Additions and corrections to their books are welcome, especially photographs of veterans, in or out of uniform. Proper credit will be given for all photos used. They can be reached at mikeannknudson@msn.com.

# Ports & Battlefields

Argonne Forest:  site of the last battle, where Corporal Richard Blue Earth was killed
Bordeaux:    major port used by American Expeditionary Force
Brest:  port
Cantigny:   battle site where Private Joseph Young Hawk was wounded
Clermont – Ferrand:  headquarters for the 337th and 339th Field Artillery
Coblenz:  headquarters for the 18th Infantry Regiment after the war
Gondrecourt:  headquarters for the 88th Division after the war
LeHavre:   port
Oudenarde:   headquarters for the 91st Division
Paris:  capitol of France
Soissons:  battle site where Private Albert Grass was killed

www.ingramcontent.com/pod-product-compliance
Lightning Source LLC
Chambersburg PA
CBHW080509110426
42742CB00017B/3050